A PASSAGE TO INDIA

THEORY IN PRACTICE SERIES

General Editor: Nigel Wood, School of English, University of Birmingham

Associate Editors: Tony Davies and Barbara Rasmussen, University of Birmingham

Current titles:

Don Juan
Mansfield Park
A Passage to India
The Prelude
The Waste Land

Forthcoming titles include:

Antony and Cleopatra
Hamlet
Henry IV
Measure for Measure
The Merchant of Venice
The Tempest
To The Lighthouse

A PASSAGE TO INDIA

EDITED BY
TONY DAVIES AND
NIGEL WOOD

OPEN UNIVERSITY PRESS
BUCKINGHAM · PHILADELPHIA

Open University Press
Celtic Court
22 Ballmoor
Buckingham
MK18 1XW

and
1900 Frost Road, Suite 101
Bristol, PA 19007, USA

First Published 1994

A catalogue record of this book is available from the British Library

ISBN 0 335 15712 2 (pb)

Library of Congress Cataloging-in-Publication Data

A Passage to India / edited by Tony Davies and Nigel Wood.
    p.   cm. — (Theory in practice series)
   Includes bibliographical references and index.
   ISBN 0–335–15712–2 (pb)
    1. Forster, E.M. (Edward Morgan), 1879–1970. Passage to India.
2. India—In literature. I. Davies, Tony, 1940– . II. Wood,
Nigel, 1953– . III. Series.
PR6011.058P3789 1994
823'.912—dc20   93–42009
                                            CIP

Typeset by Colset Pte Ltd, Singapore
Printed in Great Britain by St Edmundsbury Press,
Bury St Edmunds, Suffolk

Contents

The Editors and Contributors

PARMINDER KAUR BAKSHI was at the University of Delhi before coming to Britain in 1982. Her PhD thesis gives a homosexual interpretation of all of Forster's novels. She teaches courses in literature as well as race and gender. Some of her other works include 'Jagran: Theatre for Education and Development', *New Theatre Quarterly* (1989) and 'Homosexuality and Orientalism: Edward Carpenter's Journey to the East' in *Edward Carpenter and Late Victorian Radicalism* (edited by Tony Brown, 1990). She is at present working as a research fellow at the School of Geography and Environmental Studies, University of North London.

TONY DAVIES is senior lecturer in English at the University of Birmingham. He is the author (with Janet Batsleer and others) of *Rewriting English: Cultural Politics of Gender and Class* (1984) and of many articles on renaissance and modern writing and the theory and practice of English teaching. He has edited Milton's *Selected Shorter Poems and Prose* (1989) and *Selected Longer Poems and Prose* (1992), and is currently writing a book about humanism.

BARBARA HARLOW teaches English and comparative literature at the University of Texas at Austin. She is author of *Resistance Literature* (1987) and *Barred Women: Writing and Political Detention* (1992), as well as articles on 'Third World' literature and critical practice. Her current work, *Drawing the Line: Cultural Politics and the Legacy of Partition*, is a study of the literature of India, Ireland and Palestine.

BETTE LONDON teaches English at the University of Rochester. She is the author of *The Appropriated Voice: Narrative Authority in Conrad, Forster, and Woolf* (1990). Her articles, exploring questions of feminist theory and practice (frequently in relation to revisionist readings of canonical British authors), have appeared in such journals as *English Literary History*, *Diacritics*, and *Publications of the Modern Language Association of America*. She is currently completing a book on women's collaborative writing as it reflects and intervenes in the institution of late nineteenth- and early twentieth-century British authorship.

SARA MILLS is a senior lecturer in linguistics and critical theory in the Department of English and Drama, University of Loughborough. Her research interests are feminism and colonial discourse, and feminist linguistic and literary theory. Her main publications have been: (with Lynne Pearce, Sue Spaull and Elaine Millard) *Feminist Readings/Feminists Reading* (1989) and *Discourses of Difference: British Women Travellers and Colonialism* (1991); and (with Martin Montgomery, Nigel Fabb, Alan Durant and Tom Furniss) *Ways of Reading* (1992). She is currently working on a book on feminist stylistics and is editing a book entitled *Gendering the Reader* and one entitled *Language and Gender*.

NIGEL WOOD is a lecturer in the School of English at the University of Birmingham. He is the author of a study of Jonathan Swift and of several essays on literary theory. He is also editor of a selection from Fanny Burney's diaries and journals, *John Gay and the Scriblerians* (with Peter Lewis) and three *Theory in Practice* volumes (on *The Prelude*, *Mansfield Park* and *Don Juan*).

Editors' Preface

The object of this series is to help bridge the divide between the understanding of theory and the interpretation of individual texts. Students are therefore introduced to theory in practice. Although contemporary critical theory is now taught in many colleges and universities, it is often separated from the day-to-day consideration of literary texts that is the staple ingredient of most tuition in English. A thorough dialogue between theoretical and literary texts is thus avoided.

Each of these specially commissioned volumes of essays seeks by contrast to involve students of literature in the questions and debates that emerge when a variety of theoretical perspectives are brought to bear on a selection of 'canonical' literary texts. Contributors were not asked to provide a comprehensive survey of the arguments involved in a particular theoretical position, but rather to discuss in detail the implications for interpretation found in particular essays or studies, and then, taking these into account, to offer a reading of the literary text.

This rubric was designed to avoid two major difficulties which commonly arise in the interaction between literary and theoretical texts: the temptation to treat a theory as a bloc of formulaic rules that could be brought to bear on any text with roughly predictable results; and the circular argument that texts are constructed as such merely by the theoretical perspective from which we choose to regard them. The former usually leads to studies that are really just footnotes to the adopted theorists, whereas the latter is effortlessly self-fulfilling.

It would be disingenuous to claim that our interests in the teaching of theory were somehow neutral and not open to debate. The idea for this series arose from the teaching of theory in relation to specific texts. It is inevitable, however, that the practice of theory poses significant questions as to just what 'texts' might be and where the dividing lines between text and context may be drawn. Our hope is that this series will provide a forum for debate on just such issues as these which are continually posed when students of literature try to engage with theory in practice.

Tony Davies
Barbara Rasmussen
Nigel Wood

How to Use this Book

Each of these essays is composed of a theoretical and a practical element. Contributors were asked to identify the main features of their perspective on the text (exemplified by a single theoretical essay or book) and then to illustrate their own attempts to put this into practice.

We realize that many readers new to recent theory will find its specific vocabulary and leading concepts strange and difficult to relate to current critical traditions in most English courses.

The format of this book has been designed to help if this is your situation, and we would advise the following:

(i)   Before reading the essays, glance at the editor's introduction where the literary text's critical history is discussed, and

(ii) also at the prefatory information immediately before the essays, where the editor attempts to supply a context for the adopted theoretical position.

(iii) If you would like to develop your reading in any of these areas, turn to the annotated further reading section at the end of the volume, where you will find brief descriptions of those texts that each contributor has considered of more advanced interest. There are also full citations of the texts to which the contributors have referred in the references. It is also possible that more local information will be contained in notes to the essays.

(iv) The contributors have often regarded the chosen theoretical texts as points of departure and it is also in the nature of theoretical discussion to apply and test ideas on a variety of texts. Turn, therefore, to question and answer sections that follow each essay which are designed to allow contributors to comment and expand on their views in more general terms.

A Note on the Text

All quotations from Forster's novels are taken from the Abinger editions (full publication details supplied in the references), and titles have been abbreviated in the text as follows:

HE   *Howards End*
LJ   *The Longest Journey*
LN   *The Lucy Novels: Early Sketches for A Room with a View*
LTC   *The Life to Come and Other Stories*
M   *Maurice*
MPI   *The Manuscripts of a Passage to India*
PI   *A Passage to India*
WA   *Where Angels Fear to Tread*

The editions and abbreviations for Forster's non-fiction are:

AH   *Abinger Harvest* (Abinger)
AN   *Aspects of the Novel* (Penguin)
HD   *Hill of Devi and other Indian Writings* (Abinger)
TCD   *Two Cheers for Democracy* (Penguin)

Where the Penguin edition of *A Passage to India* is cited, this is referenced Forster (1989). Quotations from the letters are given the wording in the secondary text in which they have been located and then the Calendar number from Mary Lago's *Calendar of the Letters of E.M. Forster* (1985).

Introduction

TONY DAVIES

Surveying E.M. Forster's career for a North American magazine in 1927, Virginia Woolf found in his most recent novel, *A Passage to India*, signs of a new maturity and promise. In spite of 'ambiguities in important places, moments of imperfect symbolism, a greater accumulation of facts than the imagination is able to deal with', she noted the sharper clarity of purpose and execution, as if 'the double vision which troubled us in the earlier books was in process of becoming single . . . Mr Forster has almost achieved the great feat of animating this dense, compact body of observation with a spiritual light'. But above all, she concluded, 'it makes us wonder, What will he write next?' (Gardner 1973: 328).

A Passage to India, begun in 1912, worked on intermittently and often despairingly for more than a decade and published in June 1924, was Forster's fifth novel, and his first for nearly fourteen years. Reviews were almost uniformly good, often glowingly so, and the novel sold well: in the United States alone, 30,000 copies were bought before the end of July, and by the end of the year, most of the first printing of 17,000 British and 54,000 American copies had been sold. The *Observer* reviewer, 'beginning to fear that *Howards End* . . . was to be Forster's end', hailed the new novel as 'far greater, more spiritual, less insolently bored' than its predecessor. The *Manchester Guardian* welcomed Forster's 'reappearance as a novelist', and praised the novel's 'imagination and humour'. The *Birmingham Post* noted 'the admirable self-restraint by which Mr. E.M. Forster has limited his output'. There is, it is true, a hint of cosiness about these early reviews, since so many of the reviewers – Rose Macaulay, Leonard Woolf, H.W. Massingham (who took Woolf sharply to task for ignoring the novel's political argument), Ralph Wright – were friends of Forster himself (hardly an unusual phenomenon on the English literary scene). Even so, the reception, for a novel on a subject so much more controversial and ambitious than anything he had attempted before, was remarkably friendly. The novel was praised for the delicacy of its characterization, the effectiveness of its humour, the evenhandedness of its portrayal of Indians and 'Europeans' alike. Of the twenty-eight contemporary notices, English, American and Indian, collected by Gardner (1973: 196–287), all but two or three are highly favourable.

The exceptions are all by 'Anglo-Indians' – Britons who have lived and worked in British India – among whom the novel evidently caused a good deal of offence. Stories were told of old India hands, returning to the subcontinent after leave in the home country, hurling their copies of the book overboard in disgust. An otherwise sympathetic review in the Calcutta *Statesman* condemned the account of the trial of Dr Aziz as 'so full of technical error – indeed, so preposterous, that it cannot even be called a travesty'; and in an interesting correspondence in the British *New Statesman*, the editor (and probably author) of the Calcutta review, S.K. Ratcliffe, amplified his catalogue of factual errors in response to another correspondent who had noted 'a slight air of unreality' in the Anglo-Indian scenes of the book (Gardner 1973: 244–53). And the Calcutta *Englishman*, declaring a preference for 'the historical romance placed . . . in the time of the Moguls' as exemplified by the novels of Flora Annie Steele, unsurprisingly condemned the whole performance as a farrago of slander and prejudice (Gardner 1973: 271–2).

The book's first Indian reviewers, by contrast, praised the documentary accuracy of the narrative. St Nihal Singh, predicting correctly that the Anglo-Indians, 'not being used to being talked about in this manner . . . will hate Mr Forster for giving them away', hoped none the less that it would open the eyes of British readers to the political realities of British India and convince them of the need for 'the political elevation of Indians' (Gardner 1973: 269). The novel enjoyed a wide readership in India, and established Forster's reputation among middle-class Indians not just as a novelist but as a kind of benefactor. 'When I read *A Passage to India*', wrote one a few years later, 'I was filled with a sense of great relief and of an almost personal gratitude to Mr. Forster.' That reputation survives to the present day, though not all Forster's Indian readers were to be so well disposed. Some felt that Forster, by centring his narrative on the friendship between the Englishman Fielding and the Muslim Aziz, had misrepresented the social and political complexion of Indian nationalism. Nirad Chaudhuri, in a celebrated article published exactly thirty years after the novel itself, attacked it for sublimating the brutal realities of the conflict between independence and the Raj to the tame Bloomsburian pieties of 'personal relationship', and argued that 'with such material, a searching history of the Muslim destiny in India could have been written but not a novel on Indo-British relations, for which it was essential to have a Hindu protagonist' (Chaudhuri 1954: 19, 22). *Passage* is certainly vulnerable to such a reading, as Forster was aware. The suggestion, for instance, that 'one touch of regret . . . would have made [Ronny Heaslop] a different man, and the British Empire a different institution' might be taken to imply, in its second proposition, that the injustice and brutality of British rule in India, from the suppression of the so-called 'Mutiny' of 1857 to the massacre of civilians at Amritsar in 1919, could all have been avoided if only people had been a bit nicer to each other – a graphic demonstration, to the sceptical, of what Frederick Crews (1962), in an otherwise broadly sympathetic account of Forster, has called the 'perils of humanism'.

Chaudhuri, though he held the book responsible for helping to create 'that mood which enabled the British people to leave India with an almost Pilate-like gesture of washing their hands of a disagreeable affair', was reacting as much to the Indian canonization of Forster as a liberal saint as to the political implications of the novel itself; a similar exasperation to that which, a decade later, prompted the American novelist Pete Hamill to record his 'increasingly nauseous reaction to the totemization of E.M. Forster' and to protest at the critical elevation of this 'writer of light entertainments in the distant past' to 'the greatest living novelist . . . on the peculiar grounds that he had the courage to abandon the novel in 1924', after the publication of what Hamill calls 'this grim nanny of a novel' (Gardner 1973: 425–7). For by 1965, with Forster well into his seventies, it had become clear that the answer to Virginia Woolf's question, 'What will he write next?', was to be 'nothing'.

Curiously, this self-imposed novelistic purdah seems, as Hamill suggests, to have increased rather than diminished the tendency to venerate Forster as a sage. Of course, the answer to Virginia Woolf's question is not really 'nothing'. After *Passage* in 1924, Forster published some lectures on literary criticism, some essays on politics, literature and related topics, a memoir of a visit to India before the First World War and a couple of biographies, of a Cambridge friend, G.L. Dickinson, and of his great-aunt, Marianne Thornton. Not negligible, certainly; but, unless we count the early stories, all written before 1914 but not published until 1928, in *The Eternal Moment*, the homosexual romance *Maurice*, also pre-war but not published until 1971, and the opera libretto he wrote for Benjamin Britten, Forster, who was forty-five when *Passage* was published, produced no further fiction in the forty-six years that remained to him until his death in 1970. It was as if the rocks, the birds, the sky that had imposed their veto ('No, not yet') on the possibility of friendship between the Indian Aziz and the Englishman Fielding continued, too, to embargo those ethical and imaginative connections and resolutions that his fiction had worked so hard to achieve.

With some writers, of course, this silence of half a lifetime would not have any particular resonance. They lose the imaginative urge or need or opportunity, and turn to criticism or commerce or drink or ordinary provincial obscurity. The notion of an *oeuvre*, a lifelong body of writing maturing according to its own mysterious organic laws, is in any case a recent one (I mean post-Renaissance), and loaded with unexamined assumptions, reflecting, on the one hand, an idea of career or calling rooted in the 'Protestant ethic' of early capitalism, and, on the other, a Wordsworthian sense of moral and psychological development, the 'growth of the poet's mind'. But in Forster's case there remained, for his contemporaries, a strong sense of unfinished business and unredeemed promise, a sense that Forster himself seems to have shared. Reviewing the Indian memoir *The Hill of Devi* in 1953, another fellow-novelist, L.P. Hartley, observed that 'one of the saddest gaps in the bookshelves of contemporary literature is the space that should be occupied by the unwritten works of Mr E.M. Forster' (Gardner 1973: 416); and if the 'not yet . . . not there' that so tantalisingly defers the narrative closure of the last novel seems inevitably to prompt the question 'when, and where?', it was a question never to be answered in Forster's writing.

This lack of 'closure', of the satisfying finality and the tying-up of loose ends that we find in at least some of the novels of Fielding and Austen and Dickens and Hardy – what Henry James called the 'distribution at the last of prizes, pensions, husbands, wives, babies, millions, appended paragraphs, and cheerful remarks' (James, 1968: 82), though it can also take the form of a tragic catharsis – need not be seen as a problem, and certainly not as a problem specific to Forster. Such endings, in which the problems of the characters and the complexities of the plot are all resolved in the last chapter into a neat pattern of marriages and deaths and unexpected inheritances and retributions, have, for many readers, a perfunctory and unconvincing feel even in the most complacent Victorian fictions. In many novels, the effort of containing the manifold contradictions and dissatisfactions of contemporary life, the tension between the resolution the text is working for and the sheer unresolvability of the situations it is forced to represent, strain the narrative structure of 'classic realism' to something near breaking point, and a reading that is attentive to those tensions will detect many signs of unease and breakdown.[1] Forster had attempted just such a 'happy ending' in the last novel he published before *Passage, Howards End* (1910), and again in *Maurice* (1914, but unpublished in Forster's lifetime). In the first, the reunion of two families in an ancestral house, haymaking and the birth of a child combine in an attempt to persuade the reader imaginatively that the problems with which the text has grappled, the class conflict, the sexual exploitation, the violent death, the relentless suburbanization of country life, have all been somehow magically suspended, to disclose the immemorial rhythms and continuities of a timeless England. In the second, the agonies, uncertainties and real dangers of homosexual love are resolved in the escape of the two lovers to a 'greenwood' whose very name connects it not to the realistic contemporary milieu of the novel but to the folk-tale settings of Shakespearian comedy (though the lovers and greenwood exiles of *As You Like It* and *A Midsummer Night's Dream* have to return before the end to the realities and responsibilities of court or city). Such endings, which many readers (including this one) have found stagy and implausible, testify to the strength of the realist forms to which Forster, for all his interest in the modernist experiments of Woolf and Joyce, remained devoted. But they also derive from his personal commitment to the possibility of closure and resolution, in life as in art: to what he called 'connection'. 'Only connect the prose and the passion', declares Margaret Wilcox in *Howards End*, 'and both will be exalted, and human love will be seen at its height. Live in fragments no longer, only connect' (*HE*, 183–4); and the words 'only connect' supply a motto for the novel as a whole, as they do, some would say, for Forster's entire project as a writer. Here, the requirements of a particular literary form, the realist novel, converge with the values of a tradition and an ideology of which Forster has become a sort of secular saint: liberal humanism.

In the influential essay in which he described *A Passage to India* as 'a classic of the liberal spirit', F.R. Leavis provided his own 'rather commonplace' definition of the liberal tradition in the earlier part of the twentieth century. Forster, he maintained, was a spokesman for the finer consciousness of our time, the humane tradition as it emerges from a period of 'bourgeois' security, divorced from dogma and left by social change, the breakdown of traditional forms and the loss of sanctions embarrassingly 'in the air'; no longer serenely confident or self-sufficient, but conscious of being not less than before the custodian of something essential.

(Leavis 1962: 277)

The essay surveys all Forster's writings up to 1938 (when it was written); but it was in *Passage* above all that Leavis found

an expression, undeniably, of the liberal tradition; it has, as such, its fineness, its strength and its impressiveness; and it makes the achievement, the humane, decent and rational – the 'civilized' – habit, of that tradition appear the invaluable thing it is.

(Leavis 1962: 277)

The critic's own endorsement of the values he finds in the author is clear enough; and the liberal tradition, which he described as 'the indispensable transmitter of something that humanity cannot afford to lose' (Leavis 1962: 277), is intimately linked with the notion of 'civilization', and of the role of literature within it, that Leavis himself did so much to establish. 'The Schlegels', he wrote about *Howards End*, 'represent the humane liberal culture, the fine civilization of cultivated personal intercourse, that Mr Forster himself represents; they are the people for whom and in whom English literature . . . exists' (Leavis 1962: 269). Behind this seemingly rather parochial claim lies a view of civilization threatened on all sides by the commercialism and vulgarity of contemporary society, and dependent for its very survival on the preservation, by the 'cultivated' few capable of perceiving and embodying 'the finer consciousness of our time', of a selective canonical literature.[2] Forster does not, as a matter of fact, find a place in Leavis's celebrated 'great tradition' of English fiction. Perhaps the weaknesses that the critic found in the earlier novels, and the failure to build on the success of *Passage*, cost him a place alongside Austen and George Eliot, Conrad and Lawrence in the pantheon of the indisputably great. But he embodied, more than any of these (for there is nothing very 'liberal' about Conrad or Lawrence, nor, arguably, about Austen) the values on which the great tradition itself was built.

Leavis, writing in the shadow of the Second World War, claimed Forster for a liberal humanism that, for all its hesitancies and self-doubts, could be presented as the only alternative to the militant implacability of communism and fascism and to the no less repugnant imperialism of Americanized mass entertainment. But the critic who finally installed him as a landmark and touchstone of the liberal consciousness was the American Lionel Trilling, whose book on Forster first appeared in 1943, at the height of the war. For Trilling, too, Forster must be read in relation to 'what, for want of a better word, we may call the liberal tradition', a tradition he defines as 'that loose body of middle-class opinion which includes such ideas as progress, collectivism and humanitarianism' (Trilling 1944: 13). That definition suggests some of the distance between a North American liberal and an English one. In contrast to Leavis's 'free play of critical intelligence . . . humane, decent and rational', Trilling's liberalism sounds like a kind of Fabian socialism, with economic and social planning ('progress'), nationalization ('collectivism') and welfare for the needy ('humanitarianism'). In fact, Forster, a lifelong supporter of the British Labour Party, subscribed to all those things, which Leavis certainly did not. But the latter's appropriation of *A Passage to India* to his own campaign for the liberal decencies seems none the less closer to the grain and texture of Forster's thinking than Trilling's does; and that may be why the American critic can conclude that, in terms of his own understanding of the word, Forster is at once a liberal novelist and one 'deeply at odds with the liberal mind' (Trilling 1944: 14). Trilling's liberalism, indeed, sounds remarkably like the confident Victorianism that Forster satirized in his early novels and his friend Lytton Strachey pilloried in *Eminent Victorians* (1918). It is 'sure that the order of human affairs owes it a simple logic: good is good and bad is bad'. Against this, it is no surprise that he finds a profound ambivalence: 'For all his long commitment to the doctrines of liberalism, Forster is at war with the liberal imagination' (Trilling 1944: 14).

Nevertheless, Forster remains, for Trilling, a liberal novelist (which is something much more, clearly, than a novelist who happens to be a liberal), and more than a novelist. For him, as for Leavis, he is a beacon for the dark days, a talisman against fanaticism, hate and 'that acrid nationalism that literary men too often feel called upon to express in a time of crisis' (Trilling 1944: 23). The uncertainties and contradictions in his writing, the odd tensions and slippages between the everyday and the numinous, social comedy and transcendental insight, become, in this reading, merely the surface signs of his deep scrupulousness, his refusal of easy solutions and reach-me-down ideological nostrums, including liberal ones. Indeed, Trilling is concerned to vindicate precisely those apparent weaknesses against earlier critics, like

I.A. Richards, Rose Macaulay and Leavis himself, who saw them as failures of nerve or technique; a vindication he sets about by claiming ambivalence as itself a kind of integrity – the only kind possible, perhaps, in a world torn by competing ideological certainties. It is not difficult to see that such a view would appeal strongly to liberal intellectuals in the later 1940s and 1950s, the period of the cold war, the McCarthy witch-hunts of dissident intellectuals and the 'balance of terror' between aggressive North American capitalism and Stalinist state socialism; and Trilling's book was very influential in establishing a Forster congenial to their sensibilities. Even his failure to publish any new fiction after *Passage*, and what Trilling called his 'irritating refusal to be great' (Trilling 1944: 10), could be seen as a kind of heroism, a silent protest against the coercions of conformity and the treacheries of success.

Trilling's liberal-humanist Forster, a comic ironist with deeply serious commitments ('tolerance, good temper and sympathy', he wrote in 1939, 'they are what matter really') but only provisional convictions – the same essay, 'What I Believe', offered only 'Two cheers for Democracy . . . Two cheers are quite enough: there is no occasion to give three' (*TCD*, 75, 78) – this remained the dominant view of the novelist, in mainstream criticism at least, for three decades or more. It is a Forster not only humanist and agnostic – 'My law-givers are Erasmus and Montaigne, not Moses and St Paul' (*TCD*, 75) – but also, as those commitments imply, an aesthetic traditionalist, whose writerly affinities lie with Edwardian realism (or even earlier, with the admired Jane Austen) rather than with the mould-breaking experimentalism of modernists like Joyce or Woolf. Yet Forster's own criticism, and in particular his lectures on fiction published in 1927 as *Aspects of the Novel*, suggest a highly equivocal attachment to the deployments of character and incident typical of realist narrative. For the realist, fiction, however selective or complex or self-consciously organized and narrated, is essentially *story*. The lives of the characters, and the relationships between them, acquire meaning only through sequences of events organized in place and time. Time is the medium of memory, development, identity; place its inescapable location in a world the reader is asked to accept as real. Without the times and places in which their fictional lives unfold, the characters of realist novels, the Robinson Crusoes and Fanny Prices and David Copperfields and Maggie Tullivers, would be nothing but names; and the 'metonymic' titles of novels of this kind, which are almost invariably either personal names (*Jane Eyre, Tess of the D'Urbervilles*) or places (*Mansfield Park, The Mill on the Floss*), signify the genre's commitment to and immersion in the experience of time.[3]

For Forster, too, story, in which 'there is always a clock', is 'the fundamental aspect of the novel'. But it is an aspect acknowledged with misgiving, as in the famous opening disclaimer: 'Yes – oh dear yes – the novel tells a story.' And to the clock-time of story he opposes other narrative 'aspects': 'plot', which organizes the materials of the story not sequentially but causally; 'pattern', which gives a sense of timeless completion and wholeness; and 'rhythm', which conveys an underlying pulse and movement, 'time' in the musical rather than chronological sense (*AN*, 34 and *passim*).

Already in 1950, E.K. Brown had developed this last idea into a non-realist reading of *A Passage to India* in his *Rhythm in the Novel*, stressing not the obvious narrative sequences but recurrences (often seemingly trivial ones), analogies, repeated figures. Noting that the novel is divided into three sections or movements, Brown suggests that they 'warn of a meaning which goes behind story, people, even setting', a meaning expressed not through character or incident but through symbols (Brown 1950: 57–8). A few years later, Frank Kermode, while conceding with a Forsterish deprecation that *Passage* 'certainly tells a story', could argue that its author was none the less 'a kind of Symbolist', and attribute to him a litany of modernist convictions: 'for the autonomy of the work of art; for co-essence of form and meaning; for art as "organic and free from dead matter"; for music as a criterion of formal purity; for the work's essential anonymity' (Kermode, in Bradbury 1966: 90–1). A new interest in the formal structuring of Forster's fiction followed in the 1960s: its symbolism, its approximations to musical form, its syntax. But although this attention to form, symbol and structure, in a decade whose central critical concerns were defined by the neo-Aristotelian formalism of a book like Wayne C. Booth's *Rhetoric of Fiction* (1961) and the first stirrings of literary structuralism in the newly translated writings of Roland Barthes,[4] made Forster accessible to a modernist critical idiom schooled in Eliot and Joyce, the underlying subtext remained ethical and humanist. 'To pass beyond character, story, and setting' meant, for Brown, not to enter some Eliotic world of impersonal forms and ghostly intuitions, still less to reflect on the political and social forces invisibly but irresistibly shaping character and story, but 'to feel that numinous element so constantly present in the experience of the great man whom in these discourses I have wished to honour' (Brown 1950: 115); while for Kermode, the symbolism of *Passage* recalls us to 'the truth of imagination which Mr Forster calls "love" ', through which 'muddle turns into mystery: into art, our one orderly product' (Bradbury 1966: 95).

Here criticism threatens to pass into hagiography, with undertones of religiosity that might have surprised and would certainly have embarrassed the agnostic Forster. But even when the reverential tone is absent, the same tendency to find a formal-symbolic unity and integration in the text, a structural patterning that reconciles all its conflicts and muddles, has continued to characterize much British and American criticism. George H. Thomson, one of the first writers on Forster to have access to the manuscripts of *Passage* acquired by the University of Texas in 1960, draws on Jungian notions of archetype to claim the novel for a tradition of 'mythic' narrative, motivated not by the relationships and conflict of individuals in historical place or time but by the search for ecstatic transcendence (Thomson 1967). Wilfred Stone's *The Cave and the Mountain* (1966), perhaps the dominant academic Forster book of the 1960s, as Trilling's was for the 1940s, makes an influential case for the overall unity of the novel, beneath the failures of connection and fallings-apart of the narrative (Stone 1966). All such readings, playing down the book's ostensibly 'realist' preoccupations with character and story – Thomson declares flatly that Forster does not 'belong in the realist tradition', (Thomson 1967: 16) – in favour of an integrative 'deep structure' of myth, symbol or archetype, inevitably minimize the political dimensions of the text. John Colmer, indeed, detecting a shaping dialectic of 'promise and withdrawal', dismisses politically motivated criticism of the novel such as Chaudhuri's as irrelevant, 'confusing the difference between the facts of history and the truths of art', and asserts that 'the three-part symphonic form finally reconciles the opposites' (Das and Beer 1979: 128).

Colmer would no doubt quote Forster himself in support of at least the first part of that statement. In 'Three Countries', an unpublished essay, Forster wrote:

> the book is not really about politics . . . It's about something wider than politics, about the search of the human race for a more lasting home . . . It is – or rather desires to be – philosophic and poetic.
>
> (*HD*, 298)

It might be retorted that a novel, without being expressly 'about politics', can have political implications and effects quite unintended and unforeseen by the novelist, and that Forster was writing here simply as another reader, albeit of his own text, a reader not necessarily more (or less) authoritative than any other. In any event, to describe the novel as a 'search' falls well short of claiming that it 'reconciles the opposites'. During the 1970s a new critical emphasis begins to emerge, marked by a concern for precisely those features of the text that remain problematic, open-ended, unreconciled. An interesting transitional case is the collection of centenary essays edited by G.K. Das and John Beer, *E.M. Forster: A Human Exploration* (1979), in which Colmer's 'promise and withdrawal' piece appeared. The title, like the occasion (the centenary of Forster's birth) holds out the promise of another undemanding ramble around the liberal-humanist pieties, complete with affectionate anecdotes and perhaps even a few nostalgic snapshots of 'Morgan' himself, the tone of the whole thing perfectly suggested by the opening of an essay in another of the commemorative collections:

> Were Henry James to have a celestial tea party, inviting Henry Fielding, Laurence Sterne, Jane Austen, Emily Brontë, George Eliot, William Makepeace Thackeray, Joseph Conrad and E.M. Forster, no doubt, as James himself might say, contradiction would grow 'young again over tea cups and cigars'. One can imagine the restless spoons if the conversation turned to the role of the narrator in the novel . . .
>
> (Herz and Martin 1982: 167)

In fact, the Das–Beer volume turns out to be something rather different. The 1970s saw three developments, all of which were to have a major impact on the study of Forster. The first is the much greater openness, following his death in 1971 and especially the publication in 1977–8 of P.N. Furbank's two-volume biography, with which his homosexuality, and its implications for his writing, could be discussed, in a period in which the whole question of gay writing, past and present, was moving into the critical foreground for the first time. Neither *Maurice* nor the erotic stories collected in *The Life to Come* had been published in Forster's lifetime, although their existence was widely known. But now critics whose claims for 'connection' had rested on heterosexual relations (Schlegel–Wilcox, Fielding–Moore), the fallings-in-love and happy marriages that conclude romantic fiction from the Brontës to *Brookside*, had to ask how securely such resolutions of difference and conflict could be taken, from a writer unable or unwilling publicly to represent human connectedness in the form most immediately important to him.[5] At the same time, the availability of the manuscripts of *Passage*, to scholars since the 1960s but more widely in Oliver Stallybrass's Abinger edition

(1978), not only provided, at last, a reliable text of the novel but also opened up the process of its writing in ways that helped to challenge the critical fiction of a seamless textual unity. And thirdly, the practice of criticism itself was being irreversibly transformed by 'theory', above all by feminism, post-Freudian psychoanalysis and deconstruction. At the tea party convened by Das and Beer, the guests, or ghosts, are not Dickens and Thackeray but Irigaray, Lacan and Derrida, and the effect is anything but cosy.

Some of the pieces in the collection, as we have seen, cling to the familiar humanist preoccupations, still looking for a single integrative reading grounded in some fundamental human truth (if only the truth of difference, mystery or muddle). But Benita Parry, already the author of the valuable *Delusions and Discoveries: Studies on India in the British Imagination, 1880–1930* (1972), insists, in an important essay, on the historically and politically intractable nature of the material *Passage* is attempting to organize and reconcile, and on the text's own bafflement and helplessness in the face of it. Unlike Leavis, Trilling or Stone, Parry finds in the novel not an expression and vindication of the 'liberal spirit' but its defeated 'epitaph', and she offers her own explanation of Forster's subsequent silence as a novelist:

> He was at the height of his powers and he wrote no more novels
> . . . Forster retired to essays, criticism, biography and broadcasts,
> forms through which it was still possible to state his belief in
> liberal values, in full knowledge that the ideology sustaining these
> had been drained of vitality and was without relevance to the
> changing historical situation.
>
> (Das and Beer 1979: 141)

This analysis, which not only insists on the indispensable relevance of the 'changing historical situation' to the study of literature but also makes it integral to the structure and meaning of literary texts, recalls the priorities of Marxist criticism, from Georg Lukács, writing in the 1930s, to contemporaries like Fredric Jameson. And the influence of theoretically-informed critique is even more clearly visible in the revised version of the same essay that Benita Parry contributed to a later collection, again edited by John Beer (1985). Here, drawing on Edward Said's very influential study of the way in which the idea of 'the Orient' was constructed (by travellers, scholars, novelists, poets and administrators) and deployed as a justificatory discourse of conquest and domination (Said 1978), she is able to give theoretical and political weight to her earlier analysis of the contradictions and ambiguities in the novel, arguing that it 'can be seen as at once inheriting and interrogating the discourses of the Raj' (Beer 1985: 27). The importance of Said's book, itself influenced by the work of the French philosopher-historian Michel Foucault, lay in its contention that power was exercised not only by the direct agencies of government, law, police and military but also through the intangible reticulations of 'discourse' – the complex and pervasive interweavings of language, text, knowledge that form the basis of our understanding of the world.

Such a view restores texts – which earlier Marxisms had sometimes tended to relegate to a subordinate or 'superstructural' function, mere reflections or distortions of social reality – to an active role in the process of making and enforcing meanings. In contrast to a critical tradition which has seen Forster's novel as having, at most, a rather distanced relationship with political practice, and often as having none at all, Parry argues for 'another mode of analysis, where the articulations of the fiction are related to the system of textual practices by which the metropolitan culture exercised its domination over the subordinate periphery' (Beer 1985: 27–8). And although those dominative textual practices include the novel's occasional, seemingly inadvertent endorsements of racial stereotype – 'The celebrated oriental confusion appeared at last to be at an end' (*PI*, 122); 'Like most Orientals, Aziz overrated hospitality' (*PI*, 134) – its involvement in the discourse of the imperial power is less an effect of such incidental, if revealing, comments than of the narrative voice and genre themselves:

> Written from within the liberal-humanist ideology, and in its realist aspect using the style of ironic commentary and measured ethical judgement, the fiction does act to legitimate the authorised categories of the English bourgeois world.
>
> (Beer 1985: 28–9)

To couple liberal humanism to the very ideology it most despises through the medium of a narrative genre (realism) in this way may seem theoretically adventurous and controversial. But even for Parry, impatient as she is of claims for Forster's celebrated even handedness, the novel retains a crucial ambivalence, a critical edge, however compromised. Sharing something of the 'ontological puzzlement' of modernist writing, it enacts a 'colloquy' (a word that recalls Mikhail Bakhtin's account of the 'dialogism' of language and narrative[6]) between Western thought and language and an India neither monstrous nor exotic but simply *there*. 'What is absent', however, 'is a consciousness of imperialism as capitalism's expansive, conquering moment, and the enunciated critique of the Raj is consequently toned down' (Beer 1985: 29).

Parry's essay is informed by a developed Marxism not shared by all the contributors to the volume. For the editor, the constantly shifting idioms, registers and points of view betoken not ideological confusion or desperation but the generous abundance of 'interpretative possibilities' of a 'meditative novel that reflects not only on the world but on fiction itself'. But if this recalls a traditional critical mode, Gillian Beer finds in the novel striking confirmation of the deconstructive insights of poststructuralism and reader-response theory. The French Marxist Pierre Macherey argued, in *A Theory of Literary Production* (1978), that the meaning of a novel, its real relationship with the ideologies that determine it, is to be found not in what it says but in what it cannot permit itself to say, the critic's task being to reconstruct that hidden or repressed meaning by attending to the gaps, hesitancies, incoherences that betray the effort of repression. For the German reception-theorist Wolfgang Iser (1978), on the other hand, the 'meaning' of a text is to be found not in the text itself, in some absolute sense, but in the 'performances' through which it is activized in the minds of its readers. Thus, we may conclude, a text has not one meaning but many, no one of which – not even the author's own – can lay claim to special authority as the 'correct' one. So for Gillian Beer, *Passage* 'seemed almost too simply to confirm what Macherey, say, or Iser . . . had been telling us. *A Passage to India* is, after all, a book *about* gaps, fissures, absences, and exclusions' (Beer 1985: 45). As with Parry, there is a decisive shift here away from an author-centred reading, in which the meaning derives from or stands in a privileged relation to Forster's intentions, opinions and personality, towards a text-centred one, in which meaning is generated by the narrative and linguistic activity of the text as it is mobilized in the act of reading. Such meanings, not referable to a single authoritative source, will never be single or stable, but must always be as plural and fluid as the readers who produce them and the circumstances in which they do so. Thus there can never be, from this 'poststructuralist' standpoint, a single central truth of the kind that Forster sought and that some of his readers have hoped to find, not in texts, not in language itself. It is in these terms, rather than in any expression of opinion or presentational attitude, that Gillian Beer finds in the novel a radical questioning not only of British rule in India but also of the humanist verities themselves:

> Forster's work presages the end of Empire, not simply the end of the Raj in India (though it does that), but also the end of that struggle for dominion which is implicit in the struggle for

language and meaning – the struggle to keep man at the centre of the universe.

And that too, she recognizes, is not a 'truth' about the text but a particular reading of it, a reading available to us by virtue of our own historical difference from Forster's contemporaries:

> But it was not the readers of the 1920s who saw it thus: it is we sixty years later who can recognize this 'pressentiment collectif, projet, aspiration' [Macherey]. And we can do so by studying not what is absent, but what is there: the language of the text.
>
> (Beer 1985: 58)

This appeal to 'the language of the text' might, in another context, look like a return from ideological and historical questions to the old 'text-in-itself' preoccupations of New Criticism. But the text, for Beer, can no longer be regarded as a positive and unambiguous presence, replete with meanings waiting to be released by an attentive, sympathetic reading. What is 'there' is a tissue of self-cancelling 'negativities', inviting the reader to search for meaning in the very act of rendering all meaning unstable, as elusive and insubstantial as those mirages, echoes and hallucinations that haunt the narrative and bemuse or dispirit the characters in *their* search for closure, connection and significance. 'What could she connect it with except its own name?', wonders Mrs Moore about a town glimpsed from the train. 'Nothing' (*PI*, 199). Words and meanings slide apart, and for characters and readers alike the language of the text offers not a secure anchorage for understanding but a series of what deconstruction calls 'aporias' and Forster calls 'muddles': unanswerable questions, riddles, paradoxes, the worm that eats its own tail.

Traditionally, the paradigm of disconnection and aporia is the relation between East and West itself, the irreconcilable polarities of Kipling's poem: 'Oh, East is East, and West is West, and never the twain shall meet' ('The Ballad of East and West' (1889), Kipling 1940: 234). This view, which in the novel's Turtons, Burtons and McBrydes slides so effortlessly into assumptions of racial superiority, could not of course ever be Forster's own. The novel grew out of his love of India and testifies to it on every page; and the dedication to his one-time pupil Syed Ross Masood reminds us that his love was no touristy sentimentality but a lifelong commitment rooted in personal affections of the most intense kind. And yet the novel seems unable entirely to extricate itself from a kind of generalizing 'Orientalism' that recalls not so much Kipling as Superintendent McBryde, that 'most reflective and best educated of the Chandrapore officials' and forensic expert in 'Oriental Pathology' (*PI*, 158, 208). Some examples have already been quoted; but the symptomatic slippage from particular to general, and the attribution of contradiction and muddle not merely to this or that character but to 'the Oriental' as a whole, is well illustrated by the passage describing Aziz's suspicion that Fielding has persuaded him not to press his defamation suit against Adela Quested because she is his mistress:

> Aziz did not believe his own suspicions – better if he had, for then he would have denounced and cleared the situation up. Suspicion and belief could in his mind exist side by side. They sprang from different sources, and need never intermingle. Suspicion in the Oriental is a sort of malignant tumour, a mental malady, that makes him self-conscious and unfriendly suddenly; he trusts and mistrusts at the same time in a way the Westerner cannot comprehend. It is his demon, as the Westerner's is hypocrisy.
>
> (*PI*, 267)

Faced with a passage like this, we must ask: who is speaking here, from what point of view and with what kind of authority? The paragraph in which it occurs begins, in a recognizable realist convention, with free indirect speech – the character's thoughts rendered in third-person narrative: 'Aziz sighed. Each for himself. One man needs a coat, another a rich wife . . .'. But in 'better if he had . . .' the narrative position (and therefore the reader's, too) has shifted; Aziz is no longer the subject of the narration but the object of an explanatory commentary that views him from outside – views not only Aziz himself, as a typical specimen of 'the Oriental', but the entire East–West dichotomy from outside. For if 'the Oriental' is to operate convincingly as an explanatory category, it requires another, 'the Westerner', to operate as its antitype; and the text is thus in the extraordinary position, McBryde-like, of explaining to its 'Oriental' and its 'Western' readers alike something that neither of them can possibly 'comprehend'.

We have here a striking example of what Colin MacCabe, in his analysis of 'classic realism', calls a 'hierarchy of discourses', in which the quirks and muddles of characters unable to understand themselves are explained by an 'omniscient' narration with a privileged access to general truth.[7] But we have at the same time a graphic demonstration of the absurdity and contradiction into which the realist mode itself has been driven, since this text which offers to explain to us something 'the Westerner cannot comprehend' is itself written by a 'Westerner' for a readership, largely, of Westerners. Furthermore, the polarities established here are neither symmetrical nor reversible. The relation between East and West is not, clearly, one of mutually uncomprehending parity, since the Westerner claims the authority to understand not only the Oriental (for whom no reciprocal understanding is possible), but also *his own inability to understand*. The discourse of East and West, like all discourse, embodies both knowledge and, inextricably, power – the power to comprehend, to explain, to rule; and the text, search as it might for some humanist transcendence, connection, equality beyond politics, is trapped finally in the grim polarities and muddles of imperial power.

Ah yes, it might be said, but that reading is surely too uncompromising. The novel ends not with a 'never' but with a 'not yet', and we should not rule out the possibility that Fielding and Aziz, or their children or grandchildren, *will* be friends some day. In response it is worth quoting the whole of Kipling's famous stanza.

> Oh, East is East, and West is West, and never the twain shall meet,
> Till Earth and Sky stand presently at God's great Judgment seat;
> But there is neither East nor West, Border, nor Breed, nor Birth,
> When two strong men stand face to face, though they come from the ends of the earth!

Kipling and Forster, though not dissimilar in background and upbringing, are chalk and cheese, temperamentally and ideologically; and this kind of populist tub-thumping is as unlike the cool ironic obliquity of *A Passage to India* as can be imagined. But the two are not as far apart in some respects as is sometimes supposed. For Forster, too, the intractable oppositions of racial difference will give way only to something stronger still: the relationship between men. *Men*, we note, not *people*. Not for Forster the shrill muscular-Christian masculinity of Kipling's 'two strong men'; but as Parminder Bakshi and Bette London remind us in their essays in this volume, the bond between the widower Aziz and the bachelor Fielding is grounded in a 'homosocial' solidarity that requires for its easy intimacy the absolute exclusion of women. The former finds Mrs Moore and Adela 'easy to talk to', and is thus able, charmingly, to treat them 'like men', because they are not, for him, women at all, the first too old, the second too ugly (*PI*, 61). And the friendship between the two men is endangered, perhaps permanently damaged, by women: Aziz's suspicions, mentioned earlier, about his friend's relationship with Adela, and Fielding's marriage to Ronny

Heaslop's stepsister Stella, which makes him, in Aziz's eyes, a member of the hated Anglo-Indian ruling caste. Thus the text is able to achieve one form of connection, between Indian and Englishman, only at the cost of a greater rupture, between men and women.

If there is a 'hierarchy of discourses' here, it is not difficult to see that at its apex is a position, an authoritative point of view, that can only be described as white and male. That there is an organic affinity between these two dominative viewpoints of whiteness and maleness can be illustrated by rewriting the passage just quoted to show – as Sara Mills argues more fully in her essay later in this book – just how easily the categories of 'woman' and 'Oriental' can be substituted or super-imposed:

> She did not believe her own suspicions – better if she had, for then she would have denounced and cleared the situation up. Suspicion and belief could in her mind exist side by side. They sprang from different sources, and need never intermingle. Suspicion in a woman is a sort of malignant tumour, a mental malady, that makes her self-conscious and unfriendly suddenly; she trusts and mistrusts at the same time in a way a man cannot comprehend. It is her demon, as a man's is hypocrisy.

How easily this could come from some novelettish account of womanly jealousy – the only incongruous note, arguably, being the word 'unfriendly', belonging as it does to the vocabulary of male camaraderie.

To read the novel in this way, teasing out its unacknowledged as well as its professed anxieties, complicities and muddles, is to acknowledge the extent to which our reading has been shaped, in the years that divide us from its first publication, by practices of reading that are neither white nor male: by feminist criticism, and by what has come to be called 'subaltern studies' – the reading of the texts of the dominant imperial culture from the standpoint of those who were its victims, not its victors, who had no hand in the production of those texts and who therefore appear in them only as an absence or a misrepresentation. Those two critical practices have themselves entered into a dialogue, one not without its own tensions and abrasions but richly productive never-theless, which looks likely to shape innovative critical debate well into the next millennium. Their effects are to be seen in all the essays in this collection, which for all their diversity of idioms and perspectives share a number of common assumptions. It might be helpful to spell these out a little more clearly.

First, in a series that bears the general rubric *Theory in Practice*, it is appropriate to say something about the question of 'theory' itself. A few years ago we used to hear a lot about the supposed invasion of literary studies, and other disciplines, by an alien monster called Theory. One bite from this body-snatcher could turn a normal, decent literary critic into a rabid theorist, gabbling in an incomprehensible mid-Atlantic *franglais* about the superiority of beermats and Kellogg's cereal packets to Browning and Keats. For some, Theory was just a hot-air machine for inflating the egos and career prospects of ambitious academics who did not in fact much like reading books. For others, it was simply the old bugbear Politics (usually left-wing, just occasionally rightist) in disguise. Either way, it was a threat to civilization as we know it, and ought to be stamped out.[8] Nowadays one is more likely to be told that Theory in all its forms – Marxist, feminist, psychoanalytic, deconstructionist – is old hat, discredited, played out. We are living now, so it goes, in the age of the 'post' – post-Marxist, post-feminist, postmodern – an age that has seen the end of ideology, even of history itself.[9] As a mithridate against this sort of nonsense, it is worth remembering that the Greek word *theoria* denotes not some polysyllabic deformity of the mental faculties but the kind of thing people do in a theatre, a picture-gallery, a sports event: it means 'spectating'. This obviously implies a distinction between the spectator and those actually performing, painting or playing on the pitch, a distinction expressed in Greek by the difference between *theoria* and *praxis*, practical productive activity. Unlike the performer, the 'theorist' or spectator has a certain speculative detachment, albeit an active one informed by interest in and knowledge of what is being observed. Above all, it implies a point of view from which the activity is being observed. I do not want to press the metaphorical analogy too far, not least because there is a danger of losing sight of the fact that theory is itself a form of practice, a textualization, no less than that which it theorizes; but it should at least suggest that theory is something everybody has and does. (To paraphrase Antonio Gramsci slightly, everybody is a theorist, but only some people practise it as a specialized function.[10]) If a theory is simply a position, a point of view, then it is clear that 'not having a theory' is a theory like any other, except that it does not (or may not choose to) know that it is. Yet the hostility to theory is generally based on nothing more substantial than a sort of cheery, no-nonsense common sense (a powerful theory, that, especially in England) that imagines you can get along perfectly well without it.

Any reading, then, is positioned and informed, more or less

consciously and coherently, by a 'theory': a standpoint, a set of expectations, a mode of interest. The four essays that make up the bulk of this
volume differ from the sort of 'non-theoretical' criticism found in, say,
some of the centenary collections discussed earlier only in the explicit-
ness with which they formulate their theoretical standpoint and the
questions and implications that flow from taking that particular position in the stands or the auditorium. But it must follow from that
recognition that, although in one sense all readers are reading the same
text as all the spectators are watching the same game, that 'sameness'
is actually a rather abstract notion. In reality, texts, like football
matches or dramatic performances, can give rise in different readers/
spectators to very different ideas not only about the relative significance
of this or that part but about what actually happened; and we shall
understand those differences better if we know something of the position in the stand and the individual or collective interests and prejudices
of the people – the readings – that they represent. The defence of a
theoretically-informed reading of the kind offered here, then, is not that
theory is better or cleverer or more exciting or more politically correct
than non-theory, but that it is unavoidable, and that it is generally
better to understand what you are doing and why than not to.

Secondly, a word about *history*. Gillian Beer argued that her reading
of the self-deconstructive negativities of *A Passage to India* was possible
only because of changes to the critical agenda since the 1920s brought
about by, principally, feminism, Marxism and reception theory. This
perception of reading not as a timeless communing with great authors
but as a historically staged encounter, in which text and reader are the
product of different historical moments and of the difference between
them, has been an important aspect of the critical enterprise called,
variously, 'new historicism' or 'cultural materialism'. There was a tendency, in the 'old historicism' (in certain strands of academic Marxism,
for example, as well as in non-Marxist literary history), to assume that
although the author and text were 'historical' the critic was not; that
the historicity of the text (discernible in its language, genre, narrative
structure, thematic preoccupations and so on) could be explained from
a standpoint above or outside history, resulting in a reading that
appeared to claim for itself an absolute, transhistorical validity and
objectivity. There are interesting similarities between this kind of
criticism, which aspires to stand above the historical fray in which texts
are produced, and the Olympian impassivity of classic realism. Both, for
example, use, alongside the narrative past tense, a commentary present
tense ('Forster implies here . . .') to indicate that although the text/

narrative lies in the past, the critic/narrator's interpretation of it occupies an unchanging present. Both deploy varieties of the inclusive 'we' (something I have not always avoided myself in this introduction) to link critic/narrator and reader (*any* reader) in a shared perspective and a unified point of view. Both treat the text/story as an unselfcomprehending raw material, waiting to be released into coherence and meaning by the transformative touch of the critic/narrator's commentary. In this way do they both efface difference – historical, cultural, sexual, ideological – in the interests of identity (we *are* the same, aren't we, you and I?) and recognition (this *is* how things are, isn't it?).

The essays here, by contrast, make no bones about it: each one represents a fully conscious historical intervention, informed by a set of contemporary (1990s) concerns and interests – in ethnicity, in gender, in sexuality, in the politics of representation. None seeks to lay claim to a definitive finality; indeed, 'finality' represents the very reverse of what they offer, for which 'openness' and 'difference' suggest a better rubric. Opening the text up and out to the questions it could not or would not, historically and ideologically, ask itself, the readings they produce are able to acknowledge the plurality and difference that it both celebrates and fears without trying to reduce them to some new critical synthesis or closure; the plurality and difference that haunt the unhappy, defeated Mrs Moore, and that the novel can only represent finally, with a kind of wry regret, as incoherence and muddle:

> She would never visit Asirgarh or the other untouched places; neither Delhi nor Agra nor the Rajputana cities nor Kashmir, nor the obscurer marvels that had sometimes shone through men's speech: the bilingual rock of Girnar, the statue of Shri Belgola, the ruins of Mandu and Hampi, temples of Khajuraho, gardens of Shalimar. As she drove through the huge city which the West has built and abandoned with a gesture of despair, she longed to stop, though it was only Bombay, and disentangle the hundred Indias that passed each other in its streets. The feet of the horses moved her on, and presently the boat sailed and thousands of cocoanut palms appeared all round the anchorage and climbed the hills to wave her farewell. 'So you thought an echo was India; you took the Marabar Caves as final?' they laughed. 'What have we in common with them, or they with Asirgarh? . . .'
>
> (*PI*, 199–200)

'What have we in common with them . . . ?': the question is a political as well as an ontological one. If India is to 'rank with Guatemala and

Belgium', as Cyril Fielding sardonically puts it, is to become, that is, an independent and unified nation-state, then the question of connection, between Bombay, Marabar and Asirgarh, between Muslim, Hindu and Sikh, cannot be avoided. Aziz is, or pretends to be, confident: 'India shall be a nation! . . . Hindu and Moslem and Sikh and all shall be one! Hurrah!' (PI, 312) But Forster, like Fielding, remained sceptical – a scepticism that may seem to have been historically justified, though neither could foresee in 1924 the consequences that would follow from the decision of the retreating British to repeat the Irish tactic of partition. In any case, the continuing immediacy and intractability, seventy years later, of the issue of nationhood suggest one answer, an important though by no means the only one, to the question that is raised, directly or implicitly, by all these essays: why study A Passage to India now?

It is not the purpose of this introduction to attempt a conclusive answer to that question, even if such a thing were possible. Few, nowadays, would be likely to reply, with Leavis, that it should be studied because it is 'a classic of the liberal spirit', though its secure canonical status as such means that for many students the first answer will be 'because we have to – it's on the syllabus'. The idea of the 'classic', like the 'liberal spirit' itself, has been much contested in recent years, and the four essays that follow all start from the position that no useful understanding will follow from taking such notions at face value. But they all testify, too, to a conviction that a reading of Passage can still be both a necessary and a productive encounter: necessary, because – as the success of Paul Scott's Raj Quartet (1976) and its subsequent television adaptation as The Jewel in the Crown, which transposes several of the novel's motifs (rape, wrongful arrest, trial) and its liberal gloom at Indian 'muddle' to a post-independence setting, reminds us – Forster's novel continues to shape and inform 'Western' reflections on imperialism and its aftermath, within which we all live; productive, because the readings they offer move beyond the merely nostalgic or narcissistic 'pleasure of the text'[11] towards a critical practice grounded in the irreducibility of difference and the inevitability of change.

CHAPTER 1

The Politics of Desire: E.M. Forster's Encounters with India

PARMINDER BAKSHI

[Edward Said's *Orientalism* (1978) has inaugurated great interest in the rhetoric and practice of colonial cultural authority. In defining the Orient Westerners shore up their own identity, as 'Orientalism [is] a Western style for dominating, restructuring, and having authority over the Orient' (Said 1978: 3). In this, it resembles the *hegemonic* control described by Antonio Gramsci (see headnote to Chapter 2, this volume; and Said 1978: 7), where the Orient is a 'European invention . . . [representing for home consumption] a place of romance, exotic beings, haunting memories and landscapes, remarkable experiences' (Said 1978: 1). Its power stems from its apparently unpolitical and 'imaginative' figurative devices, and yet it is profoundly motivated, as no knowledge is ever produced in a vacuum (see Said 1978: 9–15).

In this, Said's conception of Orientalist ideology resembles the very basis of all discourses as described by Michel Foucault in *The Archaeology of Knowledge* (1972). 'Truth' is what is understood to be so according to the available linguistic and cultural formations that are tacit guarantors of its recognition; a particular discourse therefore provides the conditions in which 'truth' may be formed for a specific culture (see Foucault 1972: 23–55). For Said the differences between discourses are not merely historical ones, as they can just as crucially change when transplanted. In his essay, 'Traveling Theory' (Said 1984: 226–47), he puts the case that an idea may appear to be untranslated when received in a foreign culture, yet the purposes to which it may be put and disseminated in this new (and unpredicted) discursive formation are central issues. (It should also be noted how this forms an alternative to the more totalizing history described by Foucault. For Said any historical moment is composed of a myriad of emergent as well as hege-monic voices (see Abdul J. Janmohamed, 'The Specular Border Intellectual', in Sprinker 1992: esp. 100–20; and Said 1984: 239–41).)

For Parminder Bakshi, Said's account is suggestive rather than exhaustive, as her essay attempts to describe how the appropriation of the Orient by the West for the display and exploration of forbidden desires intersects with Forster's own (necessarily private) homosexual interests. This is more than the simple recognition that *A Passage to India*'s dedicatee is an Indian friend, Syed Ross Masood, as she notes resemblances between the Italian landscapes and cultures from previous novels and those of India. The initially alien manners observed abroad highlight as well as confront (by proxy) Anglo-Saxon atti-tudes, not just to homosexuality, but also to the enduring virtues of male friendship. Marriage is a social necessity, and, as such, is common and an obligation; friendship, on the other hand, is rare and fragile – and so more precious.

In Rana Kabbani's *Europe's Myths of Orient: Devise and Rule* (1986) this link between the sexual and the distant-exotic is examined for its often reciprocal power: the traveller's tale depicts the foreign with the heightened energy usually deployed in sexual descriptions, and the prurient often derives from metaphors of exploration. Signifier and signified are rarely distinct. One result of this preoccupation is the production of the patriarchal female, however the viewer may have encountered her in 'native' (that is, alien) contexts – all submissiveness, reduced to 'body, to possession, to physical object . . . the foreignness of the tales excusing their unseemliness' (Kabbani 1986: 64). Forster is not above describing women in this functional way. Some of the generalized portraits of worried Anglo-Indian Club life gain their satiric preci-sion from the depiction of threatened women, yet the opportunities for a sentimental herd instinct derive as much from the patriarchal defence of the status quo as from the preservation of all that may seem worthy about Anglo-India (see *PI*, 171–4), and his net comment on this surely invalidates the heterosexual authority of the McBrydes and Callendars as well as it relegates the feminine objects of their concern just to body and emotion.

For Bakshi, a reading of Forster's work is destined to be partial and often erroneous if the private narrative codes that stem from the homo-erotic are ignored.]

NIGEL WOOD

This essay attempts to illustrate how *A Passage to India* was written in the tradition of what Edward W. Said has called 'Orientalism'. While the novel displays some of the crucial characteristics of an Oriental text as defined by Said, Forster's interest in India is also specifically homo-erotic. Both in the writing and reception of the novel, *A Passage to India* was caught in the tensions between homo-erotic desire latent in the text and the overt, contemporary political context of the narrative. One implication of this tension between the political and the erotic aspects of the novel is that the position of Forster's work within Orientalism, in terms of the cultural values it conveys, is problematic.

According to Said, Orientalism is a peculiarly Western disposition, 'a style of thought based upon an ontological and epistemological distinction made between "the Orient" and (most of the time) "the Occident" ' (Said 1978: 2). The Western engagement with Orientalism, dating from Homer's time to the present day, constitutes a long tradition directed towards appropriating the Orient. Orientalism entails not just speaking *of* the Orient, but speaking *for* it and representing it. Orientalist discourse is supported by socio-economic and political institutions, which together work towards portraying the Orient as the Other to Europe while simultaneously subordinating it (Said 1978: 6). Although Said deals primarily with the Western attitudes to the Middle East and Islam, he points out that, during the early nineteenth century, the 'Orient' 'had really meant only India and the Bible lands' and until the Second World War, 'France and Britain dominated the Orient and Orientalism' (Said 1978: 4). Said's exposition, therefore, rests on the fundamental premise of the territorial, imaginative, cultural and ideological boundary drawn between the West and the Orient and the use to which this distinction is put. He argues that, while such relations have passed through numerous phases, it is a constant historical factor that 'in general it was the West that moved upon the East, not vice versa'. 'Orientalism' describes this approach in generic terms, both 'as a topic of learning, discovery, and practice' and also

> to designate that collection of dreams, images, and vocabularies available to anyone who has tried to talk about what lies east of the dividing line. These two aspects of Orientalism are not incongruent, since by use of them both Europe could advance securely and unmetaphorically upon the Orient.
>
> (Said 1978: 73)

Orientalism is thus a combined product of material and intellectual forces, and *A Passage to India* is part of this process of 'dynamic exchange between individual authors and the large political concerns shaped by the three great empires – British, French, American – in whose intellectual and imaginative territory the writing was produced' (Said 1978: 14–15).

Drawing on the complex link between Oriental texts and political circumstances, the one reinforcing the other,[1] it is notable that the Middle East or near Orient provided an exception to Western domination of the Orient. For example, the Ottoman Empire had posed a threat to Christian Europe in the sixteenth century, and during colonization the Arab countries occupied a particularly strategic place in the Western scramble for the Orient.[2] This evoked feelings of hatred and fear:

> Access to Indian (Oriental) riches had always to be made by first crossing the Islamic provinces and by withstanding the dangerous effect of Islam as a system of quasi-Arian belief. And at least for the larger segment of the eighteenth century, Britain and France were successful . . . Britain and France had fought each other in India between 1744 and 1748 and again between 1756 and 1763, until, in 1769, the British emerged in practical economic and political control of the subcontinent. What was more inevitable than that Napoleon should choose to harass Britain's Oriental empire by first intercepting its Islamic throughway, Egypt?
>
> (Said 1978: 76)

One way of overcoming this fear was to represent the figure of the Arab for Western consumption. Not just Islam, but all knowledge of the Orient as exotic and alien went through a process of domestication, of superstructural filters to provide 'a simulacrum of the Orient and reproduce it materially in the West, for the West' (Said 1978: 166).

While imperative to political control, however, Orientalism also served partly to reflect the fears and insecurity of Western society, for 'Orientalism is a form of paranoia, knowledge of another kind, say, from ordinary historical knowledge' (Said 1978: 72). Thus, it is notable that the Orient is invariably rendered in exaggerated, distorted and unreal terms. As Said explains:

> The Orient was overvalued for its pantheism, its spirituality, its stability, its longevity, its primitivity, and so forth . . . Yet almost without exception such overesteem was followed by a counterresponse: the Orient suddenly appeared lamentably underhumanized, antidemocratic, backward, barbaric, and so forth. A swing of the pendulum in one direction caused an equal and opposite swing back: the Orient was undervalued. Orientalism as a profession grew out of these opposites, of compensations and corrections based on inequality, ideas nourished by and nourishing similar ideas in the culture at large.
>
> (Said 1978: 150)

The Oriental enterprise is socially, economically, politically as well as sexually significant. The Orient frequently acted as a realm of sexual fantasy. The 'embourgeoisement' and regulation of sex in nineteenth-century Europe led Western writers to associate the Orient with licentiousness. Said remarks that after 1800, many European writers sought in the East sexual experiences that had become unobtainable in Europe: 'What they looked for often – correctly, I think – was a different type of sexuality, perhaps more libertine and less guilt-ridden' (Said 1978: 190). Thus, Orientalism in its numerous forms acts to benefit the West and is not for the sake of the countries that constitute the Orient.

An essential condition of Orientalism is that the Orientalist does not belong to the Orient. Confronted with an unfamiliar civilization, the Orientalist scholar, 'reduced the obscurity by translating, sympathetically portraying, inwardly grasping the hard-to-reach object. Yet the Orientalist remained outside the Orient, which however much it was made to appear intelligible, remained beyond the Occident.' The distance between the Orient and the Occident invariably found expression in 'metaphors of depth and secrecy, and sexual promise: phrases like "the veils of an Eastern bride" or "the inscrutable Orient" passed into the common language' (Said 1978: 222). The convergence of sexual and racial difference here is significant and one to which I will return. The crucial point is that Orientalist discourse is based on the 'exteriority' of the Orientalist to his/her subject, and as such 'the written statement is a presence to the reader by virtue of its having excluded, displaced, made supererogatory any such *real thing* as "the Orient" ' (Said 1978: 21). Orientalism is concerned not with the actual or the particular but with generalizations, flourishing 'rather on its internal, repetitious consistence about its constitutive will-to-power over the Orient' (Said 1978: 222).

Oriental discourse, therefore, is entirely self-constituting, and establishes political power by impersonalizing the Orient, 'neither interested in nor capable of discussing individuals; instead artificial entities' (Said 1978: 154). Said concludes:

> I consider Orientalism's failure to have been a human as much as an intellectual one; for in having to take up a position of irreducible opposition to a region of the world it considered alien to its own, Orientalism failed to identify with human experience, failed also to see it as human experience.
>
> (Said 1978: 328)

Said's analysis is illuminating, and he effectively confronts the issues of European and American imperialism which continue to determine world affairs today. However, it is necessary to make three main points about Said's work: first, that Orientalism is seen almost entirely in male terms; second, that the Orient is presented as a passive and silent recipient of Western constructs; and third, that Orientalism is treated as an all-encompassing, unified concept. Said addresses these matters in his recent study, *Culture and Imperialism* (1993). The book widens its scope from Orientalism to imperialism and even includes an interpretation of references to the Empire in Jane Austen's novels. Said also takes account of the history of resistance against empire and contemporary imperialism, typically in the assertion of nationalist identity. In *Culture and Imperialism* Said's focus shifts to cultural interconnections, and so he asserts that, 'for the first time, the history of imperialism and its culture can now be studied as neither monolithic nor reductively compartmentalized, separate, distinct' (Said 1993: xxiii). Orientalism is not any more a homogeneous category but consists of contradictory impulses. Said admits that:

It is no paradox, therefore, that Conrad was both anti-imperialist and imperialist, progressive when it came to rendering fearlessly and pessimistically the self-confirming, self-deluding corruption of overseas domination, deeply reactionary when it came to conceding that Africa or South America could ever have an independent history or culture, which the imperialists violently disturbed but by which they were ultimately defeated.

(Said 1993: xx)

In short, it is common to find both Orientalist and anti-imperialist strands within the same text, and Orientalism is no longer a simple concept.

This essay is concerned with Orientalism as a fractured notion comprising disparate texts to show that Forster's involvement with India is quite different from Kipling's, on the one hand, and J.R. Ackerley's, on the other. Forster adapted the general Orientalist tradition to his own purposes; for him, as for Edward Carpenter, G.L. Dickinson, T.E. Lawrence and Ackerley, Orientalism is combined with the quest for homosexual love.

Orientalism originates in the North–South divisions in Europe. For many Victorians and Edwardians, travel to the Mediterranean was associated 'with blessed escape from a painful state of mind and an oppressive society' (Pemble 1987: 149–50). The journey to Italy and Greece gave many British writers a sense of release from social and religious taboos, and they found 'in the rich art and emotional life of the South an invitation to relationships based on sympathy and sincerity rather than on rules of conduct' (Pemble 1987: 157) Also, there was a surge of interest in classical art and literature in the nineteenth century which led to a re-evaluation and modification of the Victorian response to classicism. Greek studies were disseminated in England through the works of German romantics. For instance, A.W. Schlegel talked of Greek drama as Johann J. Winckelmann had done of Greek sculpture, speaking of the influence of climate on art – thus generating the North–South oppositions which were absorbed into the writings of J.A. Symonds and Walter Pater.[3] While the English Grand Tourist visited France and Italy, Greece still remained remote and acquired connotations of the Other.

The North–South contrasts were particularly appropriate for homosexual writers in Britain because 'Ancient Greece had produced the literary treatments of homosexuality and Italy was where it was practised at the present day; in either case the imagination dwelt upon the Mediterranean world. Greece and Italy came together in Sicily . . .' (Pemble 1987: 291). Between 1885 and 1967 all homosexual acts, whether committed in private or public, were illegal under Section 11 of the 1885 Criminal Law Amendment Act, known as the Labouchère Amendment. The Vagrancy Act of 1898 made homosexual soliciting a legal offence (Weeks 1983: 15–16).[4] Over this period homosexuality was associated with crime, disease and sin. The social and religious condemnation of male love prohibited its expression in Britain. Against this context of intolerance, homosexuals were forced to look outside English society for places and ideas more conducive to male friendship.

In his search for a viable lifestyle, the nineteenth-century homosexual became an inveterate traveller to far away places, remote history and secluded regions of the psyche, as the laws on homosexuality were more lenient on the Continent than in Britain. Italy and France provided asylum to and became favourite resorts for homosexuals from England and the external journey frequently suggested an internal rite of passage. Consequently, a journey became a particularly enabling metaphor for homosexual writers. Stephen Adams discusses the relevance of the journey in homosexual fiction and says that in contrast to the present slogan of 'coming out', 'in the past "going away" was the more likely starting point in the homosexual's assertion of his or her identity'. Thus 'the image of a journey away from conventional society gives a characteristic form to the novels that deal with passage from self-concealment to self-expression' (Adams 1980: 56). Byron found sexual freedom on the Continent and chose to live in exile in Greece. Symonds managed his work in England from Davos for, as Jeffrey Weeks suggests, 'Switzerland represented for him the only hope of self-effectualization' (1983: 52). Lord Henry Somerset fled to Florence in 1879 when his wife threatened to expose his liaison with Harry Smith. From there he issued *Songs of Adieu* in 1889, about the events that had occurred ten years earlier.[5] Wilde, having served his prison sentence, migrated to France. Somerset Maugham settled in a villa in the south of France. One could also cite, in this regard, Norman Douglas and C.K. Scott-Moncrieff. Jeffrey Meyers says that, 'Forster sometimes had to go to Stockholm to find the sexual license denied to him in England.'[6]

The North–South symbols are exploited by Symonds, in *Studies of the Greek Poets* (1873), and Pater in *Studies in the History of the Renaissance* (1873), 'The Age of Athletic Prizemen' (1874), and *Plato and Platonism* (1893) (see Pater 1920a; 1920b; 1922). A German count, Baron Wilhelm von Gloeden, lived in the Sicilian village of Taormina from where he sent nude photographs of local youth for Joseph William Gleeson White's magazine, the *Studio*. Von Gloeden's photographs inspired Theodore William Graf Wratislaw's poem 'To a Sicilian Boy' in the *Artist* (1893). In *Where Angels Fear to Tread* (1905) and *A Room with a View* (1908), Forster's characters are visitors to Italy. Among his short stories, 'The Story of a Panic' (1902) is set in Ravello, 'The Road from Colonus' (1903) in Greece, 'The Story of the Siren' (1920) and 'Albergo Empedocle' (1903) in Sicily.

Once travel to Greece became easier, the East took on the connotations of the mysterious and the inaccessible, and the North–South metaphors were conflated into East–West categories. Richard Jenkyns elaborates on the process by which the North–South metaphor gradually grew into the East–West dichotomy. He points out that in *The Stones of Venice*, 'Ruskin, in fact, associates the south with the east; the very name Gothic, he says, implies a degree of sternness "in contradistinction to the character of Southern and Eastern nations"' (Jenkyns 1980: 50). To Byron in *The Giaour* (1813), the Greek islands were 'Edens of the Eastern wave . . . Far from the winters of the west' (ll. 15; 28). William Jones's *Asiatic Researches* (1799), Edward Pococke's *India in Greece: or, Truth in Mythology* (1852) and Max Mueller's 'Oxford Essays' (1856) were other works that revealed the Oriental origins of Greek myths. For writers such as Edward Carpenter, G.L. Dickinson and Forster the journey begun in the Mediterranean culminated in the East. The merging of the South and East is evident in Mr Wilcox's conversation with Margaret in Forster's *Howards End* (1910). Mr Wilcox boasts that he tips waiters everywhere he goes:

> 'Then the fellows know one again. Especially in the East, if you tip, they remember you from year's end to year's end.'
> 'Have you been in the East?'
> 'Oh, Greece and the Levant. I used to go out for sport and business to Cyprus . . .'
>
> (*HE*, 149)

The connection between desire and journey is further explicated by Said's elucidation of the concepts of 'filiation' and 'affiliation'. Said refers to the notions of home and place as integral to Western sensibility that ultimately translate into 'the exaggerated boundary drawn between Europe and the Orient' (Said 1984: 8). The language of being 'at home' or 'in place' implies the relationship of filiation. Filiation entails kinship, and instils an 'aggressive sense of nation, home, culture, community and belonging' (Said 1984: 12). Affiliation, on the other hand, arises 'from a failed idea or possibility of filiation to a kind of compensatory order', which is 'transpersonal' and often insurrectionary, 'such as guild consciousness, consensus, collegiality, professional respect, class, and the hegemony of a dominant culture' (Said 1984: 19–20).

Journey thus offers a mode of rejecting filiations and creating affiliations. While several writers found their trips abroad liberating, the conflict between filiations and affiliation is most compellingly rendered in the homosexual predicament in the nineteenth and early twentieth centuries. Travel to another country brought relationships with men of another race; Symonds's *In the Key of Blue* (1893) is a collection of essays on a journey with Augusto and the beauty of the Venetian man against various backgrounds. Symonds is said to have sent Charles Kains Jackson a young Swiss to prove to him the handsomeness of that race. Influenced by Symonds, Baron Corvo wrote *Stories Toto Told Me* (1883) in memory of the boys he had met in Italy.

For Edward Carpenter, G.L. Dickinson, Forster, T.E. Lawrence and J.R. Ackerley, the homosexual quest extended to the Orient. Some of the Oriental sources for homosexual motifs are Edward Fitzgerald's translation of *Omar Khayyam* (1859), Sir Richard Burton's translation of *The Arabian Nights* (1885), and the religious homo-eroticism of Sufi poetry, particularly the verses of Hafiz, though these translations were invariably censored. To this were added the *Bhagavad-gita* and the motif of Krishna from Indian literature. Carpenter's story *Narrayan* (1899) deals with the friendship of two Indian youths. Thomas Mann's *The Transposed Heads: A Legend of India* (1941) is another homo-erotic tale based on the Indian story *Haya Vadana*, meaning 'Half Horse'. It is a story of two men's friendship and love, mediated through a woman they both love. Ernst Haeckel's *A Visit to Ceylon* (1883) is a panegyric to the beauty of a Singhalese youth. Carpenter was on the same trail when he visited Ceylon (1890–1), and in *From Adam's Peak to Elephanta: Sketches in Ceylon and India* (1892) he praises the half-naked bodies of Singhalese men. One of his acquaintances, John Moray Stuart-Young, migrated to Africa and wrote poems on a Liberian half-caste boy, Ibrahim. Forster's first sexually consummated love affair was in Alexandria, with Mohammed el Adl, 'a young, slightly negroid-looking Egyptian' (Furbank 1977–8: II, 36–40). Of Forster's short stories, 'The Life to Come' (1922) portrays the affection between an English missionary and a young African chief, and 'The Other Boat' (1957–8) between an English soldier and a boy of mixed birth. The action of 'The Other Boat' takes place on a boat in the Red Sea, sailing from England to India. The outward voyage provides an occasion for the sexual encounter between Lionel March and the native Cocoanut.

Seen in this light, *A Passage to India* belongs to the tradition of homosexual Orientalism and provides a culmination to the Italian journeys in Forster's early novels, *Where Angels Fear to Tread* and *A Room with a View*. Although the novel was written during the Raj, unlike Kipling's work it was not inspired directly by the colonial project; it is worth remembering that *A Passage to India* is dedicated to Syed Ross Masood and 'the seventeen years of our friendship', and, as is shown in the following passages, the word 'friend' carries homo-erotic resonances in Forster's text. The very title alludes to Whitman, a poet who endorsed love between men. In his poem 'Passage to India' (1871), Whitman celebrates the opening of the Suez Canal, but the scientific achievement inspires the poet's imagination to other prospects:

> Passage indeed O soul to primal thought,
> Not lands and seas alone, thy own clear freshness,
> The young maturity of brood and bloom,
> To realms of budding bibles . . .
> Passage to more than India!

> (ll. 165–9; 224)

For Forster, too, the journey to India is not just a geographical movement, but a symbolic transition.

Forster's first real contact with India was in the form of Syed Ross

Masood, the grandson of the distinguished reformer, Sir Syed Ahmed Khan, who was the founder of the Muslim Anglo-Oriental College in Aligarh. Masood entered Forster's life in 1906 when Forster was appointed to coach him in Latin. The relationship was never fulfilled sexually, yet for Forster, it 'woke him up out of his suburban and academic life and showed him new horizons and a new civilization' (Furbank 1977–8: I, 146). Indeed, the visit to India in 1912–13 was prompted by this friendship.

Forster first went to India in 1912 with Dickinson and Bob Trevelyan, and in preparation for this trip, he read *Sakuntala* and the *Gita*. There were two further visits, in 1921 and then for three months in 1943. His accounts of India are contained in *Goldsworthy Lowes Dickinson* (1934), *The Hill of Devi* (1953) and a group of essays 'The East' in *Abinger Harvest*, one of which, 'Hymn Before Action' (1912), is on the *Gita*.[7] He also wrote articles on India to the end of his career – on Hinduism, Tagore, reviews of Kipling's work and of books on Indian architecture and sculpture.

A Passage to India has been regarded as exceptional in Forster's oeuvre in being primarily a historical novel. Since it was published in 1924, *A Passage to India* has been popularized in literary-critical practice as a comment on the British Raj. In one of the first reviews of the novel, Rose Macaulay wrote: 'Never was a more convincing, a more pathetic, or a more amusing picture drawn of the Ruling Race in India' (Macaulay, 4 June 1924, in Gardner 1973: 197). Edward Carpenter voiced a general feeling when he wrote to Forster about *A Passage to India*:

> It gives me quite the feeling of India – the Anglo-Indian life – and I think the picture of that life as shown will have a considerable and a very sane and stimulating influence upon public opinion in England. Yet you are perfectly impartial and fair, and do not take sides anywhere that I can discover . . .
> (Letter dated 14 August 1924(?), in Gardner 1973: 243)

The novel won similar praise from the Indian critics. According to a review by Nihal Singh in September 1924, the book shows 'how the British in India despise and ostracise Indians, while on their part the Indians mistrust and misjudge the British and how the gulf between the two is widening and becoming unbridgeable' (Gardner 1973, 265). Another commentator, Bhupal Singh, wrote: 'A Passage to India . . . is a clever picture of Englishmen in India, a subtle portraiture of the Indian, especially the Moslem mind, and a fascinating study of the problems arising out of the contact of India with the West' (Gardner

1973: 293).[8] Although *A Passage to India* is written in the context of Anglo-India, any discussion of Forster's historical foraging needs to be well qualified, as it is not easily identifiable with the genre of English colonial literature comprising authors such as Rudyard Kipling, Flora Annie Steele, Philip Mason, John Masters and Paul Scott. In the historical interpretations of *A Passage to India* the context overshadows the text, and this has tended to eclipse the themes that the novel shares with the rest of Forster's fiction.

A Passage to India, like all Forster's novels, works to mediate the writer's reverence for personal relations, and within this discourse the author postulates the ideal of male friendship. Relations between men in Forster are always obstructed and provoke hostility; Philip's friendship with Gino is unacceptable in *Where Angels Fear to Tread*, Rickie fails to acknowledge Stephen as his brother because he is illegitimate in *The Longest Journey*, and in *Howards End* the Wilcoxes despise Leonard Bast because he is socially below them. British rule in India offered Forster a potent situation to illustrate the barriers to male friendship. However, Forster uses the racial and political prohibitions of the friendship of Fielding and Aziz to signify a wider, universal oppression of homosexual love, so that the novel ultimately transcends contemporary politics. One might conclude that Forster's Orientalism is merely a device for advancing the theme of homo-erotic love, and is not ultimately its dominant discourse.

The success of *Howards End* blocked Forster and it was fourteen years before he published his next novel, *A Passage to India*. In *Howards End*, Forster had attempted to suppress homo-erotic desire entirely by concentrating on marriage and women protagonists, but his technique created a deadlock; the invisible desire for male love interferes everywhere with the narrative and undermines the structure of the novel.[9] Although, in *Howards End*, Forster had broadened the scope of his novel from domestic comedy to social and economic issues, he also realized that his own homo-eroticism was too pressing to be denied in his narratives. There were two options open to him – one, to write a straightforward homosexual narrative; and the other, to project homo-erotic desire on a vast canvas, thus giving it full expression. He took both those options, the first one resulting in *Maurice* and the second leading to *A Passage to India*. It is significant that *Maurice* was written during 1913–14 as a respite from *A Passage to India*, and the two novels complement each other.

The difficulties Forster faced in writing *A Passage to India* were far more intractable than those he had encountered in his earlier novels. He began the novel in July 1913, but in September 1913 abandoned it to write *Maurice*; in 1914 he again reached a dead end and declared: 'Shall never complete another novel' (cited by Stallybrass, *PI*, xii). Not finished until 1924, *A Passage to India* has the distinction of having the longest gestation history among Forster's novels. From the beginning, he sought to moderate the political tones in his narrative; however, the political issues of the time proved to be so powerful that they completely subsumed homo-erotic desire in the text. Ironically, the political situation, which provided Forster with a pretext of the British in India and gave an edge to his theme of friendship, was so powerful in itself that it threatened to take over the text. As in his previous novels, the disguise of Forster's narrative is almost too perfect to allow the author to manoeuvre the theme of homo-erotic love. Therefore, Forster constantly strove in *A Passage to India* to put politics in perspective and carefully negotiate a space for homo-erotic desire.

His most pressing problem arose when he tried to decide on the appropriate genre for his narrative. According to Stallybrass, he had initially thought of writing *A Passage to India* as a travelogue, but found the realistic mode of writing unsuitable for his purposes, and so he turned to fiction (*PI*, xi). In converting his experiences in India into a novel, Forster's central problem lay in striking a balance between politics and the theme of personal relations. He wrote of his first visit to India:

> My connection with India is peculiar and personal. It started because I made friends with an Indian, and but for him I might never have gone to his country, or written about it. His name was Masood – . . .
>
> It is on the basis of personal relationship that my connection with that strange country rests. I didn't go there to govern it or to make money or to improve people. I went there to see a friend . . . The sense of racial tension, of incompatibility, never left me. It was not a tourist's outing, and the impression it left was deep.
>
> ('Three Countries', *HD*, 297)

A Passage to India was inspired by friendship and Forster was concerned to link India and his personal experiences; the political circumstances are relevant in so far as they served to heighten his awareness of incompatibility and barriers to love between men. Such a situation provided Forster with an opportunity for projecting his total despair over personal relations, and by placing the theme of friendship in British India, he was able to give it a universal and metaphysical dimension. However, while the Indian scene enabled Forster to present the theme of male love most comprehensively, the backdrop that he chose was so big that the homo-erotic theme is lost in the novel.

A Passage to India frames the theme of friendship in the context of the British rule of India. Implicit in the narrative, from the beginning, is the question 'as to whether or no it is possible to be friends with an Englishman' (*PI*, 5). The question initially has some political content given the colonial situation of the British in India. However, as the narrative progresses, the ideal of friendship gradually loses its political charge and is presented in terms of homo-erotic desire.

Several meanings accrue to the word 'friend' as it recurs throughout the novel. Hamidullah and Mahmoud Ali discuss friendship as a political matter. The obstacles to friendship between the Indians and the English are insurmountable in the political environment of India, but Hamidullah argues that 'it is possible in England' (*PI*, 6). A little later Adela expresses a wish to know Indians and she says to Mr Turton: 'I only want to meet those Indians whom you come across socially – as your friends' (*PI*, 22). This is only consistent with the rest of the character of Adela, for whom even a sexual relationship is a rational process. When she first breaks off her engagement with Ronny, Adela is still anxious to maintain the decorum of their situation. Unmindful of Ronny's hurt, she insists that they nevertheless 'shall keep friends' (*PI*, 77). Adela tries to compensate for the bad treatment of the Indians at the bridge party by her own 'friendliness' (*PI*, 39). Her attitude is caricatured by Miss Derek, who, without Adela's honesty, is just '[a]ll friskiness and friendliness' (*PI*, 82). Then there are Aziz's Indian friends, Hamidullah and Mahmoud Ali; the Nawab Bahadur, too, is described as 'a straightforward enemy and a staunch friend' (*PI*, 31); and it is said of Fielding that 'all his best friends were English' (*PI*, 55).

Among the rather loose and scattered references, the novel generates a more specific, personal and romantic notion of a friend, as somebody with whom one shares '[t]he secret understanding of the heart' (*PI*, 14). Aziz recalls running in the rain in his boyhood: 'Then back with water streaming over you and perhaps rather a pain inside. But I did not mind. All my friends were paining with me' (*PI*, 66). This ideal of a friend is abstract and not identified solely with any individual, for it constitutes the narrator's quest in the novel.

Whereas in his 'Italian' and 'English' novels Forster uses classical allusions to denote the ideal of friendship,[10] in *A Passage to India* he incorporates references to Indian religion and mythology, and one of the central homo-erotic motifs is the reference to Krishna. In Hindu religion, Krishna is a handsome, dark, young god, desired alike by cowherds and milkmaids. In 1957, Forster reviewed W.G. Archer's *The Loves of Krishna*, and Archer in his 'Introduction' refers to 'Krishna the adored lover'.[11] The homo-erotic ideal of a friend is presented as an absence in the novel; this desire for a friend is all-consuming and expressed in Godbole's hymn to Krishna, 'Come, come, come, come, come, come'. The full context runs:

> 'I placed myself in the position of a milkmaiden. I say to Shri Krishna: "Come! Come to me only." The God refuses to come. I grow humble and say: "Do not come to me only. Multiply yourself into a hundred Krishnas, and let one go to each of my hundred companions, but one, O Lord of the Universe, come to me." He refuses to come . . .'
>
> 'But He comes in some other song, I hope?' said Mrs Moore gently.
>
> 'Oh no, He refuses to come,' repeated Godbole, perhaps not understanding her question. 'I say to Him, Come, come, come, come, come, come. He neglects to come.'
>
> *(PI, 72)*

This sense of absence is reiterated throughout the text. Ronny calls out to his peon and the whole text becomes animate with expectation at the very mention of the word 'Krishna':

> Krishna was the peon who should have brought the files from his office. He had not turned up, and a terrific row ensued. Ronny stormed, shouted, howled . . . Krishna the earth, Krishna the stars replied, until the Englishman was appeased by their echoes, fined the absent peon eight annas, and sat down to arrears in the next room.
>
> *(PI, 88)*

Impervious to the potential for male friendship, Ronny rests content with the mere echoes of the word 'Krishna'. Consonant with Godbole's song is Aziz's sentimental harping on the Mogul past and Persian poetry: 'Less explicit than the call to Krishna, it voiced our loneliness nevertheless, our isolation, our need for the Friend who never comes yet is not entirely disproved' (*PI*, 97). It is significant that these references to friendship appear, not in some direct narrational focus on male friendship, but rather as an almost metonymic deflection from its consequences. It is part, therefore, not merely of the Fielding–Aziz dialogues, but of the very fabric of the novel.

A friend attains to divine stature not only in Godbole's hymn to Krishna, but also in Aziz's religion, 'The Friend: a Persian expression for God' (*PI*, 265). Against so magnificent an ideal even the empyreal sun is devoid of majesty:

> All over the city, and over much of India, the same retreat on the part of humanity was beginning . . . The sun was returning to his kingdom with power but without beauty – that was the sinister feature. If only there had been beauty! His cruelty would have been tolerable then. Through excess of light, he failed to triumph, he also; in his yellowy-white overflow not only matter, but brightness itself lay drowned. He was not the unattainable Friend, either of men or birds or other suns, he was not the eternal promise, the never-withdrawn suggestion that haunts our consciousness; he was merely a creature, like the rest, and so debarred from glory.
>
> (*PI*, 106)

These poetic allusions to the friend relate not to the political aspect of the novel, but to the homo-erotic theme of male love that pervades all of Forster's fiction. Forster's absolute commitment to friendship is voiced, of course, in his famous declaration that if he had to choose between betraying his country and betraying his friend he hoped that he would have the guts to betray his country ('What I Believe' (1939), *TCD*, 76).

Although contemporary racial and political issues constantly impinge on the text, Forster strives at every stage to dissociate friendship from politics. Aziz is bored by political discussion and as 'The elder men had reached their eternal politics, Aziz drifted into the garden' (*PI*, 8). He could not care less about the relations between the Indians and English and says to Hamidullah and Mahmoud Ali: 'Why talk about the English? Brrrr . . . ! Why be either friends with the fellows or not friends? Let us shut them out and be jolly' (*PI*, 7). All the main characters, not only Aziz, are detached from the political scene of the novel. Fielding expresses the same weariness with political issues as Aziz. When asked 'how is England justified in holding India?', Fielding's response is carefully framed:

> There they were! Politics again. 'It's a question I can't get my mind onto,' he replied. 'I'm out here personally because I needed

a job. I cannot tell you why England is here or whether she ought
to be here. It's beyond me.'

(*PI*, 102)

So also with Adela and Mrs Moore, both of whom 'had no race-
consciousness – Mrs Moore was too old, Miss Quested too new' (*PI*,
121).

The chief protagonists, however, are *deliberately* distanced from the
political situation in India; they are private individuals against the
backdrop of British civil servants and other officials. Aziz is a doctor
by profession and Fielding is principal of a small college at Chandrapore.
Fielding is 'a disruptive force' to the British rule in that he believes (here
radically) in personal relations:

> Neither a missionary nor a student, he was happiest in the give-
> and-take of a private conversation. The world, he believed, is a
> globe of men who are trying to reach one another and can best
> do so by the help of goodwill plus culture and intelligence – a
> creed ill suited to Chandrapore, but he had come out too late to
> lose it.
>
> (*PI*, 56)

Forster repeatedly pits the values of personal relations against the
political factors that divide men.

The theme of friendship and personal relations, relevant though it is
to the overall situation in India, has a homo-erotic inflection. Among
the superficial expressions of friendship, the novel moves towards
creating intimacy between Aziz and Fielding. Aziz embodies an ideal
of friendship to which Fielding must aspire. Although maturer,
Fielding belongs to Forster's category of inhibited Englishmen with an
'undeveloped heart', heroes such as Philip Herriton and Cecil Vyse. Like
Philip in *Where Angels Fear to Tread*, who is emotionally inhibited,
Fielding too feels inadequate in his response to India:

> Lovely, exquisite moment – but passing the Englishman with
> averted face and on swift wings. He experienced nothing himself;
> it was as if someone had told him there was such a moment, and
> he was obliged to believe. And he felt dubious and discontented
> suddenly, and wondered whether he was really and truly success-
> ful as a human being. After forty years' experience, he had learned
> to manage his life and make the best of it on advanced European
> lines, had developed his personality, explored his limitations, con-
> trolled his passions – and he had done it all without becoming

either pedantic or worldly. A creditable achievement, but as the moment passed he felt he ought to have been working at something else the whole time – he didn't know at what, never would know, never could know, and that was why he felt sad.

(*PI*, 181)

The passage is an indictment of Western values that repress passion; Fielding is incapable of intensity but he cannot himself know this because he stands outside such experiences. It is only against the background of India that Fielding's emotional sterility is revealed starkly.

The political circumstances give an immediacy and added urgency to the theme of friendship. Aziz stays away from the bridge party organized by the Collector to bridge the gulf between the East and West and his relationship with Fielding occurs on a different basis in the context of personal relations. On receiving an invitation from Fielding to a tea-party, Aziz 'snatch[ed] up his pen' and 'wrote an affectionate reply'. In contrast to the cynicism over the Collector's bridge party, the meeting with Fielding is full of promise: 'For he had never met the Principal, and believed that the one serious gap in his life was going to be filled' (*PI*, 54). Later, when Fielding visits Aziz, he too looks forward to establishing a relationship: 'He had liked Aziz so much at their first meeting, and had hoped for developments' (*PI*, 104). Both meetings form crucial stages in the friendship of Aziz and Fielding.

Aziz arrives early at Fielding's house and a chord of intimacy is immediately struck between the two men. Fielding 'was dressing after a bath when Dr Aziz was announced' (*PI*, 57), and the moment of Aziz's entry is significant if we recall the homosexual connotations of men bathing in Forster's previous novels.[12] The friendship of Fielding and Aziz is spontaneous; Aziz, completely at ease with his host, 'began to look round, as he would have with any old friend. Fielding was not surprised at the rapidity of their intimacy' (*PI*, 58). Aziz confesses to Fielding, 'I used to wish you to fall ill so that we could meet that way' (*PI*, 57). The sentence evokes the homo-erotic sentiment of men caring for one another common in Forster's fiction.[13] In homosexual literature, a friend's sickness provides an occasion for presenting men together in a bedroom setting, and shortly afterwards, Fielding visits Aziz in his illness. However, in *A Passage to India*, the theme of friendship is so well integrated with the rest of the narrative that it does not stand out as it did in the previous novels.

It is perhaps inevitable that descriptions of women are functional, as they are often mediators in relations between men. During Fielding's visit to Aziz, the latter reminisces about his dead wife: Aziz 'realised what he had lost, and that no woman could ever take her place; a friend would come nearer to her than another woman' (*PI*, 49). He shows Fielding a photograph of his wife and says that had she been alive she would have come out of the purdah for Fielding: 'I should have told her you were my brother, and she would have seen you' (*PI*, 108). Fielding asks whether Aziz's wife would have treated all his friends as his brothers, to which Aziz replies: 'Of course not, but the word exists and is convenient. All men are my brothers, and as soon as one behaves as such he may see my wife.' Fielding remarks: 'And when the whole world behaves as such, there will be no more purdah?' (*PI*, 108). This conversation is an example of the subtlety with which homo-erotic codes are interwoven with the customs and environment of India. Fielding's comment is clever indeed; homosexual relations imply that there would be no need to protect women from the advances of men.

Fielding is overwhelmed by Aziz's warmth and feels inadequate before the latter's capacity for emotion: 'Experience can do much, and all that he had learned in England and Europe was an assistance to him, and helped him towards clarity, but clarity prevented him from experiencing something else' (*PI*, 109). The friendship of Fielding and Aziz is largely isolated from politics, and Aziz represents the Other to Fielding's rational and restricted outlook. The name 'Aziz' itself means 'loved one' in Urdu and gives a clue to the nature of Forster's narrative.

The first part of the novel, entitled 'Mosque', is devoted primarily to establishing friendship between Aziz and Fielding and concludes with a poetic celebration:

> But they were friends, brothers. That part was settled, their compact had been subscribed by the photograph, they trusted one another, affection had triumphed for once in a way. He dropped off to sleep amid the happier memories of the last two hours – poetry of Ghalib, female grace, good old Hamidullah, good Fielding, his honoured wife and dear boys. He passed into a region where these joys had no enemies but bloomed harmoniously in an eternal garden, or ran down watershoots of ribbed marble, or rose into domes whereunder were inscribed, black against white, the ninety-nine attributes of God.
>
> (*PI*, 113)

Fielding's visit to Aziz is deeply fulfilling and Forster celebrates the attachment of Fielding and Aziz in richly sensual imagery. It is significant that the theme of friendship in *A Passage to India* is associated with

Muslim culture and symbolized in the mosque, reflecting Forster's own love for Syed Ross Masood. Indeed, the sacerdotal becomes a screen for the sensual.

Hence the narrative of *A Passage to India* evolves from the central theme of friendship and all the three parts of the novel are concerned with the relationship of Aziz and Fielding. The novel is as far removed from its political context as possible. It is notable that although the text is located in India, the 'Mosque' part deals exclusively with Muslim India; the 'Caves' are located nowhere in particular in that they have a universal, timeless quality about them; and the final 'Temple' part is placed in an independent state in India. Moreover, Forster repudiates any idea of a political conciliation. The bridge party is a humiliating experience both for the English hosts and their Indian guests, and the narrator comments, 'all invitations must proceed from heaven perhaps; perhaps it is futile for men to initiate their own unity, they do but widen the gulfs between them by the attempt' (*PI*, 32). Elsewhere, the author minimizes the importance of political issues and adopts a philosophical attitude to the political problems of India:

> It matters so little to the majority of living beings what the minority, that calls itself human, desires or decides. Most of the inhabitants of India do not mind how India is governed. Nor are the lower animals of England concerned about England, but in the tropics the indifference is more prominent, the inarticulate world is closer at hand and readier to resume control as soon as men are tired.
>
> (*PI*, 105)

The passage suggests the scale of Forster's narrative which places human concerns, such as politics, as incidental to larger global issues. Unlike Edward Carpenter, who saw socialism as a necessary condition for homosexual love,[14] Forster did not believe that any political change could ensure individual fulfilment. Fielding agrees with Aziz that an official approach to personal relations is misguided: 'It's beginning at the wrong end, isn't it? I know, but institutions and the Government don't' (*PI*, 108). Forster undeviatingly focuses on personal relations, and in *A Passage to India* illustrates the difficulties of male friendship in the adverse political climate of India.

Love between men in Forster is always defined in tension with heterosexual relations; women characters both screen and clarify homo-erotic desire. *A Passage to India* transmits a strong antipathy towards women and marriage typical of Forster's texts. The main adversaries in the novel are not Indians and the Englishmen but the Englishwomen. It is not politics but the presence of Englishwomen that is inimical to male friendship in India. Even the Collector has some vestiges of sympathy for the subjects over whom he exercises ruthless control, whereas the women are without compassion. Mr Turton

> retained a contemptuous affection for the pawns he had moved about for so many years, they must be worth his pains. 'After all, it's our women who make everything more difficult out here,' was his inmost thought, as he caught sight of some obscenities upon a long blank wall, and beneath his chivalry to Miss Quested resentment lurked, waiting its day – perhaps there is a grain of resentment in all chivalry.
>
> (*PI*, 204)

Aziz, too, feels constrained by Englishwomen and he says to Fielding: 'Here we never look at them. Oh no, much too careful' (*PI*, 109–10). Fielding, like the best of Forster's heroes, is unrefined and not prone to chivalry, which makes him unpopular among the women from his country (*PI*, 56). Forster implies that the British rule in India is complicated by the demands made by Englishwomen, and of course, relations with Indian men would be easier if the women were not there.

Where women characters are not criticized, they are instrumental in bringing men together. Adela and Mrs Moore are responsible for initiating the friendship between Aziz and Fielding. Adela's wish to see 'the real India' (*PI*, 21) and Mrs Moore's chance meeting with Aziz result in Fielding's invitation to Aziz to his house for tea. Adela and Mrs Moore are intruders at the first meeting of Aziz and Fielding. Aziz's earlier encounter with Mrs Moore is inconsequential compared with his pleasure in talking to Fielding: 'The romance at the mosque had sunk out of his consciousness as soon as it was over' (*PI*, 59–60). He resents the interruption of their conversation and 'was disappointed that other guests were coming, for he preferred to be alone with his new friend' (*PI*, 60). Although much is made of Aziz's friendship with Mrs Moore, Aziz disclaims any special feelings for the old Englishwoman. He tells Fielding: 'I do not consider Mrs Moore my friend, I only met her accidentally in my mosque' (*PI*, 60). The effect of Mrs Moore's assertions of her affection for Aziz is to cloak the friendship between two men; Fielding's attachment and loyalty for Aziz during the trial is made acceptable by Mrs Moore's categorical belief in Aziz's innocence. Aziz's wife becomes the ground on which he declares his brotherhood with Fielding. Adela and Mrs Moore later instigate the picnic to the Marabar Caves. These details should not be forgotten when Mrs Moore is later invoked as a saint.

As in all his earlier novels, in *A Passage to India* Forster detaches love from heterosexual relations and integrates it with relations between men. From the beginning of the text the theme of friendship runs parallel to the topic of marriage. Whereas friendship is an entirely male prerogative, marriage is invariably a concern of women. Both Aziz and Fielding profess to have no use for marriage. Aziz's marriage has been a means for begetting sons and, like Lilia in *Where Angels Fear to Tread*, Aziz's wife dies in giving birth to his son (*PI*, 49). The friendship of the two men is cemented by their lack of interest in heterosexual love. Having dissociated his male protagonists from any desire for a heterosexual romance, Forster proceeds to demolish marriage in the story of Adela.

Adela and Mrs Moore's visit to India is connected to the issue of marriage and the subject looms large in the text. The foreign country displaces the values of English middle-class society and in particular challenges the predominance of heterosexual relations. Marriage becomes marginal as soon as Mrs Moore and Adela step on to Indian soil and the theme of friendship becomes more important. While Mrs Moore rebukes Ronny for his behaviour towards the Indian people, she 'regretted afterwards that she had not kept to the real serious subject that had caused her visit to India – namely the relationship between Ronny and Adela. Would they, or would they not, succeed in becoming engaged to be married?' (*PI*, 46). The friction between Ronny and Aziz is evident at Fielding's tea-party and the conflict is cultural in the widest sense – Aziz stands for spontaneity and friendship whereas Ronny upholds English conventions including marriage. Hence here, and later in the Marabar Caves, Aziz inadvertently becomes a source of destruction of marriage. In Fielding's house he asks Adela: 'Why not settle altogether in India?' She replies: 'I'm afraid I can't do that' (*PI*, 66), which is the first time she voices her doubts about her marriage to Ronny.

Contact with Aziz heightens the sense of their own deficiency in the English characters. Ronny is shocked 'for he never dreamt that an Indian could be a channel of communication between two English people' (*PI*, 76). To Adela, it brings a sense of the emptiness of marriage, and as she ends her engagement to Ronny, '[h]er ordeal was over, but she felt it should have been more painful and longer' (*PI*, 76). Their relationship lacks emotional depth, and Adela feels 'that a profound and passionate speech ought to have been delivered by one or both of them' (*PI*, 77). But marriage is not allied to personal fulfilment in Forster, and he raises the issue only to expose it. Ronny and Adela patch up their quarrel and they become engaged once more as readily as they had broken off the engagement. However, there is not much difference in either state, except that marriage generates a sense of predictability. Adela

> had meant to revert to her former condition of important and cultivated uncertainty, but it had passed out of her reach at its appropriate hour. Unlike the green bird or the hairy animal, she was labelled now. She felt humiliated again, for she deprecated labels, and she felt too that there should have been another scene between her lover and herself at this point, something dramatic and lengthy.
>
> (*PI*, 85–6)

Marriage simply contributes to the mundanity of life and, much as she tries, Adela cannot feel enthusiastic over the thought of her marriage to Ronny. She admits to Mrs Moore: 'I don't feel a bit excited – I'm just glad it's settled up at last, but I'm not conscious of vast changes' (*PI*, 88). Mrs Moore, too, has to make an effort to find a suitable response to the announcement of her son's marriage:

> She reminded herself of all that a happy marriage means, and of her own happy marriages, one of which had produced Ronny. Adela's parents had also been happily married, and excellent it was to see the incident repeated by the younger generation. On and on!
>
> (*PI*, 86)

Forster uses the phrase 'happy marriages' ironically and describes marriage as an unvarying event.

The development of the theme of friendship in the novel simultaneously entails the decentring of marriage and the narrative is carefully built up to a climax as the issues of love and marriage erupt in the Caves. The trip begins badly as Fielding misses the train. The journey is dull and uncomfortable, and Aziz and his companions make ineffectual efforts to entertain the two ladies. The tour into the first cave nearly kills Mrs Moore, while the second cave turns Adela hysterical. Aziz, who has missed his friend all along, is thrilled as Fielding appears on the scene and it marks a further stage in their friendship. The arrival of Fielding suddenly changes a disaster into a memorable event. Aziz's 'heart was full of new happiness. The picnic, after a nasty shock or two, had developed into something beyond his dreams, for Fielding had not only come, but brought an uninvited guest' (*PI*, 147). The women are relegated into the background – Adela departs with Miss Derek while Mrs Moore is too ill to participate – and Aziz cannot trace anything wrong. Aziz explains Adela's behaviour to Fielding: ' "She ran to her friend, I to mine," he went on, smiling. "And now I am with my friends and they are with me and each other, which is happiness." ' (*PI*, 149).

Thoughts of marriage are uppermost in the text as the narrative approaches the Caves and the author prepares to negate one of the most deeply ingrained structures of Western society. The journey to the Marabar Caves has an element of initiation rite in that the characters shed their old beliefs and are transformed by the experience they undergo. The Caves are cut off from reality for they posit an alternative to actual life:

> Nothing, nothing attaches to them, and their reputation – for they have one – does not depend upon human speech. It is as if the surrounding plain or the passing birds have taken upon themselves to exclaim 'Extraordinary!' and the word has taken root in the air, and been inhaled by mankind.
>
> (*PI*, 117)

In Mrs Moore, Forster annihilates Christianity and the religious sanction of marriage. Before she enters the Caves, Mrs Moore's view changes radically:

> She felt increasingly (vision or nightmare?) that, though people are important, the relations between them are not, and that in particular too much fuss has been made over marriage; centuries of carnal embracement, yet man is no nearer to understanding man. And today she felt this with such force that it seemed itself a relationship, itself a person, who was trying to take hold of her hand.
>
> (*PI*, 127)

Homo-erotic love falls outside the boundaries of conventional relationships and therefore Forster argues for the supremacy of individuals over relationships. Homo-erotic desire in Forster is more concrete than the hollow conventions of marriage; marriage is allied to the pressures for propagation but it alienates men from one another and their own true instincts.

For Adela, Aziz symbolizes the Other, the alternative and the passionate. He is thus associated with all that supplements (and so threatens) marriage. It is no coincidence that Adela confronts the fact that her relationship with Ronny is devoid of love in the isolation of the Caves, away from any external, social influences: ' "What about love?" The rock was nicked by a double row of footholds, and somehow the question was suggested by them.' It then occurs to her that 'She and Ronny – no, they did not love each other.' However, love is not essential to marriage and Adela recognizes that 'If love is everything, few marriages would survive the honeymoon' (*PI*, 143). The Caves reveal to Adela the artificiality of marriage, and the awareness is traumatic for it disintegrates all the assumptions on which her life stands. Therefore the Caves dramatize the crumbling of marriage together with the religious and social mores that sustain heterosexual relations, and in so far as the breakdown is presented in relation to Aziz and India, it also has a racial and political dimension. The violence that explodes in the Caves is not primarily political but signifies a wider collapse of Western civilization and heterosexual society.

In contrast to the cynicism about marriage and heterosexual relations, the novel elucidates the theme of friendship. Marriage separates men, and only through friendship can they come together. Adela asks, 'how else are barriers to be broken down?' if not by religion, and although her question can be interpreted in the political sense, the answer Forster gives is both metaphysical and homo-erotic: 'She was only recommending the universal brotherhood he sometimes dreamed of, but as soon as it was put into prose it became untrue.' The ideal of brotherhood in Forster belongs to the domain of personal, sexual relations and is not connected to any social or political doctrines. Thus Aziz debunks any suggestion of political unity and tells Adela: 'Nothing embraces the whole of India, nothing, nothing' (*PI*, 136). The friendship of Fielding and Aziz progresses on a personal rather than a political level. As for Aziz, Fielding had become 'a friend, increasingly dear' (*PI*, 124).

In Forster's work, obstacles to friendship test and affirm the passions of men. Philip and Gino in *Where Angels Fear to Tread* achieve friendship in spite of social taboos, and in *The Longest Journey* (1907) Rickie acknowledges Stephen as his brother despite the latter's illegitimacy. The Caves incident establishes greater intimacy between Aziz and Fielding by producing a crisis that threatens to put them asunder. In the company of Fielding, Aziz insists that 'This picnic is nothing to do with English or Indian; it is an expedition of friends' (*PI*, 151). Later, Fielding asserts his staunch loyalty to Aziz when he stands by his friend against the rest of his compatriots; and although the episode unleashes opposition between East and West, the racial and cultural conflict arises from a sexual incident, and the counter-claims of friendship over heterosexual relations.

Adela's allegation that she was assaulted by Aziz in the Caves produces massive instability in the text. However, the enmities are only partly political and stem also from an underlying conflict between heterosexual values and homo-erotic love. As in *The Longest Journey*, the battle lines between the characters are drawn along sexual conflict, and the British and Indian camps are also rendered in terms of heterosexual relations versus male friendship. This opposition is irreconcilable and acquires racial and political overtones in that the British uphold the medieval code of chivalry, while it is the Indians who endorse the validity of friendship. The British outlook is depicted in the ultra-feminine figure of a railway official's wife who 'was generally snubbed; but this evening, with her abundant figure and masses of corn-gold hair, she symbolized all that is worth fighting and dying for' (*PI*, 172). The English officials turn fanatical over Adela's cause which is not just political, but forms the core of heterosexual society: 'They had started speaking of "women and children" – that phrase that exempts the male from sanity when it has been repeated a few times' (*PI*, 174). Aziz and Adela turn into types as everybody avoids mentioning their names and it is Fielding who reminds that the incident involves two individuals.

Although it is Adela who withdraws her charges against Aziz, her courage and sacrifice are marginalized so that she does not overshadow male friendship. Adela's gesture is rejected by India because she has transgressed against affection:

> For her behaviour rested on cold justice and honesty; she had felt, while she recanted, no passion of love for those whom she had wronged. Truth is not truth in that exacting land unless there go with it kindness and more kindness and kindness again, unless the Word that was with God also is God.
>
> (*PI*, 233)

Adela is not capable of love because the novel is concerned with relations between men. Although Fielding is grateful to her for his friend's release, heterosexual relations do not have any potential in Forster's texts. As Fielding bids Adela goodbye:

> A friendliness, as of dwarfs shaking hands, was in the air. Both man and woman were at the height of their powers – sensible, honest, even subtle. They spoke the same language, and held the

same opinions, and the variety of age and sex did not divide them. Yet they were dissatisfied.

(*PI*, 252)

Forster consistently reduces Adela in stature and it is the friendship of Fielding and Aziz that survives and is extolled in the book.

The adventure in the Caves is a process of unlearning, for it deconstructs the mores of heterosexual society. However, the outcome of the events in the novel is described in the philosophical terms that Forster reserves for the microcosm. Adela observes after her tribulation in the Caves:

> 'What is the use of personal relationships when everyone brings less and less to them. I feel we ought all to go back into the desert for centuries and try and get good. I want to begin at the beginning. All the things I thought I'd learned are just a hindrance, they're not knowledge at all. I'm not fit for personal relationships.'

(*PI*, 188)

The impulse to wipe out modern civilization and go back to primitive life expresses the wish for a period when homosexual love was permitted.

In the Forsterian scheme of things the heterosexual issue of Adela's rape is redundant; it is immaterial what happened in the Cave, because what matters is male friendship. According to Beauman, in her recent biography *Morgan*, it seems that Forster radically revised the Caves incident, for in the earlier drafts of the novel, Aziz clearly assaults Adela.[15] Forster's decision to blur the incident further confirms that he did not consider the issue of rape in itself as important to the plot; while what actually happened in the Caves remains ambiguous, what matters is the events that follow. Mrs Moore has no sympathy for Adela's suffering and comments:

> 'Why all this marriage, marriage? . . . The human race would have become a single person centuries ago if marriage was any use. And all this rubbish about love, love in a church, love in a cave, as if there is the least difference . . .

(*PI*, 192)

In Mrs Moore's speech, marriage comes near to being synonymous with rape, both being equally loveless. Forster separates love from heterosexual relations as Adela admits in a conversation with Fielding:

'Tenderness, respect, personal intercourse – I tried to make them
take the place – of –'
'I no longer want love,' he said, supplying the word.

(*PI*, 251)

Adela sums up her experience in the Caves as a 'hallucination' – 'that
makes some women think they've had an offer of marriage when none
was made' (*PI*, 228). The efficacy of marriage is negated completely
from the novel and it is only after Adela corrects her perspective that
she loses the echo that has tormented her from the Caves.

It is by collapsing the structures of marriage and heterosexual relations in the Caves incident that Forster clears the space for love between
men. Marriage is criticized so severely in Forster's novels because it
poses a threat to male friendship, and Forster depicts very vividly Aziz's
jealousy over Fielding. Fielding and Adela are thrown together in the
riot after the trial and Aziz cries out to him: 'Cyril, again you desert'
(*PI*, 223). The rumours of Fielding's affair with Adela gnaw into Aziz's
heart and he exclaims bitterly: 'No one is my friend. All are traitors,
even my own children. I have had enough of friends' (*PI*, 259). The
mere thought of Fielding's marriage drives a wedge in their friendship
and there is no rational explanation for Aziz's possessiveness, except for
the homo-erotic desire that haunts the text:

> But, as he drove off, something depressed him – a dull pain of
> body or mind, waiting to rise to the surface. When he reached
> the bungalow he wanted to return and say something very affec-
> tionate; instead, he gave the sais a heavy tip, and sat down
> gloomily on the bed . . .
>
> (*PI*, 266)

Aziz's flippant behaviour saddens Fielding; he 'was conscious of something hostile, and because he was really fond of Aziz his optimism
failed him. Travelling light is less easy as soon as affection is involved'
(*PI*, 268).

As in *The Longest Journey*, the prospect of the male protagonist's marriage inevitably causes estrangement between friends. Aziz is deeply
hurt by the news of Fielding's marriage; he destroys Fielding's letters
unopened and refuses to see him when he returns to India with his wife.
Although the reason given for Aziz's anger is that he thinks that
Fielding has married Adela, the explanation does not justify Aziz's emotional outburst; the misunderstanding between the two men is merely
an excuse for giving vent to homo-erotic feeling. Even after he learns

that Fielding has married Mrs Moore's daughter, Aziz never speaks to his friend's wife and remains distant, 'What does it matter to me who you marry? Don't trouble me here at Mau is all I ask. I do not want you, I do not want one of you in my private life, with my dying breath I say it' (*PI*, 293). As Aziz says, it is inconsequential whom Fielding has married; what matters is that his friend is now attached to a woman.

Forster could not conceptualize a future for the friendship of Fielding and Aziz, and this was due not just to the political circumstances but also to the social and religious condemnation of homo-erotic love. Aziz loses Fielding through marriage, and the passion and intensity of their friendship ends in a parting. In the final chapter, all the political pretexts have been stripped away and Fielding and Aziz meet as individuals, painfully conscious that they must separate, 'Friends again, yet aware that they would meet no more'. It is a sad and tender occasion, like any doomed love scene, as momentarily 'they went back laughingly to their old relationship as if nothing had happened' (*PI*, 307). The narrator identifies several reasons for discontinuing their friendship. Aziz still embodies the ideal of friendship, but it is Fielding who cannot attain it any more:

> He too felt that this was their last free intercourse. All the stupid misunderstandings had been cleared up, but socially they had no meeting-place. He had thrown in his lot with Anglo-India by marrying a countrywoman, and he was acquiring some of its limitations, and already felt surprise at his own past heroism.
>
> (*PI*, 309)

Heroism in Forster is linked with the commitment to friendship. However, while politics has remained peripheral to most of Forster's text, it becomes the last resort for terminating the relationship of Aziz and Fielding. Aziz suddenly and uncharacteristically bandies political slogans before Fielding: ' ". . . we shall drive every blasted Englishman into the sea, and then" – he rode against him furiously – "and then," he concluded, half kissing him, "you and I shall be friends" '. But, of course, the political solution is superfluous to their friendship and Fielding asks for personal intimacy: ' "Why can't we be friends now?" said the other, holding him affectionately. "It's what I want. It's what you want" ' (*PI*, 312). All distances are temporarily lifted and homo-erotic desire is for once expressed directly. It is at this suggestion of male intimacy that the whole universe, animate and inanimate, religious and secular, rises in protest, and the sheer landscape throws innumerable barriers between them. It is to the specific proposal of love between two men that the novel's ultimate denial applies and the distances generated are emotional as much as physical:

> But the horses didn't want it – they swerved apart; the earth didn't want it, sending up rocks through which riders must pass single-file; the temples, the tank, the jail, the palace, the birds, the carrion, the Guest House, that came into view as they issued from the gap and saw Mau beneath: they didn't want it, they said in their hundred voices, 'No, not yet,' and the sky said, 'No, not there.'
>
> (*PI*, 312)

There is no one factor to which the breach of friendship can be attributed, and the whole universe is to blame for the rift between Aziz and Fielding – not politics *tout court*.

Thus, from the beginning of the novel to its end, *A Passage to India*, like the rest of Forster's fiction, is concerned with the theme of homo-erotic love. The political strand in the novel gives a poignancy to the concern for male friendship but remains subsidiary to it. The colonial situation serves to illustrate the politics of desire; as such *A Passage to India* only partly belongs to the tradition of Orientalism as defined by Said, and one should question how closely the identification of its Oriental elements accounts for the whole narrative.

The opening lines of *A Passage to India* mark a break away from the Oriental narratives on India, and Forster presents a different view of the country:

> Except for the Marabar Caves – and they are twenty miles off – the city of Chandrapore presents nothing extraordinary. Edged rather than washed by the river Ganges, it trails for a couple of miles along the bank, scarcely distinguishable from the rubbish it deposits so freely. There are no bathing-steps on the river front, as the Ganges happens not to be holy here . . . In the bazaars there is no painting and scarcely any carving. The very wood seems made of mud, the inhabitants of mud moving. So abased, so monotonous is everything that meets the eye, that when the Ganges comes down it might be expected to wash the excrescence back into the soil. Houses do fall, people are drowned and left rotting, but the general outline of the town persists, swelling here, shrinking there, like some low but indestructible form of life.
>
> (*PI*, 2)

With the opening sentence Forster rejects the traditional view of India. As the passage unfolds the author systematically decentres the exotic image of India; from the Ganges to the bazaars, houses and people, everything in India is indescribably dull. In his emphasis on mud, dirt and decay, Forster puts forward a more specific version of India, calculated to achieve a specific result with his readers.

Forster's engagement with India resembles the journeys to Italy in his earlier novels. The author himself compares India to Italy:

> To regard an Indian as if he were an Italian is not, for instance, a common error, nor perhaps a fatal one, and Fielding often attempted analogies between this peninsula and that other, smaller and more exquisitely shaped, that stretches into the classic waters of the Mediterranean.
>
> (*PI*, 55)

Fielding's bungalow, 'though of wood had reminded Fielding of the Loggia de' Lanzi at Florence' (*PI*, 63). Forster parodies the tourist's idea of India; Mrs Moore does not realize that India is only 'seemingly so mysterious' (*PI*, 43) and Adela sounds naive in her enthusiasm 'to see the *real* India' (*PI*, 19). Forster shifts the focus of his narrative in Fielding's answer to Adela. In telling her to 'Try seeing Indians' (*PI*, 21), Fielding's reply echoes Philip Herriton's advice to Lilia as she departs for Italy in *Where Angels Fear to Tread*: 'Love and understand the Italians, for the people are more marvellous than the land' (*WA*, 1). As with 'Italians', by 'Indians', Forster means men, for Indian women are practically non-existent in the novel.

Having rejected the common Oriental notions about India, Forster puts forward his own idea of the country, tinged with homo-erotic emotion. Forster depicts India primarily in terms of its men, observing in detail their physical qualities. Aziz is introduced as 'an athletic little man, daintily put together' (*PI*, 12). Forster describes some youths training: 'Round they ran, weedy and knock-kneed – the local physique was wretched' (*PI*, 51). The Nawab Bahadur's grandson, Nureddin, is referred to as 'an effeminate youth' (*PI*, 90). Aziz embodies the irresistible pull of India, albeit presented through Adela's consciousness:

> What a handsome little Oriental he was, and no doubt his wife and children were beautiful too, for people usually get what they already possess. She did not admire him with any personal warmth, for there was nothing of the vagrant in her blood, but she guessed he might attract women of his own race and rank,

and she regretted that neither she nor Ronny had physical charm. It does make a difference in a relationship – beauty, thick hair, a fine skin.

(*PI*, 144)

Aziz, in his naturalness and spontaneity, represents a homo-erotic ideal in Forster, similar to the heroes of his other novels such as Gino, George Emerson, Stephen Wonham and Alec Scudder.

Increasingly, the homo-erotic and a remade Orientalism converge. This accounts for the symbol of masculine beauty in the courtroom, the man who pulled the punkah: 'Almost naked, and splendidly formed . . . He had the strength and beauty that sometimes come to flower in Indians of low birth' (*PI*, 207). Spellbound by the dignity of the man, Adela withdraws her accusations against Aziz, 'Something in his aloofness impressed the girl from middle-class England, and rebuked the narrowness of her sufferings' (*PI*, 207). The antithesis between middle-class England and a person of lower class is familiar in Forster, and delineates an inhibitive as opposed to a permissive culture. Accordingly, the influence of the punkah-wallah in the novel is sexually liberating. The lure of the East is manifested again in Aziz and his friends as they celebrate victory after the trial:

> Fielding, who had dressed up in native costume, learned from his excessive awkwardness in it that all his motions were makeshifts, whereas when the Nawab Bahadur stretched out his hand for food, or Nureddin applauded a song, something beautiful had been accomplished which needed no development. This restfulness of gesture – it is the Peace that passeth Understanding, after all, it is the social equivalent of Yoga. When the whirring of action ceases, it becomes visible, and reveals a civilization which the West can disturb but will never acquire.
>
> (*PI*, 239)

As the above passages demonstrate, the images of beauty in India relate to men and hint at the homo-erotic desire in the text.

India is, therefore, constructed in the narrative not so much as a historical, geographical entity, but as the Other to the English society. As opposed to the 'chilly English' there are the 'flabby Hindus' (*PI*, 18) and the efficiency of the English is offset by 'slack Hindus', who have 'no idea of society' (*PI*, 62). However, beneath the cultural stereotypes, the contrasts Forster sketches are not political but emotional and sexual. The English are depicted as rational and organized, with 'everything ranged coldly on shelves' (PI, 59). Aziz pities them, for 'he knew at the bottom of his heart that they could not help being so cold and odd and circulating like an ice-stream through the land' (PI, 64). Aziz himself, on the other hand is 'incapable of administration' (PI, 64), and sentimental and melodramatic. Not accurate over 'verbal truth', he rather represents the 'truth of mood' (PI, 65). Unlike the stiff Englishmen, he is 'sensuous but healthy' (PI, 5), and often dwells on 'the Bottomless Pit' (PI, 92) without guilt. Aziz embodies an ideal of homo-erotic desire, and childish tantrums and displays of affection actually *qualify* him for male friendship.

It is no accident that the political in Forster's own brand of Orientalism is removed, at the narrative level, from the erotic. As he was to point out in 'What I Believe', human relationships were 'a matter for the heart, which signs no documents'. The claims of the state 'can run counter' to 'love and loyalty' (TCD, 76–7). Consequently, *A Passage to India* derives its metaphorical power from the specific aptness of narrative colonial signifiers to figure individual crises of desire. It is the particular colonial context that throws up dramatic and central problems as to how to equate the One and the Many, private fulfilment and public responsibility, and the truly cathartic event and communal ritual.

The contact between the English and the Indians in *A Passage to India* is rendered in emotional rather than political terms. As Aziz walks up to Major Callendar's bungalow, 'depression suddenly seized him' and 'this not because his soul was servile but because his feelings – the sensitive edges of him – feared a gross snub' (PI, 11). According to Aziz the solution to India's problems does not lie in politics. He says:

'. . . Mr Fielding, no one can ever realize how much kindness we Indians need, we do not even realize it ourselves. But we know when it has been given. We do not forget, though we may seem to. Kindness, more kindness, and even after that more kindness. I assure you it is the only hope.'

(PI, 108)

On his part, Fielding is wary of Aziz's statement because he believes that India calls for a more passionate response, 'kindness – yes, that he might supply, but was that really all that the queer nation needed? Did it not also demand an occasional intoxication of the blood?' (PI, 109). Forster projects qualities of warmth and spontaneity on to India and the Indian people. During Aziz's meeting with Mrs Moore in the Mosque, the old Englishwoman comments: 'I don't think I understand people very well. I only know whether I like or dislike them.' To this Aziz retorts: 'Then you are an Oriental' (*PI*, 17). The pattern occurs again at the end of the book when Ralph says to Aziz that he can always tell whether a stranger is a friend, and Aziz repeats: 'Then you are an Oriental' (*PI*, 301).[16]

As in Forster's other novels, the theme of friendship is reinforced by various allusions and motifs in the text, except that in *A Passage to India* the homo-erotic codes are derived from the history and customs of the country. Aziz's favourite Mogul emperor is Babur who exemplifies male love, for 'never in his whole life did he betray a friend' and 'He laid down his life for his son' (*PI*, 135). Then there is the enigmatic legend of the 'Tank of the Dagger', which has no connection with the plot of the novel, except that it tells a story of a Hindu raja who killed his sister's son, but the dagger with which he murdered the man remained stuck to his hand until he showed compassion to a thirsty cow and was himself forgiven in return (*PI*, 170). The richest symbol of homo-erotic love is of course Lord Krishna, a mischievous, pastoral deity, 'the universal lover' (*PI*, 278) beloved of men and women alike, and in some ways similar to the classical god Pan.

Therefore Forster's journey to India is romantic, and indeed, homo-erotic. The women characters do not participate in the novel's imagery of beauty and passion – Mrs Moore is too old and Adela is too plain. Aziz cannot think of her as sexually desirable: 'she was not beautiful. She has practically no breasts, if you come to think of it' (*PI*, 111). Homo-erotic desire in Forster is subversive of dominant social norms, and in *A Passage to India* he overturns the political hierarchy. The conventional plot of colonial fiction, the rape of a white woman by a native, is parodied in the novel. At the trial Mr McBryde expounds on 'Oriental Pathology' and reiterates the well-known fact 'that the darker races are physically attracted by the fairer' (*PI*, 208). In reply to which, someone shouts back: 'Even when the lady is so uglier than the gentleman?' (*PI*, 208), so comically dismissing the suggestion as soon as it arises.

The undercurrents of homo-erotic desire break loose in the Temple scene. The religious festival of the birth of Krishna, with its message of 'God is love', is described as a pagan revelry that combines spiritual with physical ecstasy. The worshippers emulate Krishna in 'innocent frolic':

> They removed their turbans, and one put a lump of butter on his forehead, and waited for it to slide down his nose into his mouth. Before it could arrive, another stole up behind him, snatched the

melting morsel, and swallowed it himself . . . Having swallowed the butter, they played another game which chanced to be graceful: the fondling of Shri Krishna under the similitude of a child . . . The child is restored to his parents, the ball thrown on, and another child becomes for a moment the World's Desire.

(*PI*, 279–80)

The 'divine mess' (*PI*, 280) generated by the ritual is a sublimation of sexual energies, 'Not an orgy of the body; the tradition of that shrine forbade it. But the human spirit had tried by desperate contortion to ravish the unknown, flinging down science and history in the struggle, yes, beauty herself' (*PI*, 278). The impact of the scene is purely symbolic, and while a vision of universal, spiritual love is accomplished by Godbole, the ideal of personal love and brotherhood between men remains unrealized in the novel.

Forster's journey to India is above all homo-erotic in that, as in all his preceding novels, the act of crossing thresholds and changing vistas involves the covenant of love, the ceremonies of friendship and brotherhood. A journey in Forster is an emblem of flight and signals the author's expectation of finding personal relations away from English middle-class constraints. Forster takes a narrative that would be hampered in a certain context and transfers it elsewhere, whether it be to a foreign country or an Arcadia or a realm of fantasy. Consequently, journeys in Forster entail a break away from a particular social order and invariably point to the society left behind. The geographical shift becomes metamorphosed into an abstract passage, with the rites of initiation and regeneration contingent upon outward movement.

Forster wrote in his 'Personal Memorandum' in 1935: 'I want to love a strong young man of the lower classes and be loved by him and even hurt by him. That is my ticket, and then I have wanted to write respectable novels' (cited by Stallybrass, *LTC*, xiv). The comment elucidates the fundamental incompatibility in his narratives between respectability and desire. In 'Notes on the English Character' (1920), Forster says that the major drawback of Englishmen is 'An undeveloped heart – not a cold one' (*AH*, 5). Forster saw English middle-class men as self-conscious and inhibited, and so the possibility 'to love a strong young man' and 'be loved by him' always exists outside the middle-class boundaries, with men from 'the lower classes'. In so far as the ideal of homo-erotic love lies beyond the structures of respectable society, distance in Forster is inseparable from desire.

A journey in Forster is a mechanism for introducing distances, for the author conceives of relations between men as a distant desire. Distance, paradoxically, becomes a means of attaining desire, for it offers a way of overcoming personal sanctions and censorship in order to achieve forbidden love. Furbank observes that Forster 'achieved physical sex very late and found it easier with people outside his own social class, and it remained a kind of private magic for him'. Furbank continues:

> he never expected an *equal* sexual relationship. His chief feeling towards anyone who let him make love to them was gratitude. Intense gratitude led him to romanticise them, at least with one part of his mind, and by romanticising them he managed to keep them at a distance.
>
> (Furbank 1970: 62)

Desire, joined as it is with the dynamics of the journey, breeds several paradoxes in Forster's texts. In his essay on Conrad, Forster mentions the 'constant discrepancies between his nearer and his further vision'. The obscurity in Conrad is due to his failure to reconcile his own world with those other lands to which he travelled: 'If he lived only in his experiences, never lifting his eyes to what is beyond them: or if, having seen what lies beyond, he would subordinate his experiences to it – then in either case he would be easier to read' ('Joseph Conrad: A Note' (1920), *AH*, 137). A similar kind of contradiction exists in Forster's narratives, too, where the narrator accommodates the ideal of male love, not available in his immediate surroundings (his nearer vision), by recourse to journey into some remote space or time (his further vision). However, Forster not only approximates desire by imposing distances but also pre-empts the fulfilment of homo-erotic love.

The desire and the capacity for friendship are projected on to and ascribed to the Other, which the characters must leave behind. Forster could not ultimately envisage lasting relations between men in any society, and in *A Passage to India* the colonial situation as well as the geographical distance between them offer a convenient reason for ending male friendship.

Therefore, homo-erotic desire is never fulfilled in *A Passage to India* and a friend remains an elusive ideal. Unable to relate to so alien a culture, Forster surrenders to the sense of complexity about India:

> How can the mind take hold of such a country? Generations of invaders have tried, but they remain in exile. The important towns they build are only retreats, their quarrels the malaise of

men who cannot find their way home. India knows . . . of the whole world's trouble, to its uttermost depth. She calls 'Come' through her hundred mouths, through objects ridiculous and august. But come to what? She has never defined.

(*PI*, 128)

Ultimately, India resists being cast in the homo-erotic mould and disappoints the desire for male love. Ronny and Adela drive across the country with the Nawab Bahadur and the characters' emotional sterility is reflected in the landscape: 'the whole scene was inferior, and suggested that the countryside was too vast to admit of excellence. In vain did each item in it call out, "Come, come." There was not enough god to go round' (*PI*, 79). The religious allegories of love do not translate into relationships and India does not endorse homo-erotic desire. For all the author's impulse to the contrary, politics impinges on friendship and Forster finally admits that 'every human act in the East is tainted with officialism' (*PI*, 178), and the relationship of Fielding and Aziz is untenable outside the political boundaries.

Forster was unable to express homo-erotic desire directly and language itself became oppressive rather than therapeutic. *A Passage to India* reflects the writer's weariness with his medium:

Most of life is so dull that there is nothing to be said about it, and the books and talk that would describe it as interesting are obliged to exaggerate, in the hope of justifying their own existence. Inside its cocoon of work or social obligation, the human spirit slumbers for the most part, registering the distinction between pleasure and pain, but not nearly as alert as we pretend. There are periods in the most thrilling day during which nothing happens, and though we continue to exclaim 'I do enjoy myself' or 'I am horrified' we are insincere. 'As far as I feel anything, it is enjoyment, horror' – it's no more than that really, and a perfectly adjusted organism would be silent.

(*PI*, 125)

Words in the text are divorced from meaning in that they do not encompass the deepest desires, and hence everything in the novel is reduced to an echo: 'If one had spoken vileness in that place, or quoted lofty poetry, the comment would have been the same – "ou-boum" ' (*PI*, 140).

Gillian Beer has pointed to the negative sentence structures of *A Passage to India* (Beer 1985: 44–58). Language indeed operates in the novel to negate the norms of English society. Mrs Moore loses her faith and is struck dumb in the Caves:

> Religion appeared, poor little talkative Christianity, and she knew that all its divine words from 'Let there be light' to 'It is finished' only amounted to 'boum'. Then she was terrified over an area larger than usual; the universe, never comprehensible to her intellect, offered no repose to her soul, the mood of the last two months took definite form at last, and she realized that she didn't want to write to her children, didn't want to communicate with anyone, not even with God.
>
> (*PI*, 141)

In the Marabar Caves, Mrs Moore felt that something 'settled on her mouth like a pad' which strangled the 'poor little talkative Christianity' (*PI*, 138, 141). With her faith shattered, Mrs Moore retreats into a permanent silence. When Adela wants to consult her about what happened in the Caves, Mrs Moore's reaction is unduly harsh:

> 'Say, say, say,' said the old lady bitterly. 'As if anything can be said! I have spent my life in saying or in listening to sayings; I have listened too much. It is time I was left in peace . . .'
>
> (*PI*, 190)

Forster incorporates pauses and silences into his narratives to produce equivocation. This technique is perfected in *A Passage to India*, where nothing ever gets cleared up – whether the accident of the Nawab Bahadur's car is caused by an animal or a ghost, whether the object that Adela sees on the way to Marabar Caves is a snake or rope, and whether Adela was assaulted in the Caves or not. Forster uses the philosophical and religious dimensions of India to heighten his own sense of despair and futility, and in Fielding's words 'A mystery is a muddle' (*PI*, 62).

Meanwhile, for all his preoccupation with friendship and personal relations, Forster's novels won acclaim for their social and political aspects. Having broached the theme of friendship from different angles in his novels, he lapsed into complete silence after *A Passage to India*, at least as far as writing novels was concerned. He is reported to have said that he stopped writing novels because he had nothing more to say (King 1978: 76). Forster's silence implies his rejection of fiction as a means of communication; his own novels had inevitably been read as heterosexual texts, in spite of their central theme of friendship.

The growing popularity of his novels, for the wrong reason, necessarily brought to Forster an increasing sense of his own failure as a novelist. He wrote to Virginia Woolf on 28 June 1927, protesting against her review of his novels: 'My novels will be either almost-successes or failures: – probably in the future almost-successes, because experience enables one to substitute cleverness for force with increasing verisimilitude' (cited by Furbank 1977–8: II, 145; Lago W542). The price Forster paid for his cleverness in coding the theme of friendship was that it went unnoticed; in *A Passage to India* he combined homo-erotic desire with universal and metaphysical issues, and hence his emotional despair attains nihilistic dimensions.

To read *A Passage to India* merely as an Orientalist text, depicting the author's stance on colonial India, detracts from the subtlety of Forster's narrative. It is rewarding to read the novel as a homosexual text, and one must take at least some cognizance of the author's strenuous objections to the political interpretations of his work. In a letter to Edward Arnold, dated 8 June 1924, Forster emphasized that he 'had been careful not to allude to contemporary politics' in *A Passage to India* (cited by Stallybrass, *PI*, xiii, fn 14; Lago A1200). Six months after the novel was published, Forster complained of the response the book had aroused, in a letter to Joe Ackerley, dated 27 June 1924: 'I am complimented on my fairmindedness until my soul is numbed' (cited by Heine, *HD*, xvi; Lago A44). Forster constantly repeated that the novel:

> is not really about politics, though it is the political aspect of it that caught the general public and made it a sell. It's about something wider than politics, about the search of the human race for a more lasting home, about the universe as embodied in the Indian earth and the Indian sky, about the horror lurking in the Marabar Caves and the release symbolized by the birth of Krishna. It is – or desires to be – philosophic and poetic.
>
> (*HD*, 298)

Indeed, the themes of *A Passage to India* are wider and more fundamental than political ones *tout court*. In 1960, Forster said to Furbank that *A Passage to India* was not 'about the incompatibility of East and West', but 'was really concerned with the difficulty of living in the universe' (Furbank, 1977–8: II, 308). Needless to say, the 'difficulty' Forster refers to includes that of being a homosexual, which in *A Passage to India* is magnified to philosophical and religious dimensions, and related to the general predicament of humanity.

Forster's transcultural novels are impelled by homo-erotic desire, and in this sense they are no different from those based in England. Whereas in the short stories Forster creates fantasy worlds, in the novels he gives his narratives a contemporary setting and immediacy, but the countries to which the characters are transported are fictional places that in many ways resemble the fantastic settings of the short stories. While the foreign culture is broadly identified as Italy or India, within the historical-geographical country 'Monteriano' and 'Chandrapore' are fictitious places. The foreign country in Forster's fiction is conceived as the Other, designed to offset the English character and identity. Italy and India represent the strange and exotic, the 'romantic' against the 'suburban'.

In a paper read before an Italian audience in November 1959, Forster confessed of *Where Angels Fear to Tread* that he knew 'very little of the class structure' or the 'economic problems' of Italy when he wrote the novel (*HD*, 291). Similarly, the depiction of India could hardly have corresponded with the realities of the country. He recalls of his second trip to India in 1921 that 'between the India I had tried to create and the India I was experiencing there was an impassable gulf. I had to get back to England and see my material in perspective before I could proceed' (*HD*, 298). It is unsurprising that Forster could not finish his novel in India and could continue with it only after returning to England; England provided Forster with a vantage point from which he could present India as an aesthetic construct. Moreover, the benefit of the cultural encounters is for the English characters alone. At the end of the Italian adventures in *Where Angels Fear to Tread*, Philip 'had reached love by the spiritual path', while Gino 'never traversed any path at all' (*WA*, 141–2), and in *A Passage to India* it is the English characters who are changed as a result of their experiences in India.

In so far as India is used to displace and expose English values and way of life, Forster appears to be sympathetic towards Indians. In his criticism of British society against the Indian setting, Forster overturns the notions of Western superiority, and to that extent *A Passage to India* subverts the cultural hegemony exercised by traditional Orientalist texts. While Forster does contrast Indians and the British, the cultural stereotypes that the author adopts are provisional and ultimately abandoned. Thus while *A Passage to India* apparently belongs to the Orientalist tradition of English literature, the Orientalism in the text is constantly redefined by homo-erotic desire. In the final analysis Forster does not endorse either British or Indian culture, but remains outside both societies. Therefore the controversy as to whether *A Passage to India* is pro-British or pro-Indian is never likely to be settled. Forster himself, in a letter to Masood dated 27 September 1922, disclaimed any part in promoting racial harmony:

When I began the book I thought of it as a little bridge of sympathy between East and West, but this conception has had to go, my sense of truth forbids anything so comfortable. I think that most Indians, like most English people, are shits, and I am not interested whether they sympathize with one another or not.

(Cited by Heine, *HD*, xv; Lago M183)

Forster's last novel, like the rest of his fiction, is an allegory of distance and desire.

SUPPLEMENT

NIGEL WOOD: Are you claiming, ultimately, that Said's model of interpretation, highlighting 'Orientalist' discourses, falls some way short of the mark, in that it cannot account for the personal codes that follow from Forster's own preoccupations?

PARMINDER BAKSHI: Said's elucidation of Orientalism falls short only in so far as any theoretical framework is inadequate for fully comprehending life and literature. Theories are useful as tools and provide different perspectives on a text, but they are not always in themselves either consistent or comprehensive. If theories enhance our interpretation of literary texts, literature in turn constantly modifies theory. What we must remember is that although writers may be strongly influenced by certain beliefs and ideologies, they do not necessarily write to make their texts fit into a predefined mould, unless, of course, it is propagandist or polemical writing.

In my interpretation of *A Passage to India*, I have used two main analytical frameworks – Orientalism and homosexuality – and it was not the theories that led to the novel, but the novel that illustrated the theories. So Forster's novel remained primary, not the theory, and my chapter presents a close reading of the novel. I believe that many of the readings of *A Passage to India* and Forster's other novels have been misguided precisely because the critics stray away from a close reading of the text, and the interpretation offered is impressionistic. Therefore, against the assertions of postmodernism, I do believe that a definite and precise reading of the text is possible, without being reductive, and this is possible only by following the text itself.

NW: You point out on p. 38 that Forster goes to some lengths to 'dissociate friendship from politics', even though 'contemporary racial and political issues constantly impinge on the text'. How do they 'impinge', if Forster excludes them? Does our reading inevitably import these issues, from a knowledge (post-1948) that Forster could not possibly have? Or does he actually involve the public world only to deny its validity?

PB: The political issues impinge on *A Passage to India* in spite of Forster's emphasis on the personal in that the text is not a pure entity, but evolves out of a context, and Forster chose the political context of colonial India to elucidate, very effectively, the difficulties of male friendship. So to that extent, the political was not and could not have been excluded from the text; any novel written during that period would have carried some political resonances. However, the irony in Forster's case was that while a political setting provided him with an excellent occasion for projecting the theme of friendship and personal relations, it proved to be almost too perfect a disguise so that the unmentionable theme of homo-erotic love is almost swallowed up in the larger political context of the novel.

Texts are loaded, and so are the minds of readers; we carry an intellectual and theoretical baggage that determines our understanding and response to the text. Forster and his contemporaries must have been aware of similar political issues; what the writer did not share with his readers and critics was a homosexual sensibility, and hence political concerns came to dominate the reception of *A Passage to India*. Forster's novel, like Salman Rushdie's *Satanic Verses*, serves as a salutary reminder of the fact that often the context and readership can dominate the text over the author's intent or even the actual content of the work.

NW: Why do you think Forster wrote no extended fiction after *Passage*?

PB: I think silence was the only recourse left to Forster after writing *A Passage to India*. From his first novel, Forster had experimented with several genres for depicting the theme of homo-erotic love, and each time he was more effective than before in coding homo-erotic desire. The success of his novels hinged upon the failure, on the part of his reader, to recognize the homo-eroticism underlying his narratives. By this time, he had written an overtly homosexual narrative in *Maurice*, but he could not publish it. Therefore, it is understandable that he should lapse into a silence as far as writing novels is concerned, as he could not really express the themes he felt most strongly about. Also, he met Bob Buckingham in 1930, with whom he at last found a fulfilling relationship, and that, too, may have taken away the urgency to write novels.

NW: You mention the similarities between Forster's depiction of Italian landscapes and culture and those of India. Is *Passage*, though, separated from his earlier novels by twelve or more years, a different enterprise?

PB: It is dangerous to call *A Passage to India* a different enterprise from his previous novels, a mistake that has already been made too often. *A Passage to India* is the product of the same preoccupations as the rest of Forster's work, and there are certain themes and techniques that run through all his novels. There is a sense of the author's development from one novel to the next, and so *A Passage to India* is mature and a sophisticated work. It is interesting that the protagonists in both *Howards End* and *A Passage to India* are older than the central characters in the first three novels. *A Passage to India* has had greater appeal than Forster's other novels perhaps because it is transcultural, and covers a vast canvas.

CHAPTER 2

Law and Order in
A Passage to India

BARBARA HARLOW

[The current distrust of global explanations for historical change has promoted the rise of competing 'histories'. Replacing the notion that history can embody certain recurrent tendencies, or even laws (loosely termed 'historicism'), there is a renewed emphasis on discrete and focused histories of certain localized topics, each with its own dynamic. Louis Althusser is most noted for this stand against a 'Hegelian' concept of history as the gradual unfolding of some World-Spirit, with its reliance on linear development (see Althusser 1971: 121–73). Such grand narratives ignore the specific agencies (and agents) of repression or discrimination, and imply that present political and social inequalities are merely part of a transhistorical, even metaphysical, pattern.

An abstract pattern may seem to be deduced from the facts to hand, but this is still a *constructed* framework. Barbara Harlow's study of the notions of law and order in *A Passage to India* stresses the way such ideas have been manifested in colonial discourse as part of a universal standard. Far from natural, this touchstone is a coercive appropriation of language and is thus ideological, the imposition of the colonialist perspective in the deepest recesses of language. Such 'British discursive legitimations' (p. 68) of colonial rule aspired to be a master-reading of history that inevitably carried in their wake appeals to 'common sense' and 'realism'. It just as inexorably defined such perceptions for its own ends, both consciously and unconsciously.

Forster's work derives authority from such ideology and yet at the same time unsettles a complacent belief in its truth. By emphasizing the split between an 'official' and 'unofficial' Forster account, criticism may well be involved in a perverse 'reading against the grain' and yet, as Gayatri Spivak indicates, it is only through the 'deconstruction' of these received notions of historical truth that deeper changes in people's lives can be mapped, colonial 'truths' analysed and the 'subaltern consciousness' retrieved (see Spivak's essay, 'Subaltern Studies: Deconstructing Historiography', in Guha 1985: 330–63).

As defined in the *Concise Oxford Dictionary*, the term 'subaltern' means not only 'of inferior rank' but also, in a technical sense derived from formal logic, 'the particular, not universal'. There is an irony at work in the title, *Subaltern Studies*, given to the several collections of radical essays on Indian history, for, (a) there is no inferiority implied in the choice to view history from the 'bottom up', and (b) it was only the colonial administrator who was content to regard individual acts of 'insurgency' as unconnected criminal actions motivated by purely personal mendacity.

The work of Ranajit Guha has done much to redefine our view of colonialist historiography and also its semantics. In his *Elementary Aspects of Peasant Insurgency in Colonial India* (1983a) he analyses the colonialist need to depict revolutionary peasant activity as sporadic breaches of law and order. Causal explanations were sought for ready-made conclusions, an induced 'historical truth', which was really just an 'apology for law and order – the truth of the force by which the British had annexed the subcontinent' (Guha 1983a: 3; see also Guha 1983b: 1–42). Underpinning Guha's account is Antonio Gramsci's perception that there is no such thing as spontaneity in history. As Guha understands it, 'this is precisely where they err who fail to recognize the trace of consciousness in the apparently unstructured movements of the masses' (Guha 1983a: 5). While such opposition was (and continues elsewhere to be) a 'negative and inversive procedure', this does not 'put it outside the realm of politics' (Guha 1983a: 9). For Gramsci, in his 'History of the Subaltern Classes: Some Methodological Criteria' (1934–5; excerpts in Gramsci 1971: 52–4), the very term 'subaltern' (the original use of the term as taken up by Guha and contributors) designates those who do not enjoy the collectivity of class consciousness. Their 'instrumentality' is still a historical force capable of definition.

This has an immediate application in the analysis of colonialist literary texts, for it is precisely this submerged 'voice' which needs amplifying, if such writing is to be given its fullest context, for not only do we listen to the repressed, but we can also identify the 'staged' *conceptual* power of Imperialism. In Gramsci's work, there was a significant distinction between the material 'rule' of a presiding power, and the 'hegemony' of the active, and so dominant, social and cultural forces that keep it in place (see Williams 1977, 108–14; Said 1984, 168–72; and, for an influential application of Gramsci to subaltern studies, Asok Sen's 'Subaltern Studies: Capital, Class and Community', in Guha 1987: 203–35). In becoming canonical, it is often the case that literary texts are used for the dissemination of residual 'hegemonic' images.

As Gauri Viswanathan has demonstrated (Viswanathan 1989), it is specifically the study of literature, never free of a particular cultural situation, that, far from ignoring the marginal or heterodox, actually 'contains' it. Mental production has the capacity to exert as material an effect on culture as the economic base. It is not that the premises that Forster recognizes in *Passage* are either 'wrong' or 'right', but rather that they stem from a class or even racial interest. Spivak has recently suggested further opportunities for turning the colonial power relation upside down when we realize that the writing of history may always be a strategy. A crisis in political authority accompanies a 'functional change in a sign system', which is a 'violent event' (Guha 1985: 331–2), not a gradual evolution towards more sophisticated and 'textual' perceptions: it bears directly on lived experience. The process of reading invoked by Spivak is a transactional one, where the critical sense is fortified by the need to question, and so displace, accepted systems of meaning, the Forster we have been encouraged to 'know' (see also Young 1990: 157–62). The elaboration of a text need not be, therefore, a wilful evasion of what seems 'there' in the words on the page, because those very words never signify innocently or autonomously. 'Elaboration', for Gramsci, meant ordering 'in a systematic, coherent and critical fashion one's own intuitions of life and the world, and to determine exactly what is to be understood by the word "systematic", so that it is not taken in the pedantic and academic sense [as a natural law, impervious to changes wrought by human agency]' (Gramsci 1971: 327; see also Said 1984: 169–72). A politically aware criticism thus sets the text against past *and present* perceptions of reality (which in any given culture are never unitary or consistent) so as to withstand and so analyse the particular strategies any writing performs.]

NIGEL WOOD

In fact, I do not know of any fictional work in Urdu, in the last roughly 200 years, which is of any significance and any length . . . and in which the issue of colonialism or the difficulty of a civilizational encounter between the English and the Indians has the same primacy as, for example, in Forster's A Passage to India *or Paul Scott's* The Raj Quartet.
(Ahmed 1987: 21)

You can only read against the grain if misfits in the text signal the way.
(Gayatri Chakaravorty Spivak: 'Deconstructing Historiography', in Guha and Spivak 1988: 21)

In his enumeration of 'some aspects of the historiography of colonial India', the Indian historian and participant in the Subaltern Studies Group Ranajit Guha argues: 'The historiography of Indian nationalism has for a long time been dominated by elitism – colonialist and bourgeois-nationalist elitism' (Guha and Spivak 1988: 37). Guha further claims that:

> the poverty of this historiography is demonstrated beyond doubt by its failure to understand and assess the mass articulation of this nationalism except, negatively, as a *law and order problem*, and positively, if at all, either as a response to the charisma of certain elite leaders or in the currently more fashionable terms of vertical mobilization by the manipulation of factions.
>
> (Guha and Spivak 1988: 39; emphasis added)

E.M. Forster's novel, *A Passage to India*, published in 1924, five years after the 1919 massacre of Indian civilians by British troops firing on a crowd gathered at Amritsar, might be read as a literary contribution to that elite historiography and its negative emphasis on the maintenance of 'law and order' as characterizing the British discursive legitimations of the administration of colonial India. *A Passage to India*, that is, narrativizes the political conflict between colonizer and colonized and the failed efforts at individual reconciliations as a crime, one that is figured in the alleged 'rape' of an Englishwoman, Adela, by an Indian man, Aziz. This incident, which occupies the central space of Forster's novel – and much of the critical attention to it ever since – is prepared in the text by the desires of the two visiting Englishwomen, Mrs Moore and Adela, her future daughter-in-law, to see the '*real* India' (*PI*, 19). The alleged crime is then adjudicated at a criminal trial that ends, as eventually will the novel itself, abruptly, if irresolutely, without a conviction and the dismissal of the charges. The allegation of sexual assault allowed the British to confront their Indian subjects. The trial, in frightening contrast, had it been permitted to continue, would have allowed in turn those subjects to confront their accusers.

I

'While ostensibly about the relations of the British with the native populations of India, [*A Passage to India*] is fundamentally a highly organized work of art, a limited world commenting on the tragedies and mitigations of the larger one' (Kermode and Hollander 1973: 622). This appreciation of Forster's final and arguably most famous novel, provided to students and anthology users in one standard version of 'modern British literature', is such that the author himself might have assented to. Indeed, as one of his biographers noted in commenting on the significance of Forster's last visit to India in 1945, on the eve of Indian independence in 1947, 'The Indians seemed to him to be inordinately concerned with politics, politics, politics' (King 1978: 98). According to Forster himself, discussing that same visit: 'When I spoke about the necessity of form in literature and the importance of the individual vision their attention wandered . . . Literature, in their view, should expound or inspire a political creed' ('India Again', *TCD*, 328). Not even Francis King the biographer, however, who otherwise also displays a certain, not atypical,[1] defensive sympathy for the 'Turtons and Burtons' of his subject's novel, in his own lengthy passage on *A Passage to India*, can altogether maintain the enforced separation of literature and politics:

> At the time of its publication, the book was acclaimed both as a triumphant work of art (which it was) and as an accurate delineation of the teeming life of the Indian subcontinent (which it was not). Unlike Maugham, who had travelled to the Far East to learn about his compatriots, Forster had travelled to India to learn about Indians. The Muslims are drawn with marvellous skill, the Hindus with only a little less so; but the Anglo-Indians are complete caricatures. The absurdity of the scenes in which the Anglo-Indians are involved ranges from the farcical elements of the trial scene (the case against Aziz is, for example, conducted by the Superintendent of Police instead of by the Government Prosecutor) to everyone on every occasion, in the original edition, addressing the Collector as 'Burra Sahib.' (Forster was subsequently to make some alterations.) Such ignorance is astonishing. Fielding, the liberal principal of Government College, and the man who in part suggested his character, Sir Malcolm Darling, were, in fact, in no way unique in the India of the time, as Forster seems to have believed. Since the majority of those who passed out top in the civil service examinations of the day opted for the Indian rather than the English civil service, it would be surprising if they had been. After such misrepresentation, my father's story of fellow passengers on their way out to India by boat beginning to read Forster's novel and then chucking their copies overboard in disgust and fury is only too credible.

(King 1978: 78)

Although the English travellers to India do not seem to have been persuaded by arguments and appreciations of art and form here, the canonical issues that exercise these other, but not unrepresentative, critics and anthologizers of *A Passage to India* assume, even as they conflate, a set of well-schooled dichotomies and cordons, both disciplinary and historical, that have conventionally underwritten a received Western literary tradition: literature/politics, English/Indian (or colonizer/colonized), and 'larger world'/'limited world'.

That canonized tradition, however, of which Forster's novel is now a recognized classic, is itself rather less long-standing than was British colonialism in India – from the East India Company's mercantile activities under Elizabeth I, through the Raj, and until the partition of the subcontinent into India and Pakistan in 1947. That tradition of exemplary literary works, of the 'canon', as Gauri Viswanathan has argued, was already constituted as such by British colonialism. In *Masks of Conquest* (1989), an examination of 'literary study and British rule in India', Viswanathan

> sets out to demonstrate in part that the discipline of English came into its own in an age of colonialism, as well as to argue that no serious account of its growth and development can afford to ignore the imperial mission of educating and civilizing colonial subjects in the literature and thought of England.
>
> (Viswanathan 1989: 2)

English literature, that is, 'appeared as a subject in the curriculum of the colonies long before it was institutionalized in the home country'. That institutionalization was not a disinterested, or even a purely aesthetic process. On the contrary, as Viswanathan goes on to propose, the curriculum and its select components were designed in the nineteenth century as 'education for social and political control' (Viswanathan 1989: 3) and necessarily excluded then, as now, from their purview any inquiry into their political and historical context, or the distorted relations of power that characterized the colonial educational setting. But if English literary study 'had its beginnings as a strategy of containment' (Viswanathan 1989: 10), that strategy had consequences beyond the 'civilizing' of the 'natives' and the eventual acculturation of some select few of these subjects. According to Viswanathan:

> [t]he self-presentation of the Englishman to native Indians through the products of his mental labor removes him from the place of ongoing colonialist activity – of commercial operations, military expansion, and administration of territories – and de-actualizes and diffuses his material reality in the process. In a

parodic reworking of the Cartesian axiom, the Englishman's true essence is defined by the thought he produces, overriding all other aspects of his identity – his personality, actions and behavior. His material reality as subjugator and alien ruler is dissolved in his mental output; the blurring of the man and his works effectively removes him from history.

(Viswanathan 1989: 20)

As if a continuation of the truncated trial in Forster's *A Passage to India, Masks of Conquest*, like Ngugi's *Writers in Politics* (1981) or George Lamming's *The Pleasures of Exile* (1960) and within the decolonizing tradition established by such intellectuals as Frantz Fanon, C.L.R. James, and Amilcar Cabral, participates actively in that contemporary and interventionist project of post-colonial critique[2] of colonial and colonizing education, culture, history and politics.

Edward Said, the author of *Orientalism* (1978), itself a critical reading of the history of Western constructions of the 'Oriental', has similarly described the recent work of the Subaltern Studies Group in Delhi, six volumes of which have been edited by Ranajit Guha, as an 'alternative discourse'. According to Said, in his foreword to the 1988 collection of selected *Subaltern Studies* essays,

the work of the Subaltern scholars can be seen as an analogue of all those recent attempts in the West and throughout the rest of the world to articulate the hidden or suppressed accounts of numerous groups – women, minorities, disadvantaged or dispossessed groups, refugees, exiles, etc. And like all the authors of those other histories the Subaltern group in its work necessarily entails an examination of why, given numerical advantage, the justice of their cause, the great duration of their struggle, the Indian people *were* subaltern, why they were suppressed.

(Guha and Spivak 1988: vi–vii)

Ranajit Guha had introduced the work of the group, in his preface to the first volume of its essays published in Delhi in 1981, as a project that would 'promote a systematic and informed discussion of subaltern themes in the field of South Asian studies, and thus help to rectify the elitist bias characteristic of much research and academic work in this particular area'. The titular term 'subaltern', derived from the work of the Italian Marxist intellectual Antonio Gramsci, and which was defined by Guha in that preface as 'the general attribute of subordination in South Asian society whether this is expressed in terms of class, caste, age, gender and office or in any other way' (Guha and Spivak 1988: 35), forcefully characterizes the subsequent five volumes of essays that continued the discussion of 'subaltern functions' over the next seven years. Those essays by participants in the group's proceedings and forums included rereadings of peasant insurgencies, critiques of modes of power, revisionings of Gandhi, and literary critical analyses of court cases, Indian short stories and British philological scholarship.

Both subject matter and methodology reciprocally distinguish the Subaltern Studies project. The emphasis, as Guha (1983b) describes in the preface to the second volume of essays, on 'the primacy of the subaltern as the subject of historical and sociological enquiry', demanded from the contributors to the project the elaboration of new methodological strategies and programmes necessarily different from those that had been sanctioned by official and elite accounts of Indian history that were in turn both cause and effect of existing and available archives, sources and documentation. In response to his own question in *Elementary Aspects of Peasant Insurgency in Colonial India*, 'How then are we to get in touch with the consciousness of insurgency when our access to it is barred thus by the discourse of counter-insurgency?', Guha raised the imperative that it 'should be possible to read the presence of a rebel consciousness as a necessary and pervasive element within that body of evidence' (Guha, 1983a: 15). In particular, he suggested two features of that element that the subaltern critic might retrieve and refashion in an interventionary reading of the official sources. The first of these was 'intercepted discourse', the reporting of peasant and insurgent propositions and activities that warranted colonial containment. The second element, 'indices within elite discourse', required a more activist translation on the reader's part: interpreting 'dacoity' (or banditry) as itself a colonially opportunistic translation of politically motivated acts; 'contagion' stood for solidarity; 'fanaticism' for determination; and 'lawlessness' for insurrection. The project of colonial historiography was, and continues still to be, that is, to 'identify peasants as rebels and their attempt to turn the world upside down as crime' (Guha, 1983a: 17). A critical, indeed alternative, rewording or recoding could begin to establish some of the parameters for an oppositional theory and practice.

While *Elementary Aspects of Peasant Insurgency* remains perhaps Guha's fullest elaboration of both the theory and practice of subaltern studies, its work is given useful summary in the two essays, 'On Some Aspects of the Historiography of Colonial India' and 'The Prose of Counter-Insurgency', which appeared in volumes I and II of the group's publications. 'Some Aspects' articulates sixteen propositions concerning colonial historiography that identify the historiography of Indian nationalism as 'dominated by elitism' (Guha and Spivak 1988: 37) in both its colonialist and bourgeois-nationalist versions. According to the colonialist historian, Indian nationalism was a 'sort of "learning process" through which the native elite became involved in politics by trying to negotiate the maze of institutions and the corresponding cultural complex introduced by the colonial authorities in order to govern the country'. The bourgeois-nationalist Indian historian who, if identified with India rather than the Raj, was no less elitist than his colonial master teacher represented 'Indian nationalism as primarily an idealist venture in which the indigenous elite led the people from subjugation to freedom' (1988: 38). In both narratives, however, what was evident was the 'ideological character of historiography itself' determined by the 'class outlook' (1988: 38) of the historian that, wittingly or unwittingly, served to overlook the 'politics of the people' (1988: 39) and the 'conditions of exploitation to which the subaltern classes were subjected in varying degrees' (1988: 41).

The 'failure', then, 'of the Indian bourgeoisie to speak for the nation' (1988: 41) is further analysed in the following essay on 'the prose of counter-insurgency', as a discourse that perpetuates the myth of 'peasant insurrections being purely spontaneous and unpremeditated affairs' (1988: 45) and thus denying historical agency – and possibility – to the subaltern. Guha in this essay delineates three types of historiographical discourse. 'Primary discourse' is 'official in character . . . written concurrently with or soon after the event . . . by the participants concerned' (Guha and Spivak 1988: 47–8). 'Secondary discourse', either memoirs or histories, 'follows the primary at a distance and opens up a perspective to turn an event into history in the perception not only of those outside it but of the participants as well' (1988: 51). Both discourses, written according to an unreconstructed 'code of pacification which, under the Raj, was a complex of coercive intervention by the State and its protegés, the native elite, with arms and words' (1988: 59), display upon examination the 'optics of a colonialist historiography' (1988: 61) that makes of the insurgent 'not a subject of understanding or interpretation but of extermination, and the discourse of history, far from being neutral, serves directly to instigate official violence' (1988: 64). What colonialist historiography celebrates by design is, according to Guha, 'continuity – that of British power in India' (1988: 71). 'Tertiary discourse' – or the bourgeois-national, however, differs from the two preceding historicizing languages in that its 'effort to break away from the code of counter-insurgency' leads to a 'recognition of the wrongs done to the peasants [that in turn] leads directly to support for their struggle to seek redress by arms' (1988: 72). But, Guha continues, 'since every struggle for power by the historically ascendant classes in any epoch involves a bid to acquire a tradition', even this attempt to 'retrieve the history of insurgency' remains caught in the 'mediation of the insurgent's consciousness by the historian's' (1988: 77).

If peasant uprisings are seen both by their instigators and perpetrators and by their targets, whether colonial administrators, moneylenders or landowners, as 'turning the world upside down', then, according to Guha in the epilogue to *Elementary Aspects of Peasant Insurgency*, 'the documentation on insurgency must itself be turned upside down in order to reconstitute the insurgent's project aimed at reversing his world' (Guha 1983a: 333). Given this imperative, of both subject and methodology, the critical, radical even, work of the Subaltern Studies group might be read as itself the plotting of an insurgency, at once academic and geopolitical – or perhaps rather taken up as an assault that seeks to demolish the fortressing barriers that divide the one arena from the other, the academy, and its literary traditions with it, from the makings of national and international political policy. As Guha prefaced the fourth volume of Subaltern Studies essays published in 1985, deploying a vocabulary that resynchronizes these historic and traditional cordons,

> nothing throws the established procedures of knowledge more out of gear than the postulate that questions do not derive their validation from answers in all instances, that on the contrary such uncoupling can open up new *continents* of doubt, push back the familiar disciplinary *frontiers* and stir up a new *restlessness* in settled epistemological *outbacks*.
>
> (Guha, 1985; emphasis added)

Subaltern Studies, that is, according to Edward Said, mobilizes its participants in a '*crossing of boundaries*, a *smuggling* of ideas across lines, a *stirring up* of intellectual and, as always, political complacence' (Guha and Spivak 1988: x; emphasis added).

II

At least one of those boundaries is decidedly drawn by E.M. Forster in the brief but ideologically marked opening chapter of *A Passage to India* in its Fanonian[3] description of the divisions that separate the 'native town' from the 'civil station'. The territorial boundary, however, has direct implications for that other separationist agenda – the division drawn between literature and politics – that informs the standardized literary critical tradition to which Forster's novel has contributed. *A Passage to India* opens with a narrative partition of the town of Chandrapore, the novel's setting, into two sites: the historicized display, as if of a natural phenomenon, of the superimposition of topography and demography. On one side:

> So abased, so monotonous is everything that meets the eye, that when the Ganges comes down it might be expected to wash the excrescence back into the soil. Houses do fall, people are drowned and left rotting, but the general outline of the town persists, swelling here, shrinking there, like some low but indestructible form of life.
>
> *(PI, 2)*

On the other side of the divide, there is 'laid out the little Civil Station':

> it provokes no emotion. It charms not, neither does it repel. It is sensibly planned, with a red-brick Club on its brow, and farther back a grocer's and a cemetery, and the bungalows are disposed along roads that intersect at right angles. It has nothing hideous in it, and only the view is beautiful; it shares nothing with the city except the overarching sky.
>
> *(PI, 3)*

Despite the ill-conceived, and even more unfortunately executed, efforts to stage transversals across that divide, in Major Callendar's bridge party, Fielding's tea-party, and Aziz's picnic, or to challenge the partition in the trial and its attendant riots, the line remains drawn between the two arenas until, at the end of the novel, the very earth and heavens cry out against unity and for partition:

> But the horses didn't want it – they swerved apart; the earth didn't want it, sending up rocks through which riders must pass single-file; the temples, the tank, the jail, the palace, the birds, the carrion, the Guest House, that came into view as they issued from the gap and saw Mau beneath: they didn't want it, they said in their hundred voices, 'No, not yet,' and the sky said, 'No, not there.'
>
> *(PI, 312)*

The passage in India, from one side to the other, is never quite accomplished and the divide remains central even at the end of the novel whose escalating narration of projects, more and less well intentioned, and proceeding through all three structural sections of 'Mosque', 'Cave' and 'Temple', to traverse it, culminate in this final scene where Aziz and Fielding go their separate ways. Those projects begin with Collector Turton's bridge party – 'not the game', as he explains to Miss Quested who has expressed her desire to meet Indians and whom he is patronizingly obliging with this social event, 'but a party to bridge the gulf between East and West' (*PI*, 22). The occasion fails, however, or, as the novel reports even before it tells of the party itself, 'at least it was not what Mrs Moore and Miss Quested were accustomed to consider a successful party' (*PI*, 33). The guests and hosts are unable to mingle or circulate with each other and remain tensely gathered in their respective closes on the club grounds. The one attempt at a conversational exchange, to which Mrs Turton, unwilling and recalcitrant, is exhorted by her husband, exhibits only the inadequacy of what Bernard Cohn has described as the 'command of language' to function as a 'language of command' ('The Command of Language and the Language of Command', in Guha 1985, 276–329):

> Advancing, [Mrs Turton] shook hands with the group and said a few words of welcome in Urdu. She had learnt the lingo, but only to speak to her servants, so she knew none of the politer forms and of the verbs only the imperative mood. As soon as her speech was over, she inquired of her companions, 'Is that what you wanted?'
>
> 'Please tell these ladies that I wish we could speak their language, but we have only just come to their country.'
>
> 'Perhaps we speak yours a little,' one of the ladies said.
>
> 'Why, fancy, she understands!' said Mrs Turton.
>
> 'Eastbourne, Piccadilly, High Park Corner,' said another of the ladies.
>
> 'Oh yes, they're English-speaking.'
>
> 'But now we can talk; how delightful!' cried Adela, her face lighting up.
>
> 'She knows Paris also,' called one of the onlookers.
>
> 'They pass Paris on the way, no doubt,' said Mrs Turton, as if she was describing the movements of migratory birds. Her manner had grown more distant since she had discovered that

some of the group was westernized, and might apply her own standards to her.

(*PI*, 36)

Cohn traces the discriminatory history of Indian language learning – Persian, Sanskrit and 'Hindustani' (or Urdu) – by British officialdom in India that resulted in the 'complex and complicated forms of knowledge created by Indians [being] codified and transmitted by Europeans' (Guha 1985: 276). In addition to ' "discoveries" of the wisdom of the ancients' and the 'patronage of institutions and religious and literary specialists', a knowledge of Indian languages was, according to Cohn, considered necessary to the English administrators and their companions as 'instruments of rule' (Guha 1985: 316), for, indeed, 'without the knowledge of languages, the European is delivered into a "helpless and dependent thraldom" of a native servant' (1985: 309). That command is challenged at Collector Turton's bridge party, a challenge that contributes to its 'failure', by the unanticipated linguistic prowess of several of the women guests, but it is a challenge that Forster himself, even as he caricatures the limitations in verb tense of Mrs Turton's Anglo-Indian Urdu, cannot permit to pass unriposted: 'High Park Corner', he has one of his guests say, as if to indicate that the Indian ladies might well know English, but they do not know England. Nor, for all their privilege, do they know English manners and etiquette, as the failure of Mrs Bhattacharya to keep her Thursday appointment with Adela and Mrs Moore, made at the bridge party, illustrates.

The bridge party, despite its shortcomings, nevertheless initiates a subsequent series of attempts at social interaction and is shortly thereafter followed by a tea held by Fielding at his garden house on the grounds of the Government College where he is the schoolmaster and to which he has invited not only the two English women visitors but also Doctor Aziz and Professor Godbole. If language was the code breached by the Indian guests at the bridge party, at Fielding's tea that transgression will be enacted against the protocols of dress when Aziz's offer of his own gold collar-stud, 'part of a set that his brother-in-law had brought him from Europe' (*PI*, 58), to Fielding who had stamped on his last stud, is misconstrued by Ronny, City Magistrate, Mrs Moore's son and Adela's soon-to-be-betrothed, who interrupts the tea party as unseemly and inappropriate company for the women under his care. Aziz's very attendance at the social function is itself a challenge to the codes of decorous behaviour that maintain East as East and West as West, but more importantly it is his appearance in European attire that threatens eventual usurpation of the assigned social spaces and the relations of power that they represent and maintain. All part of the 'bungalow-compound complex' (Guha, 1983a: 69), the body and its ornaments and garments as well as places of residence, function, according to Guha, as integral to the 'struggle for any significant change in existing power relations in the countryside [that] often appears as a contest between those who are determined to retain their traditional monopoly of such status symbols and others who are keen on appropriating them – that is, as a cultural conflict' (Guha, 1983a: 61). Disturbed, then, at the new and unwonted associations of his mother and future wife, Ronny Heaslop relocates the basis of his self-interested trepidation in a mocking critique of Aziz's apparent abuse of the dress code. 'Aziz was exquisitely dressed,' he declaims to his female relations, 'from tie-pin to spats, but he had forgotten his back collar-stud, and there you have the Indian all over: inattention to detail; the fundamental slackness that reveals the race.' (*PI*, 74).

Meanwhile, Fielding's tea party, ultimately no more 'successful' than the bridge party that preceded it, has resulted in plans for an excursion for the women, proposed now by Aziz, to the Marabar Caves. And Ronny, apprised of these plans, concludes his denunciation of Aziz's dress with a commentary on the different sense of time and timing of history and geography, that same 'fundamental slackness', that separates the two 'races': 'Similarly,' Ronny goes on, 'to "meet" in the caves as if they were the clock at Charing Cross, when they're miles from a station and each other' (*PI*, 74). Nevertheless, and although Aziz's own friends are no less adamant than Ronny that it was 'most unwise to mix himself up with English ladies, and warned him to take every precaution against unpunctuality' (*PI*, 120), the venture is planned and executed, complete with an English 'breakfast' and an Indian elephant. Aziz was momentarily satisfied at having for now, 'turned the world upside down': 'They were dependent on him for a few hours, and he felt grateful to them for placing themselves in such a position' (*PI*, 134). But the sense of 'gratitude' written into even this temporary social upheaval belies its revolutionary potential and ultimately negates the gesture of independence for which Aziz had prematurely congratulated himself. Although Aziz might have felt 'like the Emperor Babur' (*PI*, 135) leading his minions across the hills, to the English ladies he remains the 'oriental guide whom they appreciated' (*PI*, 136).

Even Aziz's tentative and self-contained gesture at 'turning the world upside down', however, cannot go thus unrequited, and the picnic at the Caves, the third attempt at 'passage' in India, marks what for many critics is the central incident of Forster's novel: the (alleged) rape (attempt) in the Marabar Caves. A wounded Adela is escorted back to Chandrapore by car – neither elephant nor train, it seems, will any longer provide adequate protection for English womanhood; Aziz is unceremoniously arrested and duly charged with the assault; and the wounded pride of the Raj rises manfully to Miss Quested's defence. The citizenry of the 'Civil Station' collect at the club to reassure the ' "women and children" – that phrase that exempts the male from sanity when it has been repeated a few times' (*PI*, 174) and to consider how best to mount its proceedings. The year 1857 is invoked – what the colonial historians remember as the 'great mutiny' but which the insurgent historians of subaltern studies identify differently as the 'sepoy rebellion' – and colonial officialdom redraws the lines of its territorial imperatives and their practical implementation. There are those who want immediate revenge, but the allegations, it is determined, will be decided more appropriately – and officially – in a court of law.

The legal adjudication of the alleged violation by an Indian of English womanhood and thus of English honour is deferred, however, in *A Passage to India* when the purported victim of the attack unexpectedly retracts her charges on the witness stand. Some few of the Anglo-Indian women community present in the courtroom protest in confusion. 'And then the flimsy framework of the court broke up . . .' (*PI*, 219). Later, Aziz, the defendant, the victim's victim, withdraws, largely at the behest of his friend Fielding, even his demand for compensation of 20,000 rupees for the personal and professional injuries suffered from the stain on his character and the time that he spent in prison. The trial scene and the courtroom in *A Passage to India* define, however, that immanent space, narrative and institutional, in which a political analysis and a historical critique of British rule in India might have entered the novel's plot as constitutive of the conflict – and contradictions of literature/politics, English/Indian (colonizer/colonized), larger world/ limited world – on which the story is premised. The threat to those premises is represented in the courtroom, exemplified briefly in the efforts of the British attendees to assume a position, outside the crowd and on the platform, that are rebuffed by the presiding magistrate: 'And the party, including Miss Quested, descended from its rash eminence. The news of their humiliation spread quickly, and people jeered out- side' (*PI*, 211). The world of colonial rule, it seemed, was being 'turned upside down' – not by a peasant insurrection but by a trial of its own making. In view of such an impending catastrophe, it is as if, at this point, the novel, like the English rule it represents, must, as soon as it has initiated the proceedings, bring them to a summary close.

Meanwhile, and most alarmingly, just as the Anglo-Indian community had been able temporarily to overcome its internal differences and consolidate itself in defence of what it saw as the aggrieved Miss Quested now elevated to a symbol of its pride of position, the Indian population too, both Hindu and Muslim, had collected and organized its efforts in defence of its own, the accused Aziz. This organization itself, as Fielding warned his Indian acquaintances it would be, was necessarily construed by the English as an intolerable threat to their sovereignty. But:

> To drag in everyone was precisely [Hamidullah] the barrister's aim. He then suggested that the lawyer in charge of the case would be a Hindu; the defence would then make a wider appeal. He mentioned one or two names – men from a distance who would not be intimidated by local conditions – and said he should prefer Amritrao, a Calcutta barrister, who had a high reputation professionally and personally, but who was notoriously anti-British.
>
> Fielding demurred; this seemed to him going to the other extreme. Aziz must be cleared, but with a minimum of racial hatred. Amritrao was loathed at the Club. His retention would be regarded as a political challenge.
>
> (PI, 165)

Furthermore, given Ronny Heaslop's 'interest' in the case as Adela's fiancé, but no less offensive for that to the colonial sensibilities, an Indian judge, Mr Das, would be presiding over the trial.

> Das was Ronny's assistant – own brother to the Mrs Bhattacharya whose carriage had played them false last month. He was courteous and intelligent, and with the evidence before him could only come to one conclusion; but that he should be judge over an English girl had convulsed the station with wrath, and some of the women had sent a telegram about it to Lady Mellanby, the wife of the Lieutenant-Governor.
>
> (PI, 186).

The trial, then, unless it were to be effectively managed and controlled, might well provide the site and the occasion – both in Forster's novel and in the history of British India – for initiating a challenge to the very foundations of British rule in the subcontinent, a fear expressed for the entire 'Civil Station' community by Collector Turton: 'The case might go up from court to court, with consequences that no official could foresee. Under his very eyes, the temper of Chandrapore was altering' (*PI*, 203).

Adela's abrupt retraction, then, of her charges against Aziz in the middle of the trial thus functions in Forster's narrative to forestall such a fundamental challenge. The 'flimsy framework of the court' might break up, but the larger administrative structures and political bases of dependency of British India remain for the meanwhile intact. No Indian judge has pronounced the verdict, even a positive one, a verdict that would legitimate her accusations and give them the force of law, over the case of an Englishwoman. No less importantly, the nationalist lawyer has been denied the courtroom as a public forum for the expression of an Indian liberationist agenda. Popular demands for independence, the Quit India movement, are relegated to the street and expressed only as the incoherent fanaticism of unruly mobs. Prosecutor McBryde's theories of Indian criminality, that 'all unfortunate natives are criminals at heart, for the simple reason that they live south of latitude 30' (*PI*, 158) are allowed to stand, uncontradicted by any articulate alternative except the vulnerable and fragile ambivalences of a young and unfortunately impressionable Englishwoman. Indeed the only challenge to McBryde's courtroom excursus on 'Oriental Pathology, his favourite theme', that the 'darker races are physically attracted by the fairer, but not vice versa – not a matter for bitterness this, not a matter for abuse, but just a fact which any scientific observer will confirm,' comes from 'nowhere, from the ceiling perhaps': 'Even when the lady is so uglier than the gentleman?' Someone, anyone, but not the anonymous commentator in any case, is quickly and forcibly removed from the courtroom and a semblance of order is restored (*PI*, 208). Nor, at the trial's end and with the charges summarily dropped, have the narrative reconstructions of villainy and degeneracy proffered by the prosecution of Aziz's character, that of his deceased wife, and the romance of their relationship, been righted in any constructive way for the official record. Politics has been excluded from the courtroom and the novel alike.

Even as it pretends to expose the stratagems of control and containment and their limitations as practised by British officialdom in India, *A Passage to India* can be read, against a certain grain, as participating literarily, in the name of 'art' and the proprieties of 'form', in what Ranajit Guha has analysed as the 'prose of counter-insurgency' and its perpetuation of the myth that 'peasant insurrections are purely spontaneous and unpremeditated affairs' (Guha and Spivak 1988: 45). As Guha has pointed out in *Elementary Aspects of Peasant Insurgency in Colonial India*, the resource materials for the reconstruction of an otherwise systematically suppressed history of subaltern opposition are available from the official records and elite historiographies themselves, whether as 'intercepted discourse', the 'direct reporting of such rebel utterances as are intercepted by the authorities' (Guha 1983a: 16), or as a 'set of indices within elite discourse' that perform the 'function of expressing the hostility of the British authorities and their native protégés towards the unruly troublemakers in the countryside' (Guha 1983a: 16). Forster had visited India twice when he wrote *A Passage to India*, once in 1912 and again in 1921 as private secretary to the Maharajah of Dewas State Senior. Those years had witnessed not only the First World War, but local resistance in India to colonial and class exploitation and irregular but insistent insurrections across the subcontinent that recalled the still awfully remembered example of 1857. Their story, written in official historiographies as crime, factionalism, fanaticism and lawlessness, and backgrounded in Forster's novel as the anonymous street violence of the Muslim festival of Mohurram that turns into popular, if disorganized, protest on behalf of Doctor Aziz, is retrieved in *Subaltern Studies* essays, such as David Hardiman's 'The Indian "Faction": A Political Theory Examined' (Guha 1982: 198–232), Gyan Pandey's 'Rallying round the Cow: Sectarian Strife in the Bhojpuri Region, *c*. 1888–1917' (Guha 1983b: 60–129) and 'The Colonial Construction of "Communalism": British Writings on Banaras in the Nineteenth Century' (Guha 1989: 132–68), Shahid Amin's 'Gandhi as Mahatma: Gorakhpur District, Eastern UP, 1921–2' (Guha 1984: 1–61), Sumit Sarkar's 'The Conditions and Nature of Subaltern Militancy: Bengal from Swadeshi to Non-Cooperation, *c*. 1905–22' (Guha 1984: 271–320), Ramachandra Guha's 'Forestry and Social Protest in British Kumaun, *c*. 1892–1921' (Guha 1985: 54–100) and David Arnold's 'Touching the Body: Perspectives on the Indian Plague, 1896–1900' (Guha 1987: 55–90).

As if deliberately oblivious to the history of these political incursions against colonial and elitist exploitation, however, all of the projects devised, by British and 'natives' alike, to provide Adela Quested and Mrs Moore with the appropriate opportunities in *A Passage to India* to see the '*real*' India' and to 'meet Indians' are social events – the bridge party, Fielding's tea, Aziz's picnic at the Marabar Caves – and orchestrated at an elite level. As such, they organize and reaffirm not only the codified social structures, along race and class axes, of colonial India but also the niceties of the narrative structure, in their management and containment of the 'unruly troublemakers in the countryside' – and the streets of Chandrapore. The classic plot of sanctioned romance in an exotic land, the betrothal, that is, and even its termination, of Adela and Ronny, is foregrounded and developed through the socially acceptable, albeit politically marked, peripeties of Aziz and his friends, a political marking to which the trial itself calls an end. Decisively backgrounded, in as strict a partition as that which separates the 'native town' from the 'civil station', to this conventional emplotment and its rigorous enforcement is the political turmoil of British India and the threatening insurgency of both 'subaltern' peasant protest and bourgeois nationalist demands for independence. The subaltern 'sounds' of India remain just that, sounds, inarticulate, inchoate and – for the novelist – inexpressible, voiced only in the cave's echo that haunts Adela until she has retracted her allegations and the garbled chanting of the crowd outside the courtroom calling in a way that for Ronny was 'revolting to hear':

'Esmiss Esmoor
Esmiss Esmoor
Esmiss Esmoor
Esmiss Esmoor. . . .'

(*PI*, 214)

Like this chant that 'erupts' (to use a lexical convention often invoked to account for the 'inexplicable') in the streets, however, subalterns also make inconsequential, if threatening individual appearances in Forster's story, as if even the most carefully calibrated narrative is finally unable fully to manage all of its resources. There is, for example, the incident of Godbole's unintelligible singing at Fielding's tea when '[t]he man who was gathering water-chestnut came naked out of the tank, his lips parted with delight, disclosing his scarlet tongue' (*PI*, 72), and the 'group of itinerant musicians' playing in the compound during Hamidullah's discussion with Nawab Bahadur and Mahmoud Ali of Aziz's legal representation. And there is the punkah-wallah in the courtroom who Forster, no more than could Adela, was unable to ignore:[4]

Almost naked, and splendidly formed, he sat on a raised platform near the back, in the middle of the central gangway, and he caught her attention as she came in, and he *seemed to control the proceedings* . . . This man would have been notable anywhere; among the thin-hammed, flat-chested mediocrities of

Chandrapore he stood out as divine, yet he was of the city, its garbage had nourished him, he would end on its rubbish-heaps . . . The punkah-wallah . . . *scarcely knew that he* [the presiding assistant magistrate] *existed and did not understand* why the court was fuller than usual, indeed he *did not know* that it was fuller than usual, *didn't even know* he worked a fan, *though he thought* he pulled a rope.

(*PI*, 207; emphasis added)

The ambivalence in this description of the punkah wallah, torn between an emergent recognition of the potential political agency of the man, his capacity to 'control the proceedings', and the attendant need to contain that agency by reinscribing him in a prerational, primitive, almost bestial, state of being, concludes with the cautionary perception that he might just be able eventually, an alarming eventuality, to make the causal, historical, connection between the rope and the fan. And that would be a 'crime', to 'turn the world upside down'. It, too, like Aziz's alleged excesses in the Caves, perhaps even more so, would have to be punished. As Guha explains:

causal explanation used in the West to arrive at what its practitioners believed to be the historical truth, served in colonialist historiography merely as an apology for law and order – the truth of the force by which the British had annexed the subcontinent.

(Guha 1983a: 3)

The 'riotous' and fanatical crowd, then, celebrating the Muslim religious festival of Mohurram outside the courtroom during the trial of Aziz, like the Hindu celebrants in the Native State in the novel's third and final part, 'Temple', are denied by Forster's narrative any political efficacy beyond that of criminal disorder, the implied threat to the British rule of 'law and order'. No more than the nameless and muted man with the scarlet tongue gathering water-chestnut in Fielding's garden, the itinerant musicians, or the punkah wallah, are these inarticulate Indian 'mobs' given a coherent, consistent or conscious role to play in Forster's Anglo-Indian narrative. And Aziz's wife remains finally but a photograph, a precious fetish guarded by Aziz, to be appreciated by Fielding and depreciated by McBryde.

III

The subject of Aziz's wife had come up between Aziz and Adela as they climbed to their momentously doomed visit to the Marabar Caves. Mrs Moore, fatigued and claustrophobic, had remained behind near the lower caves. Adela, meanwhile, was reflecting during the ascent on her impending marriage to Ronny, even though, as she admitted to her 'Oriental' guide, 'no, they did not love each other' (*PI*, 143). Asked in turn about his own marital status, Aziz lies, with still another social invitation. ' "Yes, indeed, do come and see my wife" – for he felt it more artistic to have his wife alive for a moment' (*PI*, 143). Adela, then, her ignorance compounded by her limited knowledge of Indian/ Muslim customs, trespasses, although she is excused for doing it in her 'honest, decent inquisitive way': 'Have you one wife or more than one?' (*PI*, 144). Unaware of the offence she has just caused to her host, who had already shared his wife with his new friend Fielding (*PI*, 107–8), Adela 'went into a cave' (*PI*, 144).

Aziz had already revealed his wife's photograph to Fielding in a moment of extravagant gratitude after the schoolmaster had visited him at home in his sickbed, announcing that 'All men are my brothers, and as soon as one behaves as such he may see my wife.' Fielding responds in kind: 'And when the whole world behaves as such, there will be no more purdah?' (*PI*, 108). Women are – discreetly – placed as central to the conflict that is growing ever more violent between England and its colonial subjects. But, as Gayatri Chakravorty Spivak has argued, it is necessary to 'raise the question of woman as a structural rather than a marginal issue' (Guha and Spivak 1988: 30). In her reading of the work of the Subaltern Studies Group, Spivak, looking well beyond the immediate setting of *A Passage to India*, maintains:

> If the peasant insurgent was the victim and the unsung hero of the first wave of resistance against territorial imperialism in India, it is well-known that, for reasons of collusion between pre-existing structures of patriarchy and transnational capitalism, it is the urban sub-proletarian female who is the paradigmatic subject of the current configuration of the International Division of Labour.
>
> (Guha and Spivak 1988: 29)

Aziz's wife, however, the narrative prefiguring perhaps of that 'permanent casual', remains finally and fully absent from Forster's novel, presented in the text only as the sublimations of photograph and poetry.

It is she, though, who interrupts the trial proceedings, as both its cause and its effect, as Adela and her absent, unnamed, 'Other' implicitly compete with each other for the loyalty of the Indian male. Adela, unable in the end to sustain her charges against Aziz, disempowers instead Amritrao, the nationalist lawyer. For her recusation, she in turn is rejected by the Anglo-Indian community, the 'Civil Station', as treacherous to its very principles and continued existence. The trial, that is, the moment when the political could have entered as constitutive of both the literary and the historical conflict, concludes significantly with the depoliticization of women – both Indian and Anglo-Indian – and thus, too, of the Indian struggle for national independence. It forecloses as well the eventual and necessary intersection of women's and national liberation struggles.

The trial over, with scurrilous but unsubstantiated rumours circulating about Fielding and Miss Quested, Hamidullah is reporting to Aziz on the current activities of the unreliable Indian women and advising his friend: 'if you want a subject for a poem, take this: The Indian lady as she is and not as she is supposed to be' (*PI*, 259). Later, then, having retired to join Professor Godbole in the Native State, Aziz, who has dropped his countersuit against Adela and dismissed Amritrao, and who is now remarried, takes his friend's advice:

> His poems were all on one topic – oriental womanhood. 'The purdah must go,' was their burden, 'otherwise we shall never be free.' And he declared (fantastically) that India would not have been conquered if women as well as men had fought at Plassy. 'But we do not show our women to the foreigner' – not explaining how this was to be managed, for he was writing a poem.
>
> (*PI*, 284)

Like Aziz's poetry, and no less 'fantastically', Forster's novel then can be read as participant, by its very conceptualization of the 'aesthetic' as the identification of 'art and form', and the cordoning off, in the interests of 'law and order', of literature/politics, English/Indian (colonizer/colonized), the 'larger world'/the 'limited world', in reinforcing the official 'prose of counter-insurgency' with its calculated control and misrepresentations of an emergent insurgent discourse. If it is anathema to the Anglo-Indian community to speak disrespectfully of an English-woman, Indian women are no less, if differently, disrespected, unspeaking and unspoken for, in their consignment to Aziz's deactivated discourse of poetic control in Forster's *A Passage to India*.

*

'You can only read against the grain,' argues Spivak, 'if misfits in the text signal the way' (Guha and Spivak 1988: 21). Aziz's wife, the punkah wallah, the scarlet-tongued man, the musicians, the riotous crowd, are such misfits, disruptive even to the round of social events that would seek to find a satisfactory disposition of the elite parties to the history of British colonialism in India. To attempt, then, to read *A Passage to India* through a 'subaltern studies' approach is not, however to indict, much less to condemn, the novel itself. Nor even is it to argue for a dismissal of the charges. Such a reading, symptomatically suggested here, proposes instead the insurgent, even if illicit, possibilities for dismantling the structures of 'law and order', ultimately as 'flimsy' as the 'framework of the court', that traditionally managed and controlled the separation of the political from the literary, the colonized from the colonizer, the 'limited world' from the 'larger one'. Such a reading seeks, in Guha's words, to 'open up new continents of doubt, push back the familiar disciplinary frontiers and stir up a new restlessness in settled epistemological outbacks'. According to Guha's sixteenth and final proposition from 'Some Aspects of the Historiography of Colonial India', commenting on the work of the Subaltern Studies Group and with consequences for readers of *A Passage to India*: 'We are sure we are not alone in our concern about the present state of the political historiography of colonial India and in seeking a way out' (Guha and Spivak 1988: 43).

SUPPLEMENT

NIGEL WOOD: Your reading denies the usual seriousness granted Forster's 'Victorian' liberalism, in the *Independent Review* and elsewhere, from 1903 onwards. Doesn't the adoption of a subaltern perspective, in its turn, ignore what Forster consciously felt he was doing? Does that much matter anyway?

BARBARA HARLOW: For all Forster's celebrated 'liberalism', from his pacifist opposition to the violence of the First World War, his indignation at the violent suppression, for example, by the British of the Egyptian nationalist uprising or the massacre at Amritsar – both of which occurred in 1919, to his intimate friendships with the Indian Masood or the Egyptian Mohammed, that very liberalism subscribes to the now proverbial separation of the personal and the political. That separation, a theoretical partition as it were, with no less practical consequences, functions at both the historical and the generic levels in Forster's assessment of the lines drawn by England on the world map as in the lines he himself might pen in his novels. In a letter to Masood on 27 September 1922, for example, the novelist wrote of his own disparate commitments in *A Passage to India*:

> When I began this book I thought of it as a little bridge of sympathy between East and West, but this conception has had to go, my sense of truth forbids anything so comfortable. I think that most Indians, like most English people, are shits, and I am not interested whether they sympathize with one another or not. Not interested as an artist; of course the journalistic side of me still gets roused over these questions.
>
> (Cited in Furbank 1977–8: II, 106; Lago M183)

It is just that 'journalistic' dimension – the political reporting, the processes of historical challenge and change – that the trial threatens to unleash, and which must be artistically managed by the writer. As Forster had written earlier in 'A Salute to the Orient!', '. . . we who seek the truth are only concerned with politics when they deflect us from it' (*AH*, 258) – and, he might have added, only for so long as it takes to relocate the focus on 'truth' – the time, in this case, that it takes to terminate the trial.

NW: One oft-quoted observation of Forster's, from his *Aspects of the Novel* (1927), is that the 'demon of chronology' needed exorcizing from critical evaluation, so that it might be possible to imagine the canon of novelists 'at work together in a circular room' (*AN*, 21). What do you think lies behind Forster's distrust of 'context'?

BH: There is a direct link here with my previous answer, as Forster believes he is able to 'develop' his own novel against the pressures for political change and historical redress. After all, he entitled his study of the novel *Aspects of the Novel*, as if in deliberate refusal of that other literary critical approach identified in the 'phrase "the development of the novel" ' (*AN*, 173). Indeed, Forster argued to his audience in his introductory remarks to that series of lectures: 'If the novel *develops*, is it not likely to *develop* on different lines from the British Constitution, or even the Women's Movement?' (*AN*, 27: emphasis added). The choice of the British Constitution and the Women's Movement as exemplary of historical process are themselves telling, with regard to *A Passage to India* in particular as well as to Forster's narrative ideology more generally. If the punkah wallah in the courtroom, or the 'riotous' mobs outside it, must be sublimated to the entreaties of truth, then Miss Derek (who is Miss Derek anyway?), like them, might be read – against the grain – as Forster's recontainment of the women's movement at the time. Miss Derek, that is, unlike Adela, is a 'flat character' perhaps, but one who is neither 'recognized' nor 'remembered', as *Aspects of the Novel* insists the hallmark of flat characters be. This very failure of identification, however, may well be precisely because Forster does not want that 'type' to emerge as example or even role model – the suffragette who has gone on, like Margaret Cousins, Annie Besant, and other of their comrades, for example, to participate in the nationalist movements of those peoples that their own nation state has colonized.

NW: On pp. 72–3 you outline Guha's discourses of history. Could you indicate how any other texts could be read against the grain, as you do here with Forster's?

BH: 'Reading against the grain', then, following the lead of the 'misfits in the text', the punkah wallah or Miss Derek, for example, in *A Passage to India*, or the gypsies in Jane Austen's *Emma* (1816) (remember them?), the Yahoos in *Gulliver's Travels* (1726), Kim's Irishness in Kipling's *Kim* (1901) or the Irish migrant workers in Elizabeth Gaskell's *North and South* (1854–55) . . . very often, it would seem, what doesn't 'fit' into the English novel has to do with the 'British Constitution and the Women's Movement' – as Forster well recognized, and, presciently perhaps, sought to relegate to questions of 'development', history and politics. Partition would become England's strategy for recolonization following decolonization, much as the master narrative of development and underdevelopment manages now the distorted relations of power that distinguish the late twentieth-century global order.

CHAPTER 3

Of Mimicry and English Men:
E.M. Forster and the
Performance of Masculinity

BETTE LONDON

[It is likely that the very first extended and theorized anatomy of colonialist influence was that of Frantz Fanon in his *Peau Noire, Masques Blancs* (1952; trans. 1967, as *Black Skin, White Masks*), together with his *Les Damnés de la terre* (1961; trans. 1965, as *The Wretched of the Earth*). European colonialism was not regarded as a unilateral power, but rather as a force that absorbed the colonized as well as the oppressor. In an enlarged sense, this could be expressed as primarily a linguistic problem: 'A man who has a language consequently possesses the world expressed and implied by that language. What we are getting at becomes plain: mastery of language affords remarkable power.' With a language emerges a set of preformed and habitual associations that pass far beyond a simple 'dictionary' rendering of meaning. The terms in which a 'common sense' or even nature are apprehended seem grounded on the very basis of cognition:

> Every colonized people – in other words, every people in whose soul an inferiority complex has been created by the death and burial of its local cultural originality – finds itself face to face with the language of the civilizing nation . . . The colonized is elevated above his jungle status in proportion to his adoption of the mother country's cultural standards. He becomes whiter as he renounces his blackness, his jungle.
>
> (Fanon 1967: 18)

Just as he or she learns the apparent clarity of such a civilizing force, there is the growing uncertainty about definitions as to what that *négritude* might be (gradually rendered as incomprehensible and disordered as a 'jungle'), especially so as there must inevitably be a breach between the idea or memory of a pre-imperialist order and the adulterated culture that marks the more modern (and advanced?) consciousness. The return home to a whole culture's roots is a gesture that is extremely problematic, in that the very basis for recognizing a viable future means taking broad account of the present, not a potentially idealized, and precapitalist, past.

In identifying these cultural attitudes as racial stereotypes rather than as natural formations, Fanon described them as the result of a particular history of oppression, stemming ultimately from the needs of a material economy (e.g., trade as well as the maintenance of cultural superiority). Feelings of alienation and spiritual marginalization were a necessary psychological arm of the imperialist state. What formed as a stage of colonial development was a colonizer–colonized dichotomy that Fanon termed 'Manichaeism' (see Fanon 1965: 40–5; and Young 1990: 119–26), the drive to perceive reality as composed of essential, radically opposed, qualities such as civilized–barbarian, white–black or comprehensible–mystical. Decolonization could not come about without the violence of revolution; it could not be achieved by verbal means, as the predominant discourse would always render its own 'truths' back to itself in a series of self-fulfilling performances.

Bette London's analysis of the 'Mimicry' displayed in Forster's text derives most directly from the work of Homi Bhabha, and his attempt to bring deconstructive methods to bear on this analysis of imperialism. For Bhabha (among others), a post-colonial discourse can only be attempted once the prevailing tropes of colonialism have been identified, rooted out and offered up as material against which to pit new logics and narratives. This must be a differential strategy, not one based on the possibility that a brand new discourse can be assembled *ab initio*. Bhabha often refers in this regard to the work of Edward Said, whose *Orientalism* (1978; see pp. 23–7, this volume), while undoubtedly seminal, is still prone to simplifying the workings of col-onial ideology. Orientalist discourse seems to function in Said's work as too monolithic and, even if in a preliminary way, as too unified, leading to an emphasis more on the techniques of domination than on the ambivalent way that ideology operates. (Most recently, however, Said has gone some way towards addressing this issue; see Said 1993: 1–14 and 252–64.) For Fanon, the colonizer as well as the colonized were caught up in their dependence on a mutual self-definition. Said had identified a 'manifest' as well a 'latent' Orientalism, the one a conscious political projection, the other the stuff of dreams and desires. Bhabha re-emphasizes the possible split between the two where Said had contained this threat to the Orientalist psyche by finally allowing them 'to be correlated as a congruent system of representation that is unified through a political-ideological *intention* which, in his words, enables Europe to advance securely and *unmetaphorically* upon the Orient' ('Difference, Discrimination and the Discourse of Colonialism', in Barker 1983: 200). There is, however, a crisis in definition whenever the colonizer tries to project this self-image in a foreign field. In creating or accepting a sense of Otherness, rhetorically as well as conceptually, he or she inevitably displays an ambivalence and usually therefore an anxiety about such authority (see especially Bhabha 1984). For example, the black man must be constituted as a radical and stable alternative to the white man (a Manichaean distinction), yet the need for such control is not based on a reality but rather on the needs of the colonial presence; 'black' is a projection of 'white' desire, not a direct and merely innocent recognition of differing skin pigmentation. 'White' anxieties are thus 'displaced' and visited on the 'black' and shored up by a constant process of 'repetition' or persistent ritualizing of difference that acts, as a matter of necessity, to mystify an otherwise untenable reality of exploitation and unjustified racist violence. Any reminder either that such difference is ideologically produced or that the 'black' can resemble in many respects the 'white' is unsettling. Therefore, hybridity or colonial mimicry is far less welcome than outright armed opposition. To this extent, the 'subaltern' might indeed speak through parody (see pp. 66–7, this volume).

Furthermore, colonialism *creates* hybrids and so it can be, by what might seem in colonialist discursive terms to be a perverse reading, disturbed in the act of undermining its own natural and essential claims to untroubled authority. This is potentially evasive for some commentators, for, as Robert Young and Benita Parry have both pointed out (see Parry 1987; Young 1990: 144–51), when Bhabha focuses on the double bind of such rhetoric (a syndrome where colonizer and colonized are both implicated), direct repressive agencies are not emphasized. Guilt is not as clearly depicted. In his *Critical Inquiry* essay, on the other hand, 'Signs Taken for Wonders', such mimicry becomes a potent form of resistance, marking

> those moments of civil disobedience within the discipline of civility: signs of spectacular resistance. When the words of the master become the site of hybridity . . . then we may not only read between the lines but even seek to change the often coercive reality that they so lucidly contain.
>
> (Bhabha 1985: 162)

Bette London extends Bhabha's analysis to representations of gender in colonial texts. Sexual difference is performed in a self-confirming ritual of 'civilized' social manners, yet, if one were to question and refuse the rhetoric and cultural definitions inherent in this set of repetitions, then new possibilities emerge. On p. 105 London mentions the work of Luce Irigaray on such mimicry. In *Speculum of the Other Woman* (1974; trans. 1985) and *This Sex Which Is Not One* (1977; trans. 1985) she addresses (amongst others) several topics concerning progressive possibilities for the definition of female subjectivity. What redefinitions are necessary once we focus on women apart from patriarchal forces? Post-patriarchy might function rather like post-colonialism. In her challenge to Freudian psychoanalysis, Irigaray identifies the prejudices about the role of women lingering in concepts such as 'penis envy', where Freud's assumption that women were marked by a sense of lack is regarded merely as the projected male fear of castration. The 'phallocratic order' needs to be disrupted and so modified (Irigaray 1985: 68) so that women can escape their function as commodities in a medium of masculine exchange: 'Women are marked phallicly by their fathers, husbands, procurers. And this branding determines their value in sexual commerce. Woman is never anything but the locus of a more or less competitive exchange between two men, including the competition for the possession of mother earth' (Irigaray 1985: 31-2). London's performative reading of Irigaray in this context reminds us that *Passage* is a text about female freedoms as well as India's.]

NIGEL WOOD

On Mimicry: Towards a Performative Theory of Colonial Authority

When a young Indian surgeon accosts an Englishwoman in a secluded Moslem holy place at the beginning of a widely acclaimed English novel, the scene should give us pause. Yet for most readers of E.M. Forster's *A Passage to India*, Dr Aziz's chance encounter with Mrs Moore appears what it proclaims itself to be: a respite from the relentless performance of colonial authority, a moment of sanctuary from colonialism's prevailing inhumanity. Indeed, both parties to this encounter come to the mosque in retreat: Aziz, from the 'inevitable snub' (*PI*, 12) by Major Callendar (who, having sent for his subordinate, does not even await his arrival) and Mesdames Callendar and Lesley (who steal his tonga yet do not acknowledge his existence); Mrs Moore, from the Club's suffocating performance of *Cousin Kate*, sealed off from the gaze of Indian servants. Situated 'at the edge of the civil station' (*PI*, 13), the mosque thus defines the outer limits of colonial civility.

Within the mosque, by all accounts, Aziz behaves rudely, venting his anger on some unknown Englishwoman. But if the mosque would seem to be a place beyond England's reach, colonial power asserts itself, as it always does, in the form of mimicry. For Aziz's 'rudeness' to Mrs Moore imitates, even as it inverts, the ambiguous enunciation of colonial authority, with its exclusionary codes of gender, custom, race, religion, nationality. As a woman, as English, and as Christian, Aziz implies, Mrs Moore occupies a space where she cannot be recognized: 'Madam, this is a mosque, you have no right here at all; you should have taken off your shoes; this is a holy place for Moslems' (*PI*, 14).

With the clarification of the muddle over the shoes – 'I have taken them off' – the scene assumes new configurations in which, ostensibly, the triumph of the personal over the political culminates in a moment of transcendent unity: Aziz's final address to Mrs Moore, 'Then you are an Oriental' (*PI*, 17). Yet a rereading of this scene in light of current theories of colonialist discourse might offer a more sobering view of its performance, a performance whose 'happy ending' identifies Aziz as both object and agent of what Edward Said has called 'Orientalism': the production, by and for the West, of 'the Orient' as a knowable entity. Indeed, the dialogue that produces this communion begins with the retraction of Aziz's authoritative position ('I am truly sorry for speaking'), the loss of his command of the rules of recognition (his power to confer or withhold the other's identity); and it requires that Aziz be recognized (that he recognize himself) through Mrs Moore's authority, in the terms of Mrs Moore's speech. For Mrs Moore's 'personal' disclosure of her own marital history elicits from Aziz these 'cryptic' words of identification: 'Then we are in the same box' (*PI*, 16), words that announce in their distortion of the idiom Aziz's distance from the 'common' language they speak.

Aziz's words, in fact, perform what Homi K. Bhabha has called 'colonial mimicry', proclaiming sameness even as they enact difference; in their close approximation to customary usage, they mark the speaker as 'almost the same, but not quite', the subject of a 'difference' – an ambivalence – upon which colonial power rests (Bhabha 1984: 126). Aziz's elaboration (when he learns that, like himself, Mrs Moore has two sons and a daughter), 'Is not this the same box with a vengeance?' (*PI*, 16), underlines this dynamic: the 'box' is the same and not the same, the same *with an excess*. And Mrs Moore's gentle prodding, 'What are their names? Not also Ronny, Ralph, and Stella, surely?', reminds us of the power inscribed within their respective positions. For with the naming of his children – Ahmed, Karim, Jamila – Aziz declares what is unassimilable in the lingo of Anglo-India;[1] inserting this un-English nomenclature into the language of sameness, Aziz reveals the political determinants of his mimetic dilemma where 'almost the same, but not quite' inevitably reduces to '*Almost the same but not white*' (Bhabha 1984: 130). Speaking 'inappropriately', he becomes what Bhabha calls 'a mimic man' (occupying a line of literary descent backward to Kipling and forward to Naipaul), 'the effect of a flawed colonial mimesis, in which to be Anglicized, is *emphatically* not to be English' (Bhabha 1984: 128). Indeed, the effort entailed in Aziz's acts of imitation and accommodation inevitably mark him as Other – one who must work to produce what the Englishman does naturally, what the Englishman inherits as his birthright and observes through an internalized code of behaviour.

'Is not this the same box *with a vengeance?*' (emphasis added). In these resonant words, it is as if Forster had underlined the un-English emphasis. But the phrase resonates, more generally, for a novel that turns upon a problem of identification: identification in the Caves, whose box-like sameness and resistance to differentiation produces Anglo-India's need for a vengeful agency (figured as 'India' or 'Indian'). It resonates, moreover, in the immediacy of the mosque scene, suggesting the mosque's problematic status as retreat, as a space *outside* colonial authority. And it resonates in what is edited out of the scene's normative humanist reading: the construction of Aziz's sexuality. For when Aziz surprises Mrs Moore – ' "Oh! Oh!" the woman gasped' (*PI*, 14) – there is a definite hint of sexual menace in the scene; and when Mrs Moore is unveiled as inaccessible to Aziz's sexual fantasy ('She was older than Hamidullah Begum, with a red face and white hair'), Aziz's loss is construed as disproportionately devastating: 'A fabric bigger than the mosque fell to pieces' (*PI*, 15). Here, then, as elsewhere in the text, the representation of Aziz activates familiar fantasy formations of the Other's sexuality: the Other who, as the fear of miscegenation reflects, might share desires with his fellows in the West; who desiring *inappropriately* and *in excess* reveals himself to be sexed samely/differently.

Read in this light, the episode in the Caves (never fully represented) presents 'the same box' as the mosque – but with a vengeance – rendering explicit what the earlier scene masks with its spurious unity. Mrs Moore's retreat, for example, from a space of suffocating closeness (the Club, the Caves) sets the stage for Aziz's appearance as sexual predator; what appears in the aftermath of the Caves, then, as an 'unthinkable' development (Aziz's guilty sexuality) has already been thought in colonialism's collective fantasy (in the mind of Adela and the Anglo-Indian community; in the novel's logic of representation). Moreover, if Adela's 'tactless' question about polygamy prompts the Cave's catastrophe, its point of contention has been at least ambiguously conceded in the earlier scene; for if Mrs Moore acknowledges two (dead) husbands, for Aziz, what exactly does being 'in the same box' mean?

I cite this moment of indeterminacy to return to Homi Bhabha and the problem of text and theory. For in a series of essays of imposing density and complexity, Bhabha has made 'ambivalence' the trademark of his theory of colonial mimicry – a theory reworked, refined, and elaborated in the body of his writings. As he himself explains: 'These strategies of mimicry, hybridity, incommensurability or translation, which I've been trying to variously interpret, are, I think, the unspoken, unexplored moments of the history of modernity' (Bhabha 1989: 67). Participating in the breaking of the silence about colonialism's practices and history, Bhabha's work contributes to the ongoing study of colonial discourse that has been so important to the development of what has been variously called 'cultural studies', 'culture studies' and 'cultural critique'; this study, as Gayatri Spivak explains, constitutes 'an important (and beleaguered) part of the discipline now', with its own defined and contested place in the academy ('Poststructuralism, Marginality, Post-Coloniality and Value', in Collier and Geyer Ryan 1990: 221). Cultural studies, in fact, as a recognizable academic practice and theory, has defined itself through contestation. Operating from explicitly articulated political positions, it has challenged both the traditional objects of literary study and the discipline's pose of disinterestedness; but it has also been contested from within, reflecting the inherent contradictions (and competing priorities) of an oppositional practice located *inside* the academy.

Among the workers in this new field of study, Bhabha has been the one perhaps most insistently attentive to the *discursive* construction of colonial authority, to the play of colonial power in a field of *textuality*. In this emphasis, he acknowledges two of the crucial components in his own 'hybrid position' as a critic: Derridean deconstruction and Lacanian psychoanalysis. Indeed, certain recent criticisms of Bhabha reproduce familiar critiques of Derrida's and Lacan's 'academic' theorizing: he is too distant from *real* political struggle; his work allows insufficient space for human agency (particularly the agency of those occupying marginal and oppositional positions); his project lacks historical specificity; his commitment to theory – and the theory he articulates – reproduces the 'silencing' of the Other it purportedly critiques, denying the Other an authentic identity.[2]

Yet Bhabha's particular contribution to colonial and postcolonial studies lies precisely in his effort to appropriate these critical methodologies for the work of exposing and dismantling political oppression. If Bhabha's explication of mimicry, for example, as the articulation of sameness *as* difference (where what one utters is never identical to the thing 'repeated') requires, for its underpinnings, Derrida's concepts of *différance* and 'double inscription', Bhabha deploys these concepts differently. Turning away from Derrida's *literary* emphasis on 'the vicissitudes of interpretation' in the act of reading, Bhabha introduces the crucial question of 'the effects of power' in the particular scene of enunciation he investigates: the colonial theatre (Bhabha 1985: 151). There, where power is distributed so unevenly, the production and circulation of 'identity' and 'difference' unleashed in the decisive meeting between colonizer and colonized cannot be read simply as the 'free play' of the signifier endemic to linguistic instability; rather one must ask whose interests are served and what desires fulfilled by the particular arrangement of these positions.

On the face of it, the answer would evidently be that colonial mimicry operates as the means by which colonial power shores up its authority through 'strategies of individuation and domination', through 'dividing practices' that differentiate 'us' from 'them' while covering over internal contradictions (Bhabha 1985: 151). Thus Bhabha defines colonial mimicry as

> the desire for a reformed, recognizable Other, as *a subject of a difference that is almost the same, but not quite.* Which is to say, that the discourse of mimicry is constructed around an *ambivalence*; in order to be effective, mimicry must continually produce its slippage, its excess, its difference.
>
> (Bhabha 1984: 126; emphasis in original)

By this account, mimicry works as a complex strategy for reforming, regulating and disciplining an Other it partially 'invents' through these very strategies.

To take the Anglo-Indian situation Forster writes about, the Anglicized Indian, as the ultimate product of mimicry, must impersonate the English (thereby justifying the imposition of English authority) without ultimately threatening the integrity of English identity. Thus, as Aziz explains to Fielding (when he lends him his collar-stud), he wears Western dress 'to pass the police': 'If I'm biking in English dress – starch collar, hat with ditch – they take no notice. When I wear a fez, they cry, "Your lamp's out!" ' (*PI*, 59). If the success of this mimetic performance allows Aziz to escape surveillance in the streets, the inevitable 'slippage' is produced when he comes under civil scrutiny, under the eye of Ronny Heaslop acting in his private capacity: 'Aziz was exquisitely dressed, from tie-pin to spats, but he had forgotten his back collar-stud, and there you have the Indian all over: inattention to detail; the fundamental slackness that reveals the race' (*PI*, 74). As Ronny's ill-informed judgement indicates, the native's 'slackness' serves colonialism's needs: the need to mark racial difference visibly, to uncover, as it were (to borrow Frantz Fanon's terms) the black skin beneath the white mask. For as Bhabha would read this scene, the Indian must slip up ('they all forget their back collar-studs sooner or later' (*PI*, 87), Ronny later explains) or slip out ('there you have the Indian all over') if mimicry is to remain an effective guarantee of English colonial superiority.

In this reading of mimicry, 'Colonial power produces the colonised as a fixed reality which is at once an "other" and yet entirely knowable and visible' (Barker 1983: 199); as Bhabha makes clear, such an understanding of the operation of desire and power depends upon psychoanalytic categories: disavowal, fetishism, fantasy. As an understanding of fetishism illustrates, the term 'disavowal' includes, simultaneously, both the recognition and non-recognition of difference; for the trauma of sexual difference (the discovery that the mother does not have a penis) provokes an elaborate denial – or disavowal – of that very thing. In the case of fetishism, this disavowal is achieved through the fixation on an object of substitution – the fetish (foot, shoe, etc.) – that masks that difference and thus restores the illusion of an original presence. If the mother *has* a penis, then the male subject cannot be castrated; ultimately, then, fetishism fulfils a *masculine* fantasy of wholeness and integrity that requires both the *difference* of the mother (*she* is the one who is castrated) and her *sameness*.

For Bhabha, it is the *ambivalence* of fetishism that gives it its explanatory power for colonial mimicry; thus in his rewriting of the psychoanalytic scene, Bhabha grafts racial and cultural differences on to sexual difference to produce his own hybrid categories:

> For fetishism is always a 'play' or vacillation between the archaic affirmation of wholeness/similarity – in Freud's terms: 'All men have penises'; in ours 'All men have the same skin/race/culture'; and the anxiety associated with lack and difference – again, for Freud 'Some do not have penises'; for us 'Some *do not* have the same skin/race/culture.'
>
> (Barker 1983: 202)

The racial stereotypes produced through mimicry (the native's slackness, for example, or his sexual voracity) can thus be seen as fetishistic representations, compensatory fantasies. As such, in their reconstruction of difference as inappropriateness ('slippage', 'lack', 'excess'), they protect the colonizer's illusion of an *appropriate* (i.e. non-contradictory) identity: coherent, intact, bounded.

In this reading, mimicry figures the operation by which the colonial subject (colonizer) disavows the contradictions in his own position of authority: his *lack* of originality, authenticity, self-identity. Following Lacan, Bhabha locates the recognition of this lack (and the deployment of compensatory strategies) in the subject's entry into language – the entry into social relations that both reveal and compensate for the gap between self and world, language and reality. Language (and the 'Symbolic Order' it represents), in effect, splits the subject by articulating the 'Imaginary' wholeness from which the subject now knows itself to be forever dispossessed. As a speaking subject, the self can only perform the culturally scripted fictions of identity. Bhabha, however, extends this drama to the performance of national identity; as figured in the possession of a language (English) with the power to confer reality, national identity serves as a particularly seductive script, promising the restoration of an elusive wholeness.

But as Forster demonstrates (at least when read through Bhabha's critical machinery), for the colonizer as much as the colonized, the act of enunciation betrays the crucial splitting in the self required for the mimicry of English identity. For to 'make England in India' (*PI*, 66) entails more than 'doing what comes naturally'; even on the verbal terrain, as the production of *Cousin Kate* confirms, English middle-class identity must be *performed* – and reperformed – on a daily basis. Thus Fielding, in spite of the fact that 'all his best friends were English', finds that among his compatriots *in India* he cannot pull off a successful impersonation of an Englishman: 'he appeared to inspire confidence until he spoke' (*PI*, 55–6). And Ronny can achieve this apotheosis only at the cost of authenticity: 'When he said "Of course there are exceptions," he was quoting Mr Turton, while "increasing the izzat" was Major Callendar's own. The phrases worked and were in current use at the Club' (*PI*, 28). Moreover, as the response to 'the incident' in the Caves illustrates, a united Anglo-Indian front can be maintained only through careful vigilance and repressive discipline – the type of linguistic policing (the lookout for slippages) that contains native insurgency.

If Bhabha, then, remains deliberately vague around questions of agency, relying on such terms as 'the desire of colonial mimicry' (*whose* desire?) and 'the colonial subject' (*which* colonial subject – colonizer or colonized?), this ambivalence reflects his sense that mimicry operates both ways simultaneously. Indeed, this doubleness constitutes one of the most distinctive (and controversial) features of Bhabha's theory – a theory that locates in mimicry not only the inscription of the mechanisms of colonial authority but also the site of the dislocation, disruption or subversion of that authority. To follow the metaphor of fetishism, mimicry unmasks in the process of masking the desire in which it originates. Thus Bhahba explains: 'The effect of mimicry on the authority of colonial discourse is profound and disturbing' (Bhabha 1984: 126). For mimicry, in effect, through the *fantasy* of difference it projects, continually produces and reproduces the threat against which its operation militates. Consequently, whatever *really* happened in the Caves, the emergence of Aziz as potential rapist can be understood as the logical extension of colonial mimicry, with its demand for the Other's lawlessness. In fact, at the moment of his arrest, Aziz slips up, attempting to escape rather than maintaining a stiff upper lip in the face of opposition. Acting the criminal, he stands as cause and effect of the 'normalizing' knowledge his transgression activates – in this case, the Superintendent of the Police's 'theory about climatic zones': 'The theory ran: "All unfortunate natives are criminals at heart, for the simple reason that they live south of latitude 30 . . ." '(*PI*, 158).

As this scenario demonstrates, the failure of mimicry (Aziz's inappropriate behaviour) is simultaneously the mark of mimicry's successful ability to discriminate the Anglicized from the English. If mimicry, then, lays bare the assumptions that govern colonial relations, what it exposes most emphatically are the contradictions that underwrite colonial authority. As Bhabha explains it, the mimetic performance alienates colonial authority from its own first principles, from the language of liberty and fairness, from the practice of civility. It works, then, to *split* the rhetoric of Anglo-India, by opening to view the space where the philanthropic colonial justification (the obligatory answer to uncomfortable political questions, 'England holds India for her good' (*PI*, 102)) meets its self-interested double: England holds India for *her* good – i.e. the good of the mother country. And it works to illuminate a 'civil administration' indifferent to the claims of common civility: 'We're not out here for the purpose of behaving pleasantly!' (*PI*, 43). If the 'unpleasantness' of the Caves, then, provokes extraordinary measures that unleash colonialism's sadistic fantasies ('He wanted to flog every native that he saw, but to do nothing that would lead to a riot or to the necessity for military intervention' (*PI*, 174)), these fantasies (circumscribed within the law) already inhabit colonial authority's *ordinary* operations.

Producing other knowledges of colonialism's norms, mimicry alienates colonial practice from its universalizing pretensions; exposing the contradictions that split the colonial subject, it disrupts the play of power in a single direction. For Bhabha, then, part of mimicry's subversive potential lies in its capacity to undermine colonial authority as a monolithic structure. In this operation, it opens a space for colonial resistance – a space that might tap the desire of the colonized to uncover and displace the grounds of their oppression, to turn 'the discursive conditions of dominance into the grounds of intervention' (Bhabha 1985: 154). But for Bhabha, resistance need not be 'an oppositional act of political intention' (1985: 153); it exists as 'the effect of an ambivalence' within colonial authority. While Bhabha argues that this ambivalence enables 'a form of subversion, founded on that uncertainty' (1985: 154), he resists locating the subversive agency. Aziz's remark, then, with which I opened this discussion of Bhabha's concept of mimicry, 'Is not this the same box with a vengeance?', yields up a final echo in this 'vengeance' that enters without origin and trails off so indeterminately. Yet in such vengeance – the potential for subversion that adheres to all acts of mimicry – we might locate the grounds for a performative practice of reading. Putting Bhabha's theory to Forster's text, I would like, then, in the following section to reorientate this discussion. For a theory of mimicry might illuminate not only the colonial drama Forster explicitly stages but also the one in which he participates: the performance of culture enacted in the narrative's enunciation, in the authorial voice of a reluctant Englishman.[3]

Between Men: The Performance of Masculinity

Dismayed at the poor showing of '[her] countrymen' at the Collector's bridge party ('Fancy inviting guests and not treating them properly!'), Adela Quested, new to India, confides in Fielding: 'You and Mr Turton and perhaps Mr McBryde are the only people who showed any common politeness. The rest make me perfectly ashamed, and it's got worse and worse' (PI, 40). In a strategy typical of much of the novel, Adela's plainspoken assessment of the situation – the kind of thing her compatriots regularly write off to her 'inexperience' – receives an immediate endorsement in the voiced-over narrative: 'It had. The Englishmen had intended to play up better, but had been prevented from doing so by their womenfolk, whom they had to attend, provide with tea, advise about dogs, etc.' (PI, 40). As this 'explanation' makes clear, however, the countrymen Adela attacks merely cover for her countrywomen, whose inappropriate desires disfigure the façade of English gentlemanly behaviour. Indeed, Adela's tentative approval of Mr McBryde – 'Mr McBryde did not speak much; he seemed nice' (PI, 42) – emerges quite explicitly in reaction to the disagreeable chatter of Mrs McBryde and Miss Derek. Even as she speaks, then, Adela is doubly silenced. For in the terms of Anglo-India, as Ronny painstakingly informs her, Adela's gender excludes her from first-hand knowledge of her subject:

> A public school, London University, a year at a crammer's, a particular sequence of posts in a particular province, a fall from a horse and a touch of fever were presented to her as the only training by which Indians and all who reside in their country can be understood . . .
>
> (PI, 73)

But in the alternative terms the narrative offers, Adela can no more speak *as a woman*; allowed a moment of authoritative utterance, Adela speaks to evacuate the place of women's enunciation.

That Adela must purchase narrative authority at the expense of her sexual identity proves only one of the passage's ironies; for in the relentless logic of the plot (dictated by the theatrical terms of colonial mimicry), Adela will be forced, even to the point of grotesquerie, to assume the feminine position: to enact Anglo-India's nightmare fantasy of race and sexuality. Moreover, responding to the appeal of Adela's compromised body, the very men she here invokes for their exemplary behaviour will slip into the characteristic incivility that both makes and unmakes the Englishman in India. Thus Mr McBryde, who seems nice as long as he does not speak, gives vent, once his lips are unsealed, to an unstoppable flood of 'knowledge' of Oriental Pathology. Empowered by his position of authority (Superintendent of Police) – and inspired by the scene of a crime in which Aziz embodies all that threatens English propriety – McBryde, at the trial, gives himself over to his favourite theory: 'the darker races are physically attracted by the fairer, but not vice versa' (PI, 208). As at the bridge party, a compatriot's breach of etiquette ('He wanted to keep the proceedings as clean as possible, but Oriental Pathology, his favourite theme, lay all around him, and he could not resist it') registers itself in Adela's embarrassment – this time, quite literally, in the mortification of her body. For McBryde's appeal to scientific evidence produces an unauthorized rebuttal from the Indian section of the audience that sets Adela's body trembling: 'Even when the lady is so uglier than the gentleman?'

Represented as 'the most reflective and best educated of the Chandrapore officials' (PI, 158), McBryde reveals here, through a type of reverse mimicry, the fate of all Englishmen in Forster's narrative scheme: even the best of them eventually slip up, betraying their race and national identity. Indeed, the stereotypical representations of Anglo-Indians that so enraged some of Forster's contemporaries might readily be understood in terms of Bhabha's theory of colonial fetishism; but in the novelistic reconfiguration of the structures of authority, the *difference* that must be disavowed is the *resemblance* of 'the narrator' to the Turtons and Burtons who uphold the colonial regime. For even these more extreme caricatures of authority speak the same language as the narrator. Thus when the narrator discloses Turton's 'inmost thought' – 'After all, it's our women who make everything more difficult out here' (*PI*, 204) – his words register as the 'almost the same, but not quite' to the narrator's earlier pronouncement about Englishwomen, tea and dogs. From this perspective, the narrative compulsion to make things worse and worse – McBryde, for example, must be proved as bad as the rest, not only a racist but also an adulterer – serves to sustain the differentiating fantasy. For Forster, also well educated and highly reflective, occupies the same box as McBryde – with a vengeance. In his case, as in McBryde's, the question remains whether 'niceness' can survive the entry into speech. From what position can one speak uncontaminated by national identity?

In *Passage*, this crisis at the site of enunciation finds its resolution – and its articulation – in the practice of narrative mimicry.[4] In place of the distinctly discernible Forsterian voice of the earlier novels – urbane, ironic, assured – *Passage* projects a narrative gone mad: a shifting, slippery, unplaceable voice that seems to take its timbre from whatever voice it happens to be near. This voice, split by contradictory articulations, figures a crisis in narrative authority and English identity that posits the liberal humanist author as 'mimic man': master impersonator and impersonated human being. Slipping in and out of the voices it projects, appropriating and disowning these voices with abandon, the narrative refuses to connect into the semblance of a coherent person. But if voice here functions to dislocate the narrative body, it also recuperates that difference through rearticulation in the aesthetic hybridity of the *modern* English novel.

In 'Difference, Discrimination and the Discourse of Colonialism' (Barker 1983), subsequently revised as 'The Other Question . . .' (Bhabha 1983), Bhabha argues that 'the construction of the colonial subject in discourse, and the exercise of colonial power through discourse, demands an articulation of forms of difference – racial and sexual' (Barker 1983: 194). If we take Forster's 'Indian novel' as implicated in that category (the construction of the colonial subject *in discourse*), then Bhabha's formulation might illuminate the differential and differentiating practices the novel disseminates. Up to this point, following Bhabha, I have largely concentrated on the articulation of 'race'. When, for example, the diehard colonialist and liberal critic meet in the discourse of 'woman trouble' ('it's our women who make everything more difficult' and 'The Englishmen had intended to play up better but had been prevented by their womenfolk'), I have read this alliance as the return of the culturally repressed, the articulation of 'Englishness' as the 'almost the same *because* white'. The passage, of course, admits another reading, in the space of shared masculine privilege. In fact, throughout this essay, in my discussions of colonial authority, I have deliberately preserved the masculine pronoun, if only to underline the self-evident: that colonial mimicry operates for and between men.

Indeed, if there is one thing in this troubling novel over which East and West can agree, that thing may very well be 'troublesome women'. Even before the courtroom outburst – 'Even when the lady is so uglier than the gentleman?' – it is evident that Indian men share in the disparagement of English women. 'They all become exactly the same – not worse, not better. I give any Englishman two years . . . And I give any Englishwoman six months' (*PI*, 6), Hamidullah confidently explains. But as his subsequent remarks suggest, he also feels politically stymied by *his* women's refusal to give up purdah – in his terms, their refusal to hear sense: 'For fifteen years, my dear boy, have I argued with my begum, for fifteen years, and never gained a point, yet the missionaries inform us our women are downtrodden' (*PI*, 259). And Aziz, chastened by his experience of British India, retires to a native state to write poems with one theme – Oriental womanhood: ' "The purdah must go," was their burden, "otherwise we shall never be free." And he declared (fantastically) that India would not have been conquered if women as well as men had fought at Plassy' (*PI*, 284).

In Bhabha's case, despite the clear demand he articulates for an analysis of forms of racial *and* sexual difference, his own work continues to privilege the nexus of 'racial/cultural/historical otherness', an emphasis that leaves *sexual* difference in a decidedly supplemental position. To the charge that his work does not sufficiently acknowledge a particular kind of inflection *within* representation that sexuality provides, Bhabha responds with characteristic ambivalence: 'In my case, I'm guilty and innocent at the same time' (Bhabha 1989: 79). As he subsequently explains, 'it's like the sexuality of my discourse is in a place where it assumes the position of women' (1989: 81). And although he admits (in an interview) that he 'would talk about feminism as having completely informed the problematic' of his critical project, he does not, in his theoretical investigations, explicitly acknowledge this contribution, despite the fact that feminism has been a powerful other site for the theorizing of mimicry as the performance of sexual difference (as, for example, in the writings of Luce Irigaray).[5] 'What I feel about my work is that I don't investigate the social construction of masculinity', Bhabha writes. 'Because in a sense, if you do that, it opens up the whole question: from where do you pose the question of the woman?' (1989: 81).

But, as I have tried to suggest in my preliminary treatment of Adela, if you do pose the question of the woman, then the fabric of masculinity must come under scrutiny. And in the case of Forster's *Passage*, the construction of masculinity holds particular interest, since we inevitably read the novel today with the knowledge of Forster's homosexuality. It might, then, be possible to offer yet another turn on the author as 'mimic man' – one who mimes masculine authority. From this perspective, we might expect the narrative to produce its slippages from the normative discursive positions that encode the recognized forms of masculinity. As Bhabha reminds us, however, the subject of masculinity cannot be clearly separated from the other differentials (race, class, nationality) through and against which it is constructed. Bhabha's interpretative apparatus, then, might most usefully provide us access to these intersections: to the *permutations* on the differential complex of race/sex, for example, through which authority must be purchased in Forster's English novel.[6]

In the body of his work on mimicry, Bhabha consistently highlights 'the *in-between* spaces through which the meanings of cultural and political authority are negotiated' (Bhabha 1990: 4). In my reading of *Passage*, I want to suggest that the narrative articulates precisely such a space between cultural registers: between an affected denationalization and a recalcitrant national identity; between the refusal of the compulsory heterosexual matrix (the marriage plot Forster both can and cannot do without) and the enforcement of culturally sanctioned misogyny. And I want to suggest, by reading one of the 'in-between spaces' of the novel, that in Forster's practice these spaces are negotiated within and between men. For this purpose, I want to look not at one of the famed 'impersonal' intertextual passages (the preludes to the first two sections of the novel), but at the space between 'Mosque' and 'Caves' represented *within* the narrative proper, within the interior space of Aziz's domicile (Chapters 9–11).

In a scene overshadowed by the melodramatic performances that follow it, the sick/not sick Aziz entertains a party of men in his 'shameful' bungalow. The very bungalow, then, that Aziz contemplates with horror when Adela presses him for his address (prompting his rash invitation to the Caves) here becomes the site for an alternative entertainment that markedly excludes women. For although Aziz laments his inability to see Fielding again, 'If he entered this room the disgrace of it would kill me' (*PI*, 92), Fielding's subsequent arrival confirms that it is gender, not race, that makes Aziz's rooms unacceptable to 'mixed company'. In fact, in its structural configurations, the scene anticipates the one later to be played out in an 'identical' bungalow (a replica not of Aziz's humble dwelling but of all the transient homes belonging to Anglo-India) over the body of a sick/not sick woman (the hysterical Adela). But in that later scene, the male body drops out of sight in the abstraction of Aziz into 'the person in question' (*PI*, 193).

As I want to show, however, what happens in Aziz's bungalow marks Aziz – 'before the fact' – as highly questionable. For it positions Aziz to be remarked *as a body* in an economy in which bodiliness is always suspect: only *other* races have bodily markings (colour) and only women have sexualized bodies. The prostrate form of the bedridden Aziz thus proves doubly problematic. Indeed, within the confines of Aziz's bungalow, illness is construed as a peculiarly 'Indian' phenomenon, associated with the disorders of the lower body – hence the rumours about Godbole's 'mysterious' complaint (diarrhoea/haemorrhoids) and the representation of Aziz's symptomatic proclivity 'to think about beautiful women'. As Aziz's response to the European sex manuals suggests, his 'infirmity', like Godbole's, has no place in the 'bad English grammar' that, as the schoolboy Rafi somewhat facetiously explains (excusing his own scandalmongering), 'often gave the wrong meaning for words, and so led scholars into mistakes' (*PI*, 100). But as the discourse of Anglo-India makes clear, to broach such delicate subjects as the workings of the lower body would render in bad taste even a 'good grammar'.

Aziz's desire, then ('Yes, he did want to spend an evening with some girls, singing and all that, the vague jollity that would culminate in voluptuousness' (*PI*, 92)), can be construed as pathological (as the trial will construe it) simply for being *spoken*. Indeed, speaking Aziz's desire, the narrative projects his guilt on to the succeeding scenes even as it provides the 'inside view' that could substantiate his innocence – the view that, like Adela, Aziz has 'nothing of the vagrant in [his] blood' (*PI*, 144), his desire being clearly aligned towards beautiful women of his own skin colour. Aziz's perception, moreover, of an Anglo-Indian difficulty with the necessary arrangements for his pleasure can be understood, in part at least, as a problem of articulation:

If Major Callendar had been an Indian, he would have remembered what young men are, and granted two or three days' leave
to Calcutta without asking questions. But the Major assumed
either that his subordinates were made of ice, or that they repaired
to the Chandrapore bazaars – disgusting ideas both.

(*PI*, 93)

In fact, Aziz's own discourse here gets out from under him, splitting
between some universalizing code ('what young men are') and some
essential racial/national opposition ('If Major Callendar had been an
Indian . . .'), between the projection of a uniform 'Indian' desire and
the particularizing of normal/abnormal and class-specific sexualities.

Sexuality, then, like everything else in Forster's India, appears infected
by the discursive constraints of colonial authority – the constraints as
well of the English novel; for to put sexuality into discourse inevitably
reveals the *difference* between native and non-native speakers of English,
between proper and improper Englishmen. Thus while Aziz imagines
he might find in Fielding a receptive listener to his sexual difficulties
('It was only Mr Fielding who –' (*PI*, 93)), such open communication
suffers in translation, suffers from the English language (unequally
possessed) through which it must be mediated. When Fielding, for
example, enters Aziz's sick room, crying cheerily, 'I say! Is he ill or isn't
he ill?' (*PI*, 100), the six (Indian) men gathered around Aziz's bed
(divided by age, education, religion, class, politics) react as one in their
recognition of the perfect accents of 'the Englishman', of someone at
home in the affable patter of his country: ' "An Englishman at his best,"
they thought; "so genial" ' (*PI*, 101). Even in his challenge to his own
superior (his refusal to endorse Turton's view of Aziz's 'shamming'),
Fielding appears, in the company of Indians, the perfect gentleman
(which is to say, indelibly English). Aziz, on the other hand, when he
thinks in English (presumably the way to master a foreign tongue)
dislocates his identity: 'That's India all over . . . how like us . . . there
we are . . .' (*PI*, 92). Moreover, when the wished-for private conversation with Fielding occurs, and the discussion turns to 'personal relations', Aziz falters over vocabulary ('Prig, prig? Kindly explain. Isn't
that a bad word?' (*PI*, 110)) and slips up on propriety ('She [Miss
Quested] has practically no breasts, if you come to think of it'
(*PI*, 111)).

The episode in Aziz's room closes the 'Mosque' part of the novel with
the consummation of the friendship between Fielding and Aziz: 'But
they were friends, brothers. That part was settled, their compact had

been subscribed by the photograph, they trusted one another, affection had triumphed for once in a way' (*PI*, 113). Attention to the *construction* of the scene, however, reveals the contradictions within the humanist project it illuminates, within the desire to connect that fuels the narrative. For the 'humanity' celebrated in such individualized acts of kindness does not comprehend women as active parties to the social contract. This scene not only displaces the earlier union in the mosque (between Aziz and Mrs Moore) but also seals the brotherhood of men through 'the traffic in women' (the transfer of the photograph of Aziz's dead wife).[7] But as this 'exchange' illustrates, the affection that triumphs 'for once in a way' masks the inequality of an arrangement in which, significantly, the white man does not 'trade'.

Moreover, the contradictions within masculinity that disturb Aziz's speculations on prostitutes at the opening of this episode remain intact, if hidden, at the episode's close. Indeed, Aziz and Fielding meet to consecrate their friendship only after the room has been cleared of the other visitors who so visibly proclaim that all men – even all Indian men – are *not* the same. Yet even without that audience to keep politics alive, *sexual* difference intervenes in their meeting. And it intervenes with the invocation of the very prostitutes who first summon Aziz's fantasy of Fielding's superior 'understanding': 'It was only Mr Fielding who –'. For given the opportunity, Mr Fielding categorically refuses Aziz's offer of sexual favours ('For you I shall arrange a lady with breasts like mangoes . . .' (*PI*, 111)), and we are left to speculate over the factors that determine this negative display of sexual preference (race, class, age, sexual orientation). Indeed, the narrator's 'knowing' explanation for Fielding's hostility to women ('the girl's a prig' and 'It's the old mother's doing') opens up as much as it forecloses: 'any suggestion that he should marry always does produce overstatements on the part of the bachelor' (*PI*, 111). More curiously, the construction of Aziz's emphatic heterosexuality echoes passages from Forster's suppressed 'homosexual novel', *Maurice*, written in 1913–14, when Forster abandoned his first efforts at *Passage*.[8] Between the 'licentious' Aziz, however, and the 'bachelor' Fielding, homosexuality remains, as only proper to the English novel at this time, unspoken – if not unimagined – within the narrative.

While this behind-the-scenes episode, then, offers the promise of friendship across nations, it also articulates the rifts between men that threaten such affection. Those rifts, as the bungalow scene anticipates, involve a complex set of displacements between race and sexuality. For if, after Aziz's arrest, he and Fielding come together across the body of

Adela, the trial makes explicit at what cost this 'marriage' can be saved: '[Fielding] saw that she was going to have a nervous breakdown and that his friend was saved' (*PI*, 218). In the events that follow the trial's resolution, the narrative tracks 'the tragic coolness' that develops between Aziz and 'his English friend' (*PI*, 260) – coolness attributable to the intractableness of national identity. When Aziz, for example, wants Fielding 'to "give in to the East," as he called it, and live in a condition of affectionate dependence upon it', Fielding resists Indianization: 'Yet he really couldn't become a sort of Mohammed Latif' (*PI*, 249). The narrative explains the rift as racially motivated: 'When they argued about it something racial intruded – not bitterly, but inevitably, like the colour of their skins: coffee-colour versus pinko-gray.' Yet the terms of Fielding's demurral suggest that what he fears most is the unmanliness of becoming, like Mohammed Latif, a *déclassé* 'poor relation'. Moreover, this something 'racial' that always intrudes turns out to be, I would argue, the (white) woman's body. The arguments between Fielding and Aziz thus invariably deadlock on the same issue: 'If you want to reward me, let Miss Quested off paying' (*PI*, 249).

Indeed, from the start – from Aziz's unwelcome suggestion, in the bungalow, that Fielding and Adela marry – Adela's body divides the two men, intruding itself into their most intimate moments. At the victory celebration, for example, on the night of the trial, Aziz's crude references to Adela's unattractiveness alienate Fielding. For in the 'apology' he formulates at Fielding's bidding – 'Dictate to me whatever form of words you like' – Aziz makes explicit not only that the two men do not like the same form of words but that they cannot share a discursive hold on Adela: ' "Dear Dr Aziz, I wish you had come into the cave; I am an awful old hag, and it is my last chance." Will she sign that?' (*PI*, 240). Pained by Aziz's refusal of the protocol of the gentleman, Fielding resumes the voice of the schoolmaster: ' "Oh, I wish you wouldn't make that kind of remark," he continued after a pause. "It is the one thing in you I can't put up with" ' (*PI*, 241). Ultimately, in the denouement of the Caves, 'that kind of remark' destroys the friendship. For when Aziz repeats the rumours of Fielding and Adela's 'dalliance', Fielding does not share Aziz's enraged response to this coupling of his name with Adela's. And when Aziz ventures another remark of that sort – 'So you and Madamsell Adela used to amuse one another in the evening, naughty boy' – Fielding suffers a complete breakdown of civility, addressing Aziz as 'You little rotter!' (*PI*, 262).

Although Aziz explains this incident as the usual trouble, 'Oh dear, East and West. Most misleading' (*PI*, 262), the politics of *sex* governs this breach as it does the novel's resolution. Indeed, in the novel's grim logic, woman's body continues to bear, until the very end, the weight of perpetuating colonial authority – continues to cover for all the differences (within and between men) colonialism both disavows and requires. Thus in the 'Temple' sequence Stella Moore's fertile body comes to replace Adela's sterile one. Bearing the child Heaslop already 'knows' to be Fielding's 'son and heir', Stella must fulfil the feminine condition, bringing Fielding more 'into line with the Oppressors of India' (*PI*, 298). Aziz's 'unreasonable' insistence, then, when caught out in his mistake, that it is *as if* Fielding had married Adela contains its own logic; for in the no man's land he and Fielding inhabit, women's bodies are interchangeable.

Indeed, in the brief reconciliation of Aziz and Fielding, Stella's body completes what Adela's could not accomplish. For when Fielding's and Aziz's boats collide, Stella's body passes between them, catapulting the boats and facilitating the men's reunion ('That was the climax, as far as India admits of one'): 'The shock was minute, but Stella, nearest to it, shrank into her husband's arms, then reached forward, then flung herself against Aziz, and her motions capsized them' (*PI*, 305). Completing the compact begun in the bungalow, Stella becomes, momentarily, Fielding's 'hostage' to masculine intimacy, sealing a friendship that cannot include her. Thus, in a final effort to prove his affection, Fielding, in his last conversation with Aziz, forces himself 'to speak intimately about his wife, the person most dear to him' (*PI*, 309). But in the larger scheme of things, as Fielding recognizes, he and Aziz no longer have the luxury of even Aziz's bungalow: 'socially they had no meeting-place'. Having 'thrown in his lot with Anglo-India by marrying a countrywoman', Fielding knows, even as he prolongs the fantasy of their connection, that it is Aziz who has become 'a memento, a trophy' (*PI*, 309).

When speaking confidentially to Hamidullah, Aziz, in an earlier scene, defends his decision to relinquish his claim to Adela's money; upholding the superior claims of masculine friendship, he explains, 'wink[ing] at him slowly', 'There are many ways of being a man; mine is to express what is deepest in my heart' (*PI*, 258). Yet despite his show of worldliness, the 'naughty rumour' of some impropriety between Fielding and Adela disconcerts Aziz completely, producing an 'explosion of nerves' and an exaggerated sense of abandonment: 'But who does give me assistance? No one is my friend. All are traitors, even my children. I have had enough of friends' (*PI*, 258–9). When subsequently Aziz tells Fielding of his 'dismay and anxiety' upon learning of the rumour, Fielding, quite literally, cannot imagine it: 'Don't use such exaggerated phrases' (*PI*, 261), Fielding chides, but, given Aziz's outburst, the phrases appear both an under- and overstatement.

With the incontrovertible proof of Fielding's marriage to Stella – and consequently, the definitive dispelling of the 'naughty' rumour – Aziz, in the novel's final scenario, regains both manhood and friendship. Where Fielding *offers* Stella ('the person most dear to him') in a conciliatory gesture before the inevitable parting – 'And, anxious to make what he could of this last afternoon, he forced himself to speak intimately about his wife' (*PI*, 309) – Aziz, in the flurry of reconciliation, *relinquishes* Adela (the object of his hatred). In what the narrator calls a 'charming letter', Aziz acts the gentleman: 'As I fell into our largest Mau tank under circumstances our other friends will relate, I thought how brave Miss Quested was and decided to tell her so, despite my imperfect English' (*PI*, 308). But as the narrative makes clear, this gesture comes too late. For Aziz, who has definitively abandoned British India, and Fielding, who now admits 'no further use for politeness' (*PI*, 311), the gentlemanly thing cannot articulate a binding authority. Indeed, the manly ethic Aziz now subscribes to constitutes a type of militaristic fantasy – a fantasy at least indirectly served by the magnanimous gesture of the letter. For in relinquishing the grounds of his difference with Fielding (their inability to possess a common understanding of Adela), Aziz clears the field for the projection of man-to-man combat with which the novel ends – combat performed over the body of India. Invoking his two sons (as males, the only children presumably worth counting), Aziz conjures the apocalyptic battle through which (and *only* which) their friendship can be purified:

'. . . If I don't make you go, Ahmed will, Karim will, if it's fifty or five hundred years we shall get rid of you, yes, we shall drive every blasted Englishman into the sea, and then' – he rode against him furiously – 'and then,' he concluded, half kissing him, 'you and I shall be friends.'

(*PI*, 312)

In his 'imperfect English' Aziz thus makes explicit the operation of the novel. For enacting and resisting a discourse that permits only one way to be a man, the narrative performs the act it dare not name: the mimicry that governs its own articulation.

Between Performance and Pedagogy

When *A Passage to India* was first published, rumour has it, civil servants outward bound for India, seeing themselves caricatured in the novel, threw their copies overboard, declaring that 'Anglo-Indian Society was no longer "like that" ' (Scott 1966: 15). In the classroom today (and in the institutional outreaches of the academy) the desire to 'chuck' the novel, were it to be voiced, would speak from (and for) other sites of identification: the places at the margins of traditional English studies and at the margins of British and American culture. Indeed, were we to put to the novel the question Gayatri Spivak has popularized, 'Can the subaltern speak?' (Spivak 1985), the novel would not be likely to yield up a response helpful to a politics of identity. For looking at the novel's parade of Indian figures – from the most individualized characters to the most stereotyped, from the most vocal (the chattering Aziz and the gnomic Godbole) to the most silent (the invisible women, the absent political activists) – we might ask who wants to claim a subaltern who speaks 'like that'. And the situation would not be much improved if we turned to other sites of representation: to the portrayal of women or the non-portrayal of homosexuals.

Teaching *Passage* today – to audiences formed (knowingly or unknowingly) by the postmodern discourses of a postcolonial geography – the liberal humanist rubrics that have served Forster so well (for example, the novel 'is about something much wider than politics') no longer seem adequate to ensure the text's institutional security. The challenges posed by 'minority' discourse studies – colonialist/postcolonialist analysis, feminism, gay studies – demand articulation in our practices of reading and teaching. And in this context, the model of outward-bound colonial officials boldly repudiating *Passage*, in 1924, on the grounds that the text did not reflect *their* reality, has a certain pedagogical efficacy – even urgency – for today's disenchanted readers. In fact, the unabashed theatricality of the colonial gesture (however apocryphal) – and the expressive immediacy of its theory of reading (the assumption that the text transparently reflects some pregiven reality) – provide considerably surer ground for students than the subtleties of Bhabha's laboured and infinitely mediated performative strategies.

For if the question emerges, whether we should continue to teach Forster, and if so, how, Bhabha answers both parts of the inquiry: *with difficulty*. This 'difficulty' informs Bhabha's commitment to 'theory' as a textual practice *and* a political intervention; complicating our understanding of both aesthetic practices and political referents, Bhabha demands that we see these 'objects' or 'categories' as inextricable from the discourses that construct them as intelligible. Neither race, then, nor gender nor sexuality (to choose the terms I have privileged in my reading) can lead us out of difficulty; for they do not exist as radically 'expressive' social totalities that might undergird some new position of authority; rather, for Bhabha, all 'positions of authority are themselves part of a process of ambivalent identification' (Bhabha 1990: 296) in which race, gender, and sexuality occupy shifting discursive locations, in contest with each other and with other historical dispositions.

Yet despite this difficulty – or rather, because of it – Bhabha's theories have a particular usefulness when reading familiar novels like *Passage*; for forcing us to resist the sure grounds of identity the novel so willingly offers, they block, even as they illuminate, the novel's channels of communication. In other words, they permit us to see the novel's cultural authority *as a performance* – a speech act whose efficacy requires our complicity as readers. Paradoxically, however – and somewhat problematically for the clarity of pedagogy – Bhabha figures resistance as nearly identical to complicity: almost the same, but not quite. For him, it would seem, the way to resist a text is not to chuck it, but to read it – but to read it in such a way that the accents fall differently. Indeed, mimicry, as Bhabha understands it, has certain affinities with reading, whereby the (silent) repetition of the culturally inscribed text produces inevitable slippages from the 'original'. Such a strategy of reading (and teaching) opens to view the operations of power through which 'the English book' establishes subject positions: who speaks and with what authority?

A performative theory of reading thus makes explicit that the cultural authority of the English novel is not 'natural' but 'constructed'. It offers a framework for understanding the deployment of markers of difference (such as race, sexuality, gender) as they operate within a system of power that plays them off against each other in the interest of shifting alliances of sameness and difference. Yet these alliances, and the rules that regulate them, often remain masked – even in self-consciously oppositional practices of reading. Where 'performance', then, might be most productive as a theoretical category is in what it illuminates about precisely those critical practices in which we are most implicated; indeed, it demands our recognition of the rules we play by, and hence, the particular ways we delimit and situate critical problems. In the case of *Passage*, criticism attentive to the politics and poetics of difference has been limited by its tendency to read particular sites of identity in isolation. Critics have thus been forced to choose between colonialism's false oppositions: to collude in the text's misogyny when explicating the novel's constructions of race and nationality (by leaving gender an unquestioned category) or, more rarely (given the scarcity of feminist readings), to adopt the novel's problematic racial categories to expose its sexual economy.[9] My own interest (in a reading motivated by Bhabha's theories) has been neither to label and hence dismiss the text as either racist or sexist but rather to uncover the operation of its appropriation in and through these culturally powerful categories.

In using categories like race, gender and sexuality, however, I have represented them as considerably more stable and coherent than Bhabha's problematic would allow. Indeed, the difficulty and abstraction of Bhabha's thinking remain the greatest obstacles to its usefulness in the classroom, and I have been able to appropriate it here only at the price of radical oversimplification. If the performance of this essay has been to demonstrate theory in practice, I have done this in part by putting practice (Forster's text) into (Bhabha's) theory. In my reconstructions, then, of Bhabha's project, I have used Forster's highly 'readable' articulation of the colonial scenario to render 'intelligible' Bhabha's more inaccessible theory. In this respect, I have reversed Bhabha's methodology by intersecting the display of a radically *performative* practice with the counterdemands of the *pedagogical* – the demand for something resembling an expressive reality.[10]

The encounter I have staged, then, between Bhabha and Forster operates on a variety of levels, providing students with multiple entry points and different layers of access. I have begun with the assumption that in so far as Bhabha provides a useful filter for understanding colonial discourse, his theory will illuminate the theatrics Forster represents as the 'unfiltered' product of a faithful record of the colonial scene. But in so far as texts of cultural authority (including the 'anti-imperialist' novel) also participate in the colonial legacy, Bhabha's theory might read *Passage* against itself: muddling its aesthetic of metaphysical mystery, articulating – and dislocating – the cultural power with which it invests itself. If Bhabha's emphasis on enunciation in his theories of mimicry permits us to question not only what is said but from where it is said, then 'performance' in *Passage* takes on new meanings. In other words, we may need to question *which* performances we read, distinguishing between the text (of any particular scene) *as performance* and that performance *as textual effect*. The Fielding–Aziz drama, for example, which I have spotlighted in the preceding section, can be read as a richly textured performance with complexly layered

meanings; but it can also be seen as itself the 'product' of a textual performance that produces the problems of two ultimately unimportant
individuals as *the* drama that matters. For the configuration of this
drama of personal relations erases many things, rendering the political
extravaganza of British rule of India as, as it were, a small-screen 'home
drama'. If, as Bhabha has argued, the shadow of the home nation always
falls on the condition of exile (Bhabha 1990: 292), then we might
ponder the condition of England as it infiltrates *Passage*'s posture of
an 'exiled' narrative. Read as domestic fiction, *Passage* articulates the
process – and price – of becoming familiar (family) reading matter.

Forster's reputation has always depended upon a kind of 'safeness', a
condition of 'minor' greatness. But that state of cosy familiarity is not
without its disruptions and not without its cultural power. As a text,
however, *Passage* has remained on the sidelines of the canon battles;
occupying a space largely outside the heated arguments that have flared
up around, for example, Conrad's *Heart of Darkness* (1902), it continues
to be quietly read and studied. What Bhabha brings to Forster might
be seen, then, as a type of borderline occupation. Near the end of an
essay entitled 'DissemiNation: Time, Narrative, and the Margins of the
Modern Nation', Bhabha writes: 'For it is by living on the borderline
of history and language, on the limits of race and gender, that we are
in a position to translate the differences between them into a kind of
solidarity' (Bhabha 1990: 320). If Bhabha's theory, then, offers us no
definitive readings of *Passage*, no fully formed positions of identity from
which to speak the text's meaning, it offers us a space and mechanism
of translation. Indeed, in my 'application' of Bhabha to Forster's text
I have translated rather loosely, producing a reading of the narrative
construction of masculinity facilitated but not determined by Bhabha's
theoretical premises and directives. If Bhabha's theory of mimicry,
however, is to move us beyond the dissection of the discourses of the
dominant culture to the production of 'other spaces of subaltern signifi-
cation' (Bhabha 1990: 312), we would need to intersect the English
novel (the text of language) with other texts of history. But in the
postcolonial theatre of impersonation, we also need to remember our
implication in a culture formed in and by colonial strategies. As a
practice of interventionist reading, then, Bhabha's theory has much to
teach, opening the well-thumbed passages of Forster's novel to the
echo of other voices, to new articulations – in all their complicated
embeddedness.

SUPPLEMENT

NIGEL WOOD: Your section 'Between Men' suggests new opportunities for analysing the operations of repressive discourses. Could you say a little more about the idea of performative theories of literature, especially as regards gender positions, perhaps in relation to other texts?

BETTE LONDON: In thinking about performative theories of literature, I have in mind a practice informed by the work of someone like Judith Butler, whose theoretical investigations so powerfully articulate an understanding of gender as performative (see Further Reading). If, as Butler suggests, gender is not expressive of a pregiven essence but is constituted and performed in social acts, what 'literary' theory can offer us is a means to read this performance – to read the process by which gender is produced and naturalized. More particularly, it might illuminate the structures that 'select' those particular gendered positions that align both sex and gender within familiar binary oppositions (male–female), thus enforcing the heterosexual contract. Clearly literary texts constitute one public/private space for viewing these performances, and, especially in the case of the canonical literary text, they represent a site of authority through which particular culturally sanctioned performances receive legitimation.

But performance can also be understood as a crucial part of the practice of reading, for the act of reading requires the repetition of a prescripted reality; in this scenario, the classroom mediates between the public locations of the text (in the literary marketplace, in the media, in the halls and archives of the academy) and the private space of individualized reading. The act of reading, then, particularly as it is endorsed institutionally, participates in our education into a knowledge of ourselves as gendered beings. In the case of literature, this operation works in part through the appeal of the text's available positions of identification (what, in the case of *A Passage to India*, for example, has often gone under the name of Forster's much celebrated 'humanism'). A theory of performance, however, might remind us of the sexual positions and gender possibilities excluded from a normative conception of humanity; indeed, Butler would suggest, we become 'humanized' by performing our gender properly. But a recognition of this performance opens up the possibility of reading to 'repeat differently', to inhabit other positions or, at least, to make visible the repression of positions marked as 'deviant'.

Given this context, it is perhaps not surprising that performative theory has held particular interest for some versions of gay and lesbian studies as a way of destabilizing fixed understandings of gender and sexuality. I am thinking here, in particular, of work on camp, masquerade and mimicry – practices that insist on their status as performance and hence on the contingent status of the gendered bodies they stage for us. A theory of performance, as the maker and marker of gender, might provide an especially fruitful means to read texts dependent upon a self-conscious theatricality – a text like Woolf's *Orlando* (1928), for example, immediately suggests itself. But performance theory has as much to tell us about those texts that would seem to announce their unmediated authenticity – that perform so flawlessly that the performance tends not to be seen. In this respect, performance theory challenges, among other things, feminist literary criticism's investment in gender as a stable category. To the extent, for example, that it has proved interesting for feminism to read something like *Jane Eyre* (1847) or the *Letters* of Héloïse as speaking to the truth of women's experience, we might need to rephrase the terms of our inquiry to ask what operations these texts perform that convince us to take their enactments of gender as 'the real thing'.

NW: I get the feeling that you're not convinced that Forster's liberal critique of Anglo-India is relevant today, or rather that it can't survive the exact historical conditions to which it immediately refers. Why now study Forster?

BL: I begin with the assumption that Forster continues to be worth studying (why write this otherwise?) and worth studying in part because, however outdated and inadequate its solutions, texts like *Passage* continue to speak powerfully for a compelling vision of 'humanity' – a vision reinforced by its very failure to be achieved. Because we remain inheritors of this liberal tradition, and inheritors of its practices of reading, in some sense the study of *Passage* is important precisely to interrupt and interrogate the novel's 'naturalizing' processes. What continued study of Forster might most help us see is the way we continue to be constructed by the assumptions of a liberal humanist agenda – and the way the literary canon privileges those texts that conform to this paradigm and privileges the conformist messages in them. My problem with the novel's 'liberal critique' (or rather, with our reading of it) comes from a particular defence of liberalism that would forestall criticism – or even certain kinds of close analysis – of the novel's representational politics on the grounds that such readings are somehow anachronistic. In Forster criticism, this is commonly formulated as, 'Forster was an enlightened man for his time.' But even granting that, to repeat such a position today (as sufficient and self-explanatory) seems to me problematic – in part because it erases our participation in those 'liberal' positions and makes impossible anything other than an endorsement of the novel. But how does one produce a reading enabling of alternative positions we might now want to occupy?

Teaching *Passage* to students in the United States allows the illusion, at least, of its subject's distance from *our* history. So I want to get at my uncomfortableness here in a somewhat roundabout way through an example presumably closer to my students' experience of a problematic cultural legacy. When I have taught Martin Luther King's 'Letter from Birmingham Jail' to Freshman English courses, a frequent response would begin: 'Back in the 1950s when people used to be prejudiced . . .'. For my students, born after King's death, Martin Luther King has become a 'historical figure' (appearing somewhere vaguely in a chain of notables, following closely after Washington and Lincoln). For the most part, these students lack any sense of the contestedness of King's historical position and of alternative positions – from both the Right and Left – through and against which King defined himself. What is lacking is a sense of the conditions under which a particular programme and political agenda gains ascendancy and legitimacy. These concerns seem relevant to the teaching of Forster – especially, since for many students, Forster may be their primary source of access to British colonial rule – an access supplemented by David Lean's film and the PBS version of *The Jewel in the Crown*. Indeed, if literary representations have cultural power – in their time and beyond – *Passage's* power is perhaps even greater today as the 'authorized' story of India.

It seems important, then, to study Forster today in such a way as to understand the particular place of Forster's work in resisting and reinforcing British colonial supremacy. Certainly, there are projects I would see as complementary to my own undertaking that would put Forster's text into play with a set of historically contiguous discourses that articulate alternative possibilities. But to produce and enact alternative responses, we need to understand our own situatedness. This does not necessarily mean that we must dismiss Forster's liberal critique (or Forster's text), but we can question its sufficiency. In doing so, we might unleash alternative positions *within* Forster that have been obscured by ruling traditions of reading. We might, for example, read the novel for the access it offers us into the chilling process by which 'authority' is achieved. And we might read it for what is silenced by its explicit political emphases – by its liberal critique of Anglo-India. As I tried to suggest in the 'Between Men' section of my essay, Forster is also of interest today to students of the history of gender and sexuality; continued study of Forster could do much to uncover the intersections of that history with the colonial project. Continued study of Forster, moreover, might shift emphasis from the author/text's regulatory message to our practices of reading – practices that can illuminate, disable and disrupt particular messages of cultural authority.

NW: Just as Forster's fiction expresses a *hope* of civilized coexistence he usually portrays an antagonistic reality, especially true of the world outside, for example, what lies outside Howards End. Couldn't it be the case that he is quite aware of the cosmetic attempts to disguise states of affairs by the culture he depicts?

BL: That Forster might be aware of 'the cosmetic attempts to disguise states of affairs by the culture he depicts' seems to me beyond question. In so far as his novel does function as liberal critique, he explicitly attacks Anglo-Indian society for precisely those cosmetic gestures; that his more idealized liberal spokespersons might be caught in another ameliorating fantasy would seem to enter the consciousness of the text in the novel's insistent sense of fatality. It would hardly require much stretching of the biography to say that some such recognition provoked Forster to give up writing novels altogether after the completion of *Passage*. If I were to speculate in these terms, however, I would want to argue for differing levels of 'awareness'. And I would want to argue that on the question of awareness, much of the interest of the novel lies in the fact that so much seems undecidable. For the novel consistently produces an excess of effect, contradictory effects, 'unreadable' moments of narration, and disruptions of narrative authority. It would be possible to argue, moreover, that the emphasis on cosmetic cover-up, on a civilized 'hope' that cannot hold up against antagonistic reality, ultimately serves to preserve that hope, to leave it unquestioned as a lost ideal – or ideal under threat. Consequently, a question remains about Forster's investment in that fantasy of civilized coexistence and its status as ahistorical utopian dream.

But at another level, Forster's awareness is not really my concern. What interests me in uncovering the texts of mimicry is the operation of power (and the underlying cultural assumptions) that link the besieged liberal hope to the acts of colonial authority. That Forster remains delimited by the historical conditions of his writing should not be surprising; one could not imagine Forster 'aware' of the particular implications of his practice in colonial mimicry – as defined by the likes of Homi Bhabha – any more than one might assume that the acts of 'resistance' Bhabha locates in the Delhi natives' reading of the English Bible (under a tree outside Delhi, May 1817) would necessarily be understood, in precisely those terms, by their historical agents. Part of the point of this type of analysis – and this type of application of a theoretical machinery – is to see what, by definition, the particular historical agents could not possibly see (or see as coherently and systematically). This is not to dismiss Forster as uncritically naive or some 'dupe' of ideology, but to suggest that our distance – historically, culturally, ideologically, methodologically – allows a framing of these acts unlikely to be available to Forster. From this perspective, then, what Forster 'knew' is ultimately less important than what is written in the text and what is received by its audiences. My analysis concerns itself not with the final 'truth' about the text – or its politics – but rather with what the text can now be made to yield by virtue of our particular positionings and our particular motivations for reading.

NW: You suggest on p. 115 a further direction criticism could take, using Bhabha's readings, namely the consideration of 'the condition of England' in the midst of an apparently 'exiled' narrative about life thousands of miles away. Could you expand on this?

BL: In raising the question of 'exile', I want to suggest some of the ways *Passage* both participates and does not participate in the condition of exile. The narrative, it seems to me, works through a pose of self-exile, a fantasy of denationalization; it is this fantasy of a radical and definitive break from home that permits the disembodiment of the narrative voice – a voice markedly disorienting in its slippage from 'us' to 'them' in its relations to 'British' identity. At the same time, if, as Bhabha suggests, narratives of exile are always shadowed, even overshadowed, by 'home', Forster affirms his exile in the protracted doubling of his identity. Moreover, if colonialism attempts, in Forster's words, to 'make England in India', Forster could be said to make the English novel in an Indian setting. In this light, one might, for example, read *Passage* more along the lines of *Howards End* (1910). What might it offer by way of class analysis? What might it say about anxieties about inheritance, property, national identity? *Howards End* poses the question of English inheritance through both a lower-class challenge – figured in terms of economic mobility and sexual promiscuity – and an upper/middle-class cosmopolitanism – figured in the Schlegel's German/Englishness. The 'condition of England' narrative thus reveals itself as implicated (as in *Passage*) in stories of 'miscegenation' – stories whose moral import resists easy categorizings. For the Other both threatens pure English identity and offers the hope of revitalizing it, of saving it from becoming nothing more than the outpost of the paradigmatic businessman. In *Desire and Domestic Fiction*, Nancy Armstrong (1987) argues that the domestic English novel characteristically displaces class conflict into romance plots, replacing class difference with sexual difference as the novel's central drama. Forster, as inheritor of this legacy, might be seen to offer a narrative domestication of the Indian political theatre. *Passage* performs this domesticating function not only in so far as it offers a space devoted to the containment of the Other but also as it provides a forum for displaced discussion of domestic concerns – domestic, in the sense of English (versus foreign) and domestic (as pertaining to home and family). In India, the English middle-class drama (the stuff of domestic comedy) appears as a performance executed in obliviousness to the changed social, political, economic, cultural realities of the British presence in India; but in England, conditions also changed to make such performances a nostalgic fantasy. *Howards End*, then, could be said to offer a fantasy of place – a wholesome, unified, English country house – to be replaced in *Passage* by the Anglo-Indian bungalow colony. Like *Howards End*, *Passage* questions the condition of an England whose borders no longer prove inviolable, encroached upon by new women, new gender relations, new unauthorized 'outbreaks' of sexuality; and like *Howards End* it ponders the need to redefine 'culture' in a hostile setting in order to heal the wounds of modernity.

CHAPTER 4

Representing the Unrepresentable: Alice Jardine's *Gynesis* and E.M. Forster's *A Passage to India*

SARA MILLS

[In a patriarchal cultural and political order it is especially difficult to use the very means of that system, its 'normal' discourses, to define or even to suggest an alternative to its operations. As Sara Mills makes clear in this essay, the 'feminine' is assigned a marginal role wherever the norm is the 'male'. Women characters in narratives that assume this division become angels or whores, victims or temptresses, Ophelias (as in Shakespeare's *Hamlet*) or Mesdames Bovary. These types are male projections that help define, not women, but the need to tame them.

Alice Jardine's *Gynesis* (1985) attempts to analyse and so unsettle this tendency. To be marginal can be recuperated as a radical force, questioning the very assumptions that construct certain qualities as 'central' and as the guarantors of a certain knowledge. What is perceived to lie beyond the reach of patriarchy is emptied of content until it is conceptualized as 'space', a completion of the pattern and thus merely part of it. It is, though, *by definition*, also outside the control of the centre, even if seen in relation to it: 'This other-than-themselves is almost always a "space" of some kind (over which the narrative has lost control), and this space has been coded as *feminine*, as *woman*'. 'Gynesis' denotes the deliberate step of putting 'woman' into discourse, which actually captures the 'condition of modernity'. Furthermore, this gender-specific manoeuvre is not merely old wine in new bottles, but actually constructs the 'modern' – not by disowning the 'historical connotations' of the 'feminine', but realizing that they are 'somehow intrinsic to new and necessary modes of thinking, writing, speaking' (Jardine 1985: 25). Gynesis does not merely invert this hierarchy, but, by embracing ambiguity and hybridity, it rather refuses to take up a position within its figural topography.

This move to opt out of patriarchy emphasizes what is, according to Jardine, occurring anyway: a 'crisis in the narratives invented by men' (Jardine 1985: 24). It is the precise position of authority (not inevitably a male preserve and which is sometimes occupied by particular women at certain times) which is being interrogated. This is why Jardine is careful to associate gynesis with 'woman', not an aggregate experience of actual 'women' under patriarchy. To adopt a term from the French psychoanalyst, Jacques Lacan, 'if man and woman exist, they do so only within the symbolic', that is, in the restraints on comprehension and identity of an inherited linguistic organization (Jardine 1985: 48). This Symbolic Order supplies the promise of an essential and recurring position that the perceiving subject takes up, the identification of the chaotic and unfixed self with the apparent fixed point of the first person in a sentence or even with the terms by which we are named.

Jardine acknowledges the influence of several French feminists, especially Julia Kristeva, in arriving at this perception. In several closely argued texts Kristeva explores the potential vacuum (and so freedoms) in definitions of 'woman'. Opposing the social distinction between male and female, she does not discount the significance of the political force that accrues whenever specific women's interests are supported by collective action. There is, however, a deeper level at which a 'woman' cannot be represented. In her interview, 'La Femme, ce n'est jamais ça' (1980), she claimed that 'a woman is not something one can "be"; it does not even belong in the order of *being* . . . By "woman" I understand what cannot be represented, what is not said, what remains above and beyond nomenclatures and ideologies' (Kristeva 1980: 137–8). As Mills points out (p. 126) Jardine's thinking is not derived directly from Kristeva's, but it shares the same determination to suggest a space that is not catered for in Lacan's Symbolic Order. In this, it is not a history of women, but a process that unsettles all models of order. Toril Moi has recently pointed out that Kristeva 'does not have a theory of "femininity", and even less of "femaleness". What she does have is a theory of marginality, subversion and dissidence' (Moi 1985: 164; see also Moi 1986: 24–33, 74–136). Against the Symbolic she poses the 'semiotic', a prerational and prelinguistic signifying process. In her doctoral thesis, *La Révolution du langage poétique* (1974; trans. as *Revolution in Poetic Language* in 1984), her first extended treatment of this process and its consequences for language, the 'semiotic' is regarded as testing the sense that all should be intelligible and is nearer to the purely rhythmic or melodious. (See also Kristeva's 'The System and the Speaking Subject', in Sebeok 1975, 47–55; Kristeva 1980; Moi 1985: 161–2; 1986: 93–109.)

Kristeva and Jardine are pronounced examples of the recent feminist project to promote an awareness both of a specific female power in reading and writing and also its necessary rupture of the accepted norms of language. As Elaine Showalter has termed it, this search is for a 'wild zone', 'a place forbidden to men . . . Experientially it stands for the aspects of the female life-style which are outside of and unlike those of men' (Showalter 1985: 262).

(See Jane Moore's 'An other space: a future for feminism?', in I. Armstrong 1992: 65–79; and Hélène Cixous's 'Sorties: Out and Out: Attacks/Ways Out/ Forays', in Belsey and Moore 1989: 101–16.)

The process of writing this summary of 'gynesis' and the 'semiotic' in this headnote could thus be regarded as an ironic gesture, given the content of the theories described. A male attempt to render the essence of these processes, or simply to embrace the objective, is exactly a move that the 'gynetic' evades; its fertility of expression and non-patriarchal conception should ensure that such a move is doomed to inaccuracy at the deeper levels of experience. If this is accepted, the hope is that this note merely performs the preliminary task of tentative suggestion.]

NIGEL WOOD

For many critics, E.M. Forster's *A Passage to India* is a book about the problematic and difficult relationship between the characters of Fielding and Aziz, at times read by critics as a dramatization of E.M. Forster's relationship with Syed Ross Masood, at other times as a symbolic enactment of Britain's colonial relationship with India.[1] To see the book as primarily about relationships between men means that the female characters such as Adela Quested and Mrs Moore are simply impediments to both types of relationship. This essay tries to focus on how a feminist might read the book. There is great diversity within feminist theory and it is conventional now to speak of 'feminisms' rather than feminism. However, it is possible to define a common denominator of feminism in the following way: by 'feminist' I mean those readers, both female and male, who have discovered that there is a systematicity in the representational (and other) practices of British and other cultures, whereby women are produced as the negative term in an opposition where the male is positioned as the norm. Feminists are those critics who analyse not only the discrimination which exists in this differential representation but also its effects, and who attempt to bring about changes in these practices and in the socio-economic, cultural and political system at large.[2] Groups of feminist literary theorists, because of their allegiances to systems of analysis such as psychoanalysis, Marxism and discourse theory, differ markedly in the way they tackle the differences in representations of women and men. For example, some feminist theorists might, when analysing *A Passage to India*, propose a critique of the notion that the book is about male relationships by a simple inversion whereby they assert that the book is really about female relationships. These feminists would concentrate their analysis on the female characters in the text. Such a simplistic inversion, while interesting, nevertheless falls into the same problematic concerns with trying to discover what the book is *really* about, and with attempting to prove that your own particular reading of the book is more valid or more comprehensive than others. Such beliefs that literary texts have unified meanings are difficult to hold in the present climate of modern literary theory, particularly feminist theory, because it is quite clear that there is more to an ambiguous and elusive text like *A Passage to India* than the relationships between characters. In many modern texts, what happens is often the subject of great critical debate, and therefore it is necessary to try to develop a model of analysis which can deal with the complexity of such texts and which will not try to impose a unitary meaning on them. *A Passage to India* is clearly a text where it is possible to develop an almost infinite number of readings, even if one focuses on one aspect rather than others. Rather than attempting to produce a feminist reading which would try to interrogate this specific text, in order to develop analysis, it is the aim of this essay to outline one theoretical model, Alice Jardine's notion of 'gynesis', which may be used to expose in a more general way some of the mechanisms whereby certain types of representational practice can be dominant within Western culture.

Alice Jardine's Gynesis: Beyond Images of Women

The representation of women in texts, both literary and non-literary, has concerned feminist critics since the early 1960s. Many feminists, such as Kate Millett, focused on the stereotypical representations of women, either as sex objects or as adjuncts to males, that are frequently found in a wide range of texts.[3] Much of this early criticism (generally labelled Anglo-American criticism) was concerned with attacking these images for their sexism, that is to say, the demeaning and inaccurate representations they produced, and, in their place, proposing more positive images of women. This type of feminist criticism went on to celebrate those positive images found in literature which could be used as 'role models' for women readers: those characters which could be seen to have positive traits, such as assertiveness or independence.[4] In order to analyse sexist representations of women in texts, many feminists were forced to adopt rather crude models of textuality, for example, assuming a fairly straightforward relationship between the textual and the real and between female characters and women readers. These feminist critics were led to assume that reading certain types of representation of women had direct effects on the way women came to form a notion of their own sense of self. While it is clear that being constantly confronted by images of women which stress their sexual nature, their fragility or their dependence must have some effect on both women and men, many feminists were uncomfortable with the notion that characters could simply be mapped on to people in this simple way. This led some feminist critics, such as Toril Moi, influenced by French psychoanalysis and modern critical theory, to pose an alternative: a focus on representations alone and an agenda for feminist critics to move from such simplistic analyses to more complex considerations (Moi 1985, esp. 42–9 and 150–73). For Moi, concern with producing images of what she termed 'female tractor drivers' to counter sexist images of women led feminist criticism into an impasse.

However, while there are problems with simply analysing representations of women and judging them to be authentic or as role models, the question of representation is still very much at the forefront of feminist debates. Like Alice Jardine, many have drawn on critical theories such as psychoanalysis in order to discuss representations without assuming that there is a simple link between the textual depiction of female characters and women in the real world. She states:

> I am more concerned about the process of [reading and writing] woman than about the representation of women in literature. I am looking for the logical and not so logical operations that organize the fictions of the 'real world', but am less interested in explicating why that world is represented in such a way.
>
> (Jardine 1985: 19)

Jardine is not so much concerned with the stereotyped representation of individual female characters in literature, as with what happens when 'woman' or 'the feminine' intrudes into a text, something which happens not just when texts seem to be explicitly 'about' female characters, but rather as an essential part in the production of any modern literary text.[5] Thus, like much modern literary theory, Jardine is concerned to develop general analytical frameworks rather than readings of specific texts.

Drawing on psychoanalytic theory, she proposes that 'the feminine' is an integral and disturbing part of every literary text. Jardine is like other feminist psychoanalytical critics, such as Julia Kristeva, in seeing the feminine as a place of disruption and marginalization. This is how it has often been described within psychoanalytic theory by Freud or Lacan, but feminist critics see the feminine as a place of positive instability, denying it the negative polarization which it has been largely accorded by male critics.[6] This stress on the feminine moves analysis away from femaleness, a term indicating a biological essence, towards the processes which individuals undergo in developing gendered roles. Both females and males have access to femininity and masculinity. For most post-Freudian psychoanalysts, the resolution of crises in children around the question of gender (the Oedipal crisis) involves a recognition of masculine authority at a symbolic level and a simultaneous entry into language. Language and masculine authority are inextricably bound, and for some theorists, such as Jacques Lacan, language is founded on the Law of the Father. The feminine is thus a position which is somehow outside masculine authority and therefore not firmly embedded within language. For theorists such as Julia Kristeva, this feminine position, which she terms 'semiotic', is the position which children occupy in the pre-Oedipal phase before they have acquired language and a clear gendered role. The 'semiotic', however, continues to have an effect on language even after the resolution of the Oedipal crisis, since it bubbles through its apparently calm surface; for Kristeva it is the place where texts quite literally do not make sense in a conventional way. The reader's attention is drawn to the materiality of language when the 'feminine' is in ascendancy, so that the reader focuses on the rhythmic qualities and repetitions of sounds rather than the content. That is not to say that the words are nonsensical, because for Kristeva this is a different kind of meaning; for her, the 'feminine' breaks through into language and forces the reader to consider the way so much is normally taken for granted in the process of making sense of texts.

Jardine's approach is slightly different, but based on the same psychoanalytical model. This feminine element she terms 'gynesis': that is, 'the putting into discourse of "woman" or the "feminine" as problematic' (Jardine 1985: 236). The feminine here should not be confused with the feminine attributes which are supposed to be ideal characteristics for women to aspire to (such as caring for others, modesty, sympathy and so on); rather, it is a space or nexus which is 'outside' representation, since the laws of representation within psychoanalytic theory are necessarily governed by the Law of the Father, that is, the Symbolic Order. The Symbolic Order is that system of language whereby language users are contracted in to a common code of meanings in order to make sense of one another's speech. In submitting to this system when learning language, children also submit to two other systems: one a system of rules and regulations which largely determine their view of the world and which appears to be self-evident or commonsensical, and the other a system of control which represses 'play' in language as well as repressing a certain play in the self.[7] The Symbolic Order is the realm of the Father, and the feminine is that space where the control exercised by the Symbolic Order does not extend – where the system of meaning breaks down or is in a state of instability or play.[8] Jardine suggests that 'that which is beyond the Father, overflowing the dialectics of representation, unrepresentable, will be gendered as feminine' (Jardine 1985: 143).

But rather than simply assuming that the feminine is always outside all forms of representation, Jardine, like Kristeva, regards this particular configuration as specific to texts written within the modern period. She sees gynesis as a form of symptom in a text, brought about by a 'crisis of legitimation' in modern narrative. Like many other literary theorists, she is concerned with the way modern texts are no longer able to call on the narrative structures and certainties that texts in the past seemed to be able to do. Notions of universal truth are now very difficult to argue for, and critical positions, even seemingly factual statements, are seen to be founded not on simple reference to reality but on very unstable ground.[9] Jardine defines this as a crisis in knowledge brought about by a realization that there are knowledges apart from that contained within the text, and these other knowledges have been repressed or excluded. Despite being repressed, these excluded knowledges are not forgotten or banished, but linger in the text itself and threaten its integrity. Jardine states that 'this . . . is almost always a "space" of some kind (over which the narrative has lost control) and this space has been coded as *feminine*, as *woman*' (Jardine 1985: 25). Thus, gender issues are one of the knowledges which have been excluded from much of Western knowledge, but in that very process of exclusion they have been repressed within the text. That moment of repression can never be complete, and thus the feminine surfaces as a moment of disruption or instability. Jardine states that gynesis is that moment in the text which:

> is perhaps only noticed by the feminist reader – either when it becomes insistently 'feminine' or when women (as defined metaphysically, historically) seem magically to reappear within the discourse. This tear in the fabric produces in the (feminist) reader a state of uncertainty and sometimes of distrust – especially when the faltering narrative in which it is embedded has been articulated by a man within a nonetheless still existent discipline.
>
> (Jardine 1985: 25)

Thus, just as Kristeva's 'semiotic' intrusion into language is a moment of possible disruption and revolution, for Jardine this intrusion of the feminine destabilizes the seeming authority of masculine voices. Those knowledges which seem self-evidently stable contain within them repressed knowledges which will lead to their overthrow. For Jardine, the notion of male symbolic power over women (and over other men) has had to repress the very process whereby that power was achieved; this leads to the claim that 'the discussion of loss of authority inevitably comes around to women, who return, empirically, as among those principally to blame for this loss' (Jardine 1985: 67). Thus, even those texts which have not repressed the subject of 'woman' themselves will code their repressions as feminine. A text which describes the power relations of one male group over another will necessarily encode that power struggle as gendered.

For Jardine modernity is the moment when familiar truths can no longer be trusted, when we can no longer be sure that it is possible to construct a true historical record, since there are so many competing voices, and when scientific enquiry seems to have left us with more questions than answers. She states: 'those writing modernity as a crisis-in-narrative, and thus in legitimation, are exploring newly contoured fictional spaces, hypothetical and unmeasurable, spaces freely coded as *feminine*' (Jardine 1985: 69). The questioning of authority which has happened in the modern period has led to a distrust of conventional writing practices. It is almost as if, in experimenting with language and with form, the only space available outside patriarchal authority is the feminine, for 'those texts of modernity attempting to work through the crises in legitimation and figuration . . . cannot avoid putting "woman" into circulation' (Jardine 1985: 102). Jardine here, like most psychoanalytic theorists, elides masculinity, authority and knowledge and thus can only place instability and crisis in the realm of the feminine: 'The demise of the Subject, of the Dialectic, and of truth has left modernity with a *void* that it is vaguely aware must be spoken differently and strangely: a woman, through *gynesis*' (Jardine 1985: 154).

Alice Jardine's work is thus an attempt to move beyond the judgemental analysis of female characters, since it is clear that texts, particularly those of the modern period, are more than simple representations of reality. What she is concerned with is the notion that texts are not coherent, cohesive entities but unsuccessful attempts to impose a coherence on material which will, by its very nature, by the fact of its being excluded or repressed, pull the text itself apart. That is why it is important that this type of analysis should not be seen as an attempt to say what the text is *really* about, since that would assume a unitary voice to the text, a unitary intention emanating from an author. Within psychoanalytic theory, texts may be the product of an author, in that they are written by particular individuals, but they always exceed the conscious intentions of that author – the unconscious comes into play in the writing process and can never be successfully excluded. Thus, it would be impossible and unproductive to try to trace the conscious intentions of the author, since the text is an unstable system of figuration where instabilities will always surface and threaten the seeming coherence. Rather than being the products of individual writers expressing themselves, texts are seen within psychoanalysis as places where individuals try to resolve certain crises, where they display more than they intend, and where can be traced certain general textual problems of that particular culture.

'Gynesis' and *A Passage to India*

A Passage to India is a text written by a white man about a supposed sexual assault on a white woman by an Indian man, a theme that recurs in numerous other texts written by British writers during the colonial period.[10] In many of the symbolizations of the Empire, the figure of the pure, white female is central, both visually and in texts, and violation of this figure is seen to be linked with loss of authority. Consider, for example, the way the so-called Indian Mutiny of 1857 is represented both in fiction and in British historical accounts, where stress is laid not on the military operations of the insurgents, but rather on the rape and murder of white women. In a similar way, the narratives of the Black Hole of Calcutta seem to have precisely that overdetermined character because this incident involved the torture and death of white women. Since this representation is repeated so often throughout British literature about the colonial context, there is clearly more to this than simply the depiction of innocent civilians who are caught in conflict. Within the imperial context, white women seem to be symbolizing far more than simply purity and innocence, as they did in the home context; they seem to stand for the moral rightness of the whole imperial enterprise. This representational practice must be considered when reading any text which deals with the problem of sexual attacks, real or imagined, on white women.[11]

The temporal placing of *A Passage to India* is important: the text is set in a period which was already for Forster the colonial past, at a moment when the British colonial presence was being called into question, but the period when Forster was actually writing was a moment when British rule was being more radically questioned, that is, the early nineteen-twenties, when Mohandas Gandhi was organizing his passive resistance campaigns.[12] The setting for the novel is that moment of a crisis of legitimation, which Forster himself draws attention to when he states in a letter to Edward Arnold of 17 November 1914: 'when all contemporary life seems crumbling I find more difficulty than ever in attempting a picture of it' (quoted by Stallybrass, in Forster 1989: 12; Lago A1182).

Many modernist texts are focused on women, and particularly crises of control over women; one has only to think of D.H. Lawrence or Henry James to notice a shift not only in writing technique from classic realist texts but also in subject matter. As noted above, many texts written within and about the colonial situation, particularly in India, are focused around women as a problem which the text tries to resolve. Modernity is seen to be a crisis of Western culture and authority, and this can be clearly seen in novels about the loss of Britain's colonial role. For Jardine, it would not be coincidental that many of the novels about the Empire are about loss, and that loss seems to be displaced on to or articulated through the problem of women. She sees these two subjects as inextricably tied within this particular moment of Western culture.

A Passage to India is modernist in the sense that it is not entirely a classic realist narrative; by that I mean that there are moments within the text when the meaning seems to be unclear, where the text seems to be having difficulties expressing what happened, or where the reader is left in doubt as to what exactly has happened. These may be moments when a number of conflicting viewpoints are presented almost simultaneously, and where the reader cannot disentangle them or decide which one is the 'true' version of the events.[13] I shall concentrate on a number of these moments in the text where there seems to be a problem of expression, and which constitute moments of gynesis; my focus will be on mysticism, female characters, the wild zone and India itself, but there are other incidents within the text which could equally well have been chosen to exemplify these moments of gynesis.

Mysticism

In colonial periods, there is very often a rigid demarcation between the ruling power and the colonized people, in terms of the places that they inhabit, the clothes they wear, the way they behave and the way that they are described in texts. As Edward Said has shown, this demarcation is brought about in order to justify the imposition of the power relation

(Said 1978: 20–4, 117–21). The colonized nation is represented as the 'Other', that is, as the exact opposite of the colonial power. Frequently, texts written in the colonial period stress the difference between the colonized people's religion, which is portrayed as barbarous, immoral and sometimes obscene, and Christianity, which is simply portrayed as logically and morally better.

Several of the characters in *A Passage to India* are prone to mysticism, that is, a non-rational religious musing which aims to see oneness rather than disparateness. This would normally be the realm of the Other, figured in the religions of the colonized people. But here mystical characters are either Indian males or British women. The characters who are most mystical are those who stray into that forbidden space which exists between the clearly demarcated borders of Indian and British societies. This mysticism is often associated with the feminine or with females, for example, when Aziz is sitting in the mosque thinking about 'Islam, his own country, more than a Faith, more than a battle-cry, more, much more . . .' (*PI*, 13). In thinking of Islam he begins to think of his own death and starts to compose the inscription he would like on his own tomb:

> The secret understanding of the heart! He repeated the phrase with tears in his eyes, and as he did so one of the pillars of the mosque seemed to quiver. It swayed in the gloom and detached itself. Belief in ghosts ran in his blood, but he sat firm. Another pillar moved, a third, and then an Englishwoman stepped out into the moonlight.
>
> (*PI*, 14)

Here the text seems to be having difficulty presenting clearly what is happening; it is at moments like this that the narrative veers towards free indirect discourse and the narrative voice seems to be neither clearly the voice of the narrator nor of a character, but rather a mixture of the two positions. Aziz is experiencing a mystical moment inspired by thinking about the quatrain on a tomb, and suddenly the realism of the text is rendered problematic by a movement of a pillar, a ghost or a person. The phrase 'one of the pillars of the mosque seemed to quiver' is a projection from Aziz within a passage which largely emanates from the narrator: these are Aziz's thoughts, and yet they are presented as being part of the narrator's commentary. Instead of a straightforward depiction of an Englishwoman, the moment of mysticism is elided with her presence. At first, Aziz reacts with anger, asserting the difference of their religious positions: 'Madam, this is a mosque, you have no right here at all' (*PI*, 14). However, once it is clear that she respects the mosque and that she is not concerned with the 'difference' of the place, since 'God is here' (*PI*, 15), they begin to talk and Mrs Moore joins Aziz's mystical musings. This mystical representation is in strict contrast to the rest of the British community, most notably her son Ronny, who on hearing of his mother's visit to a mosque states 'But, mother, you can't do that sort of thing . . . It's not done' (*PI*, 24), insisting that differences must be maintained, and then begins to interpret her encounter as a sexual one:

> 'He called to you in the mosque, did he? How? Impudently? What was he doing there himself at that time of night? – No, it's not their prayer time' . . . 'So he called to you over your shoes. Then it was impudence. It's an old trick.'
>
> (*PI*, 25)

He begins to consider the incident and decides that '[i]t was his duty to report suspicious characters, and conceivably it was some disreputable hakim who had prowled up from the bazaar' (*PI*, 27). Thus while Mrs Moore is concerned only with the similarity between herself and Aziz, Ronny is concerned with the way in which this incident fits in within a colonial system based on difference.

As the narrative unfolds Mrs Moore becomes the object of mystical speculations, and also herself the place where mysticism is located. For example, the narrator relates that: 'A sudden sense of unity, of kinship with the heavenly bodies, passed into the old woman and out, like water through a tank, leaving a strange freshness behind' (*PI*, 24). These moments of assertion of oneness are also paradoxically (or, Jardine would say, precisely) the ones where the text seems to pull apart, where the very fact of trying to assert oneness or wholeness is the point where the text cannot maintain its hold on language. Particularly in the colonial context, founded as it is on the demarcation of difference, the assertion of sameness or wholeness is difficult and almost unrepresentable. Mrs Moore's statements often seem vacillating and paradoxical, for example, when she says: 'What a terrible river! What a wonderful river!' (*PI*, 26) – here no meaning is achieved, but rather an indeterminate expression of awe. Later, during and after the trial, Mrs Moore is transformed into Esmiss Esmoor, 'a Hindu goddess'; she is deified by the Indian people. 'People who did not know what the syllables meant repeated them like a charm' (*PI*, 214) and in this sense her name loses its meaning and referentiality, its relation to the Symbolic Order, in a process of mantra-like chanting. Thus, the mysticism of Mrs Moore is elided with that of Aziz and presumably other Indians, and is set in stark contrast to the Christianity of the established British community. Mysticism is figured in female form, itself constituting a moment of gynesis, or instability within colonialism. Sameness is repressed within colonialism in order to focus on difference, but it reasserts itself, as exemplified here, in moments of mysticism where the differences between religions are presented as of little importance. Ronny and Mrs Moore are opposed here, for example, when he states: 'We're not out here for the purpose of behaving pleasantly! . . . We're out here to do justice and keep the peace' (*PI*, 43). To this Mrs Moore replies: 'The English *are* out here to be pleasant . . . Because India is part of the earth. And God has put us on the earth in order to be pleasant to each other. God . . . is . . . love' (*PI*, 45). Because of the strength with which sameness is repressed, the mere assertion of oneness within a colonial text has a profound destabilizing effect.

Women and Colonialism

This text is concerned with how to depict women within colonialism. In representational terms, it is problematic since the colonial is generally depicted from the British perspective as an almost exclusively male endeavour, even though in reality women were involved throughout the period in a wide range of activities (see especially Trollope 1983). Fielding shows that there is a mismatch between women and India when he states: 'He had discovered that it is possible to keep in with Indians and Englishmen, but that he who would also keep in with Englishwomen must drop the Indians. The two wouldn't combine' (*PI*, 56). There is no explanation given to this statement in the text; it is simply asserted as a fact, one which is validated by the fact that Fielding's voice is often elided with that of the narrator. The Indian characters likewise seem aware of this 'fact' that British women and Indians cannot coexist, for when Aziz and Fielding are talking about whether they like Englishwomen, Aziz states: 'Hamidullah liked them in England. Here we never look at them. Oh no, much too careful. Let's talk of something else' (*PI*, 109–10).

As I mentioned earlier, women exist in the colonial period much more easily as symbols than as real people. In the moment of crisis after the incident at the Marabar Caves, when there is fear of riots and revenge attacks, the text focuses on Mrs Blakiston,

> a brainless but most beautiful girl . . . The wife of a small railway
> official, she was generally snubbed; but this evening, with her

abundant figure and masses of corn-gold hair, she symbolized all
that is worth fighting and dying for; more permanent a symbol,
perhaps, than poor Adela.

(*PI*, 172)

During the anxiety following the incident, the British use 'women and
children' as a phrase to intoxicate themselves (*PI*, 174), replicating the
mantra-like effect achieved by the Indians in the repetition of 'Esmiss
Esmoor'. It is at this moment that reference is made to the Uprising or
Mutiny of 1857, although the text does not explain what happened or
what the significance of this event is: 'The crime was even worse than
they had supposed – the unspeakable limit of cynicism, untouched since
1857' (*PI*, 178).

A Passage to India displays British women as both the moment of
the most extreme symbolic value of the Empire, and as a moment of
disruption or a threat to stability. The period when the memsahib figure
appears in India is in many historical accounts the one where the British
begin to lose their colonial power. Many historians make an explicit
link between these two events.[14] The Collector himself makes this
elision explicit when he says: 'After all, it's our women who make
everything more difficult out here' (*PI*, 204), and the female Turtons
and Burtons are often portrayed as being the *real* problem with govern-
ing India. This can be clearly seen in the bridge party where the
established female members of the British community are those who
refuse to have any contact with the Indian women and men; as one
states: 'I refuse to shake hands with any of the men, unless it has to be
the Nawab Bahadur' (*PI*, 35). Here the female members of the British
community are taking up a masculine position (as is open to them
within this system of masculine–feminine difference), allying themselves to the colonial system of difference and authority. Adela, however, is unable to ally herself to this system and is clearly operating
within the feminine:

Miss Quested now had her desired opportunity; friendly Indians
were before her, and she tried to make them talk, but she failed,
she strove in vain against the echoing walls of their civility.
Whatever she said produced a murmur of deprecation, varying into a murmur of concern when she dropped her pocket-
handkerchief. She tried doing nothing, to see what that produced,
and they too did nothing.

(*PI*, 37)

Here women are presented as the problem of the colonial presence in India; either they will not have any contact with Indians or they wish to have contact but cannot achieve it. Thus, loss of authority is allied to the problem of women; British women begin to symbolize some of the problems with colonial rule itself.

As Rana Kabbani has shown in her analysis of travel writing and literature about the Empire, it is difficult to find depictions of non-British women in anything but the most stereotyped terms (Kabbani 1986). The only Indian females who are represented in *A Passage to India* are either restricted to the harem/purdah – for example, the wives of both Hamidullah and Aziz, the latter maintained in purdah even after her death through the disclosure of her photograph only to selected male friends of her husband – or they are whores, the women 'with breasts like mangoes' (*PI*, 111) whom Aziz would like to invite Fielding to visit in Calcutta. The whores are never presented as such in the text, but are only alluded to by Aziz. These female characters are presented in contrast to British females, but interestingly enough British women are represented as themselves almost in a state of purdah, for example, when they are rehearsing *Cousin Kate* at the Club: 'Windows were barred, lest the servants should see their memsahibs acting' (*PI*, 19). Thus Indian women and British women are both stereotyped into problematic roles involving hiding/protection or taboo; neither group has a simple representational role within colonialism.

The 'Wild Zone'

The 'wild zone' is a concept developed by Shirley and Edwin Ardener and later drawn on by Elaine Showalter to describe the space occupied by women which is seen to be outside the norms of society (Ardener 1978; 'Feminist Criticism in the Wilderness' (1981), in Showalter 1985: 243–70). This space, because it is positioned as non-male, is also allied to the non-human, and hence is marked as 'wild'. In *A Passage to India* the wild zone or the zone of gynesis can be seen to be that space between the Indians and the English which several key characters attempt to inhabit. Fielding, Aziz, Mrs Moore, and Adela Quested all at some stage attempt to move beyond the boundaries of their strictly defined societies. Those who enter this space are valorized – after all they are the central characters – but they are also problematized and their entry into this zone creates confusion and danger. When Adela enters this wild zone at the bridge party, as mentioned above, all that she encounters are 'the echoing walls of their civility' (*PI*, 37), recalling the echo she hears at the Marabar Caves. Whenever someone enters this zone there is misunderstanding – for example, the accident in the Nawab Bahadur's car, the confusions at the bridge party, the incident at the Marabar Caves, the collision of the boats and the final parting of Aziz and Fielding at the end of the book.

To consider a few of these incidents, let us first take the car accident which happens after Adela and Ronny have decided to break off their engagement. The car they are in collides with something, and when they investigate after the crash, they find that:

> Certainly some external force had impinged, but the road had been used by too many objects for any one track to be legible, and the torch created such high lights and black shadows that they could not interpret what it revealed.
>
> (*PI*, 81)

They decide that it was a hyena, but when they tell Mrs Moore, she states that it was a ghost. However, when questioned by Adela she denies that that was what she said. At this point the narrator intervenes with some information about the Nawab Bahadur in whose car they had been driving: he had killed a man in his car nine years before. This is posed as his 'racial secret' (*PI*, 90); the text seems to be offering a range of different information from the rational perspective of the narrator; the frame itself cannot hold all of this information to be true at the same time. Either the object is a hyena, the rational answer, or it is a general spirit as Mrs Moore suggests, or it is the ghost of the man whom the Nawab killed. The text gives no precedence to any of these 'answers' and the reader is left without a clear-cut answer as to what happened in the incident.

The Marabar Caves themselves might be thought of as a space where indeterminacy reigns. When Godbole is about to describe the Marabar Caves to Mrs Moore and Adela Quested he falls silent and Aziz understands this: 'It was . . . that a power he couldn't control capriciously silenced his mind. Godbole's had been silenced now, no doubt not willingly, he was concealing something' (*PI*, 68). There is an echo which both Mrs Moore and Adela hear:

> The echo in a Marabar cave . . . is entirely devoid of distinction. Whatever is said, the same monotonous noise replies, and quivers up and down the walls until it is absorbed in the roof. 'Boum' is the sound as far as the human alphabet can express it, or 'bououm', or 'ou-boum' – utterly dull.
>
> (*PI*, 138–9)

Mrs Moore is overwhelmed by the echo and feels that it is saying to her, 'Everything exists, nothing has value' (*PI*, 140), and she feels that it ends by calling into question the very basis of religion.

Adela – whose very name is indeterminate (is she quested, that is, sought after, or is she the one who quested?) – poses a question to Aziz as she enters the cave, which leads to indeterminacy and misunderstanding, about the number of wives he has. Aziz is shocked, but Adela, who is 'wondering with the other half [of her mind] about marriage' fails to realize that she has offended him (*PI*, 144): 'She had thought of love just before she went in, and had innocently asked Aziz what marriage was like, and she supposed that her question had roused evil in him' (*PI*, 216). When Adela is considering what happened, it is the echo which seems to be the important matter rather than the supposed sexual assault (although it must be remembered that Mrs Moore at first thinks that she herself has been sexually assaulted in the caves). The echo seems to be both to do with sexuality and about evil, for in one of several examples of free indirect discourse, the narrator/Adela says:

> The sound had spouted after her when she escaped, and was going on still like a river that gradually floods the plain. Only Mrs Moore could drive it back to its source and seal the broken reservoir. Evil was loose . . .
>
> (*PI*, 185)

Mrs Moore asks herself what it was that she had encountered in the Caves and she says: 'Something very old and very small. Before time, it was before space also' (*PI*, 198). After the incident Mrs Moore retreats into indeterminacy, talking in paradoxes and, in Ronny's terms, not making sense: 'all this rubbish about love, love in a church, love in a cave, as if there is the least difference' (*PI*, 192). However, the echo which persists inside Adela's head recedes when she considers that she might have made a mistake, that is, when she considers the matter from a rational standpoint, rather than trying to allow indeterminacy to reign.

When Forster was asked what did happen in the Marabar Caves he replied, in a letter to G.L. Dickinson of 26 June 1924:

> In the cave it is *either* a man, *or* the supernatural, *or* an illusion. If I say, it becomes, whatever the answer, a different book. And even if I know! My writing mind therefore is a blur here . . . This isn't a philosophy of aesthetics. *It's a particular trick I felt justified in trying because my theme was India.*
>
> (Quoted by Stallybrass in Forster 1989: 25; Lago D334)

The blur is one whose primary focus is woman, and this to Forster seems justified because he is writing about India, a place where power relations are at one and the same time most asserted and most challenged and a context within which the subject of woman is most closely linked with the loss or maintenance of imperial power.

Finally, there is a moment of gynesis at the end of the book. Rather than its being the colonial relations between Britain and India which prevent the friendship of Fielding and Aziz, or even personal or cultural difference, it is something much more indeterminate:

> The horses didn't want it . . . the earth didn't want it . . . the temples, the tank, the jail, the palace, the birds, the carrion, the Guest House . . . they didn't want it, they said in their hundred voices, 'No, not yet,' and the sky said, 'No, not there.'
>
> (*PI*, 312)

These disparate elements, a mixture of natural and human forces, are seen to be the cause working to prevent the relationship between Fielding and Aziz. Thus, what specifically is preventing their relationship is rendered unclear; there seems to be no real motive force in this collection of hetereogeneous elements.

India Itself

A reader of colonial fiction normally expects a text to present a clear position on the country being depicted; but the narrator here does not offer that position – India is presented in both a negative and a positive light – and it is difficult to describe the text's stance, since it replicates colonial 'truths' as well as challenging them. India is described in terms which are reminiscent of those terms used for the feminine. India is described as 'queer' throughout; the word 'queer' is constantly repeated, but it is interesting that this word is also used to describe Adela Quested – 'the queer, cautious girl' (*PI*, 19). Furthermore, India is described as a 'muddle' (*PI*, 62), a conventional colonial attitude which leads to narratorial statements such as these: 'But nothing in India is identifiable, the mere asking of a question causes it to disappear or to merge in something else' (*PI*, 78). Fielding states in a voice which is indistinguishable from that of the narrator: 'The Mediterranean is the human norm. When men leave that exquisite lake . . . they approach the monstrous and extraordinary; and the southern exit leads to the strangest experience of all' (*PI*, 270–1). Instead of Mediterranean normality, in India everything was placed wrong. He had forgotten the beauty of form among idol temples and lumpy hills; indeed, without form, how can there be beauty? Form stammered here and there in a mosque, became rigid through nervousness even, but oh, these Italian churches!

(*PI*, 270)

All of the inhabitants of India are described as vacillating, or lying, and Ronny is faced with the task in his job of deciding 'which of two untrue accounts was the less untrue' (*PI*, 44). India is portrayed as a country where there is no truth; Callendar states: 'He only knew that no one ever told him the truth' (*PI*, 48). Indians are also portrayed as vacillating between moods: Aziz will at one moment mourn his wife and then at the next be filled with ecstasy. Thus both India and Indians are portrayed as irrational, odd, eccentric and hence indeterminate, as a moment of gynesis.

There is a constant attempt by various characters to discover the 'true' or 'real' India, to make a wholeness of this heterogeneity. This links with the idea of mysticism, where it is precisely that wholeness which cannot be achieved. For example, when Adela is considering what her future life in India would be like if she were married to Ronny, she knows that she would have to miss the whole vision of India:

Perched up on the seat of a dogcart, she would see them [colour and movement]. But the force that lies behind colour and movement would escape her even more effectually than it did now. She would see India always as a frieze, never as a spirit, and she assumed that it was a spirit of which Mrs Moore had had a glimpse.

(*PI*, 41)

In this way, Adela will never grasp a full, an entire image of India, nor is this presented as a possibility for any of the characters. Instead they are left with unrelated elements of colour and movement.

Thus, an analysis of gynesis in a literary text attempts to locate those moments in the text where rationality and control seem to be undermined – in Jardine's view, moments where the feminine is in ascendance. We have seen in the examples above that where there is textual indeterminacy 'feminine' elements or female characters often intervene. It is not coincidental that the moments of crisis in the text are those which are centred around the two female characters, Mrs Moore and Adela Quested. But other moments in the text such as those of mysticism are ones which are also coded as feminine, an assertion of sameness in the face of the rigid dualism of colonialism. The elision of these two elements of indeterminacy and the female/feminine produces moments of gynesis within the text.

Conclusions/Problems

One of the principal problems with this type of analysis of the instabilities in texts is that there is an assumption that all instabilities relate to gender. This is also a problem in Julia Kristeva's work, where there is a similar assumption that the feminine is always marginalized. But in much the same way that it is difficult within texts to reduce all forms of 'Othering' to the problems of racist representation, as Young has shown, it is similarly impossible to assert that all of the textual indeterminacies can be reduced to a question of gender or gynesis (Young 1990: 157–75). We would need to go on to examine those moments of indeterminacy in the text where the feminine did not seem to be dominant, for example, with the representation of Indian male characters. It is unclear whether Jardine would assert that these characters are presented in a feminine way, and indeed take up a feminine position in relation to the masculine authority of the British. These characters, such as Aziz and Godbole, do indeed create moments of conflict and indeterminacy within the text, but we would need to consider whether it is theoretically productive to code that as a feminine moment, since it seems to be the result of the negotiation of a power relation; the relation between masculine and feminine is an analogous relation, but it is debatable whether it can simply be superimposed on all other differential relations.

A further problem with this approach emerges when using a psychoanalytic model of textuality to analyse texts embedded in colonial history and discourse. Although Peter Hulme and Homi Bhabha have used psychoanalysis to analyse colonial texts in productive and insightful ways, what is being described is a relationship of power between states, and groups of people, rather than a relation between psyches – although that obviously is involved, and perhaps in *A Passage to India* more than in many other texts, the colonial is reduced to how individuals resolve their individual conflicts (Bhabha 1983; Hulme 1986). Psychoanalytic readings thus tend to analyse a conflict of states as if they were individual psyches, and perhaps in this way the very political and economic domination which is fundamental to colonialism is ignored.

Another problem which I have encountered in reading *A Passage to India* using Jardine's work is that there is a feeling of inevitability about the concept of gynesis, as if this is not only all we have at the moment, but also all we will ever have. The reader is left wondering whether Jardine is asserting that gynesis occurs in all modern Western texts or in fact all texts. If this is so, what is the hope of feminist analysis doing more than simply exposing the fact that patriarchy is imbricated in texts? There seems to be little hope that feminist criticism will be able to do anything about this problem other than describe it. Since feminism is essentially a political movement committed to changing the structures it describes, this seems rather paradoxical.

Furthermore, it is debatable whether feminist critics can find productive a theoretical position which allies the feminine to instability. Although psychoanalytic critics constantly stress that the feminine should not be confused with the female, just as they stress that the phallus should not be confused with the penis, it is hardly coincidental that a term which already has current association with femaleness is used to describe indeterminacy. Coding this instability in a positive way may not be enough to overcome the problem of women being constantly represented as outside the Symbolic Order, the rational, the centre.

Thus, while this essay has shown that the unrepresentable, the moments of gynesis, do appear in texts to occur in conjunction with the feminine, the feminist reader might ask whether this type of analysis should perhaps constitute the start of wide-ranging critique aimed at bringing about change in representational practices, rather than simply accepting that gynesis is a necessary part of textual production. Perhaps what would need to be grafted on to this analysis of gynesis would be precisely an historical account which would set the text within the context of colonial relations (see Pratt 1992). In this way it would be possible both to analyse the difficulties of figuring women within colonial texts which would result in moments of gynesis, and to set that difficulty against a full historical analysis of British women's active and symbolic involvement in the Empire. Rather than simply assuming that all moments of instability within texts are the result of the feminine, this model of textuality would need to be modified to encompass other types of power relation. Even though psychoanalytical models find it difficult to deal with politics and power relations apart from gender relations, it is essential that a wider model which can deal with the relations between groups of people should be developed. In this way, it will be possible to analyse colonial texts, focusing on the way in which 'woman' is a central conceptual problem, but also analysing the other power relations circulating in the texts, causing similar but distinct indeterminacies.

SUPPLEMENT

NIGEL WOOD: Jardine's approach to the critical process presupposes the collapse of the master-narratives of 'Man, the Subject, Truth, History, Meaning' (Jardine 1985: 25). Does this not undermine the radical alternatives as well, that is to say, how can we supplant a decadent 'logic' without better truths or meanings?

SARA MILLS: Within current thinking on this issue, it is deemed to be impossible to construct grand narratives, since the very bases for these have become unstable and open to question. Radical alternatives are usually by their very nature based on the notion of critique; that is, they do not propose themselves as full explanatory systems, but are, at least in the first instance, concerned with finding the problems with systems within which they are working. The search for better 'truths' is one that few radical thinkers engage in since they have seen that this type of generalizing, globalizing move almost invariably involves the exclusion of one group or another. Most radical thinkers are content with partial visions with partial solutions, which they set very much in the context of other visions and other solutions. For me, this is a positive move.

NW: A common reading of *A Passage to India* is that it comments on 'male' imperialist ideology by shifting the narrative focus so often to Mrs Moore's and Godbole's non-Anglican behaviour. How does Forster recuperate Western meanings?

SM: This is a complex question and one to which there is no simple answer. The text does not seem to offer any single stance on any of the characters or groups. Mrs Moore's mysticism is not presented in a simple favourable light within the text, and although male imperialist ideology is often held to scorn, there are a number of moments in the text where the narrator proffers standard imperialist knowledges to the reader in unmodified form. Overall I feel that, read in the light of other British texts about India, *A Passage to India* can be seen as a fairly conventional book about Indian rule and about British women as a problem in that rule, much as Paul Scott's *Raj Quartet* is concerned with that 'problem'; however, neither Forster nor Scott seems to offer a comfortable position for the reader, and Forster presents no safe haven with Adela Quested, Mrs Moore, Fielding or in fact with the Indians.

NW: You point out that you are uneasy with Jardine's apparent identification of the feminine with instability. Could you expand here on your closing comments that feminist critics should be attempting to frame new 'representational practices' as well as noting the forces that attend all textual production?

SM: I feel rather uncomfortable with any model of textuality which critiques a system of representation but which does not offer an alternative. If 'gynesis' is a fact of textuality, then there is nothing for feminists, or for that matter anyone, to do. 'Gynesis' seems to be a moment of instability within certain types of texts, particularly those texts produced within a period of political and philosophical questioning and upheaval. Presumably, as different questions and interests assert themselves in the socio-economic sphere, there will be different textual structures. I would also like to think that it is possible for feminist creative writers to write in a different way.

NW: Is there not a sense in which we could say that Forster was not really writing about India at all, but rather the cultural stereotype that is part of Anglo-India?

SM: I don't think that any of the British writers who wrote about the colonial situation were writing about India at all; all of their books were destined for the home market, and all of them concerned themselves with the British community in India, with India really only figuring as a backdrop or as a problem. Most of the books written about the colonial context seem to be far more concerned about correct and moral British behaviour and, in that sense, India really only serves as a test. Some would argue that this is all that British writers within this particular power nexus could do.

Endpiece

NIGEL WOOD

I suspect that, when Forster is revered, it is often for the very qualities that often lead some readers to dismiss his work as outdated and hopelessly idealistic. His liberal individualism is hardly an optimistic sentiment, but it is difficult not to regard it as a rather utopian (and reassuring) accent from more balanced days. After all, it is probable that we first found pleasure in the practice of criticism at school because we were more taken with Forster than with Marx or Freud, more drawn to the memorable dicta and metaphors found in literature than to the debates over the heterogeneity of their effects on generations of readers. The personal element in literature can be described and enthused over, yet, as an object for analysis, there are clearly limitations in confining its *effects* to the severely biographical and individual traits of style or ideas and the sense of our own personality when reading them. Concepts of 'ideology', the 'unconscious' or 'patriarchy' help us now to comprehend writing in its original context which exceeds any writer's power to identify just what has fed into her or his consciousness. The obverse may also be true: that the testimony of a writer and the metaphorical complexity of what was *intended* is often neglected the better to make the writing fit some predetermined scheme, but what is at stake is not whether, say, our knowledge of the writer's intention or 'character' is a critical fallacy or not, but rather the place 'intention' has in critical assessment.

When Forster addressed students at the Government College,

Lahore, on 3 March 1913, on 'The Enjoyment of English Literature', his targets took in the 'examination habit' and the social snobbery of cultural elitism: 'Ignorance doesn't matter. That can be cured. Self-consciousness and conceit are the real enemies . . . Read [books] because you want to. That's the only true reason . . . [Identify] the frank personal response' (HD, 233). It may now seem tactless to anatomize this apparently casual and disarming credo, but it is not without its own presuppositions, some of which we may not totally agree with when identified.

The most enduring motive for coming to terms with your response to a text (being 'self-conscious' about it) is that you can test your initial and perhaps superficial reasons for liking, or disliking, a work. The passage to the 'frank, personal response' is rarely a straightforward one and can actually be aided by noting the significance of what may seem like just aesthetic preferences – in short, by Theory. We may like Indian food, feel threatened by, or interested in, homosexual culture, have just seen the latest Merchant–Ivory or just admire the artwork on the library's Forster paperback, and these are undoubtedly preliminary reasons for approaching his work in the way we do, but, in setting ourselves to the task of identifying the 'personal' and discarding the accidental, we may also discover something about ourselves, namely, that our literary preferences are never purely personal and rarely divorced from a cultural context. Moreover, you may be a reader of Forster in present-day India, or count as part of your racial inheritance relatives who remember the India of 1922, or, more significantly, the Amritsar massacre of 1919. You may be vaguely proud that Britain was once an imperial power or come from neither Britain nor India/Pakistan, and so may not be in this immediate case a nationally or racially interested individual at all and so do not compare the events described in A Passage to India with your own contemporary culture. You may also be 'self-conscious' about how you are addressed by the novel as a woman or as a man, a Christian or a Hindu, an agnostic or a believer. The point is that these considerations are worth identifying and weighing in the balance not as prejudices to be cleared before the essentially human reading shines through but rather as constitutive of the 'personal' account.

Later in this same talk, Forster ventures a definition of the novel as 'talk, glorified talk':

> the words of a man, perhaps of a man who has been dead for three hundred years and is trying to talk out of that immense darkness

to you. He talks. You listen. There is no one and nothing between
you, and you must get on with each other as best you can.

(*HD*, 233)

This desire to provide a vocative sense of immediate and shared communication, the virtues of an animated conversation, sets a much lower
priority on the ambiguities of written language where there is no shared
physical environment to help direct the words towards some correct,
'intended' goal. It also implies an exchange of views and position
between writer/speaker and audience manifestly not true of novel-
reading. While Forster does elevate his notion of 'talk' in this instance
into a 'glorified' version, set above daily conversation, his norm is an
oral one: 'Listen to the voice of the writer speaking to you; that is the
only guide. Listen to him as if he was a man, actually present in the
room' (*HD*, 235). This pleasure is distinct from mere appreciation
which might entail a knowledge of context and literary traditions.

I fear that this volume would not pass the Forster test, as it concerns
itself in each essay with all that might interpose itself between a writer
and the immense variety of her or his readers: assumptions that are
gender-specific and potentially politically divisive. For both Bette
London and Barbara Harlow, *A Passage to India* is most historical when
it appears to be ahistorical, as it attempts to replace the political with
an ethics based on the same personalized basis as informal dialogue. In
her use of the work of Homi Bhabha, London questions this goal of
an innocent, unmediated understanding of Forster's narrative, whereas
Harlow explores the proposition that, from a subaltern perspective, the
set of tacit rules and preferences that underlie his linguistic and artistic
choices, his discourse, is inevitably implicated in the far larger and more
impersonal project of colonialism – the very basis on which significant cultural differences are identified and perpetuated. Similarly, for
Parminder Bakshi and Sara Mills, the work constructs images of sexual
identity that do not derive in some uncomplicated way from observed
reality. Bakshi identifies how the ideal of male friendship affects other
depictions, of landscape and especially of relationships between the
sexes. For Mills, the episodes where Forster portrays the indefinable
aspects of India and the indefatigable quest for truth resemble moments
of 'gynesis', in Alice Jardine's coinage, where 'normal' perspectives are
rendered as unstable and as of only relative value. 'Gynesis' itself is then
examined for its limited place in a political feminist criticism.

Forster is, however, a powerful reminder that style can be deceptive.
It is often taken as characteristic of his work that it somehow represents

the Heaslop/Callendar world-order, and the ideas outlined above can be caricatured as popularly oversimplified, but they need not be completely identified with the more complex rhetoric of *Passage*. When interviewed in 1958 by David Jones for the BBC, Forster looked back on his reluctant decision to abandon the writing of novels as 'too long a story' on which to dwell, but he did state that one reason why he turned to other genres involved the great change from that date of the 'social aspect of the world':

> I had been accustomed to write about the old-fashioned world with its homes and its family life and its comparative peace. All that went, and though I can think about the new world I cannot put it into fiction.

The 'personal voice' is not entire unto itself, it would seem. Forster was entirely pleased at *Passage*'s commercial success in that it was influential in ways that may seem startling given some of his other earlier comments, 'because the political side of [the situation described in the novel] was an aspect I wanted to express, although it is not primarily a political book' (*Listener*, 1 January 1959, in Stape 1993: 39). V.S. Pritchett agreed, but with a significant difference. In his *New Statesman* article on Forster of 12 June 1970, the break in Forster's writing before *Passage* was explained as a more or less direct result of the First World War, which 'pulled the carpet from under his feet and left his early drawing rooms unbelievable'. *A Passage to India* was his only shot at capturing a world markedly different, where his comedy, 'with its rude introduction of accident, panic or mess', managed to annihilate the norms of social comfort: 'In *A Passage to India*, he saw that another ethos might exist and that it would be a chaos. A grave and didactic work, this novel was also a comedy of the perils of understanding' (Stape 1993: 223). While it may depict the aspirations of those who might celebrate friendship and connection, the narrative is unsparing in the portrayal of disappointment and *anomie*, as well as the unsettling loose ends (the Marabar Caves being only the most dramatic instance) where verbal definition is beside the point.

While the apparent realism of the text produces associations of correspondence between signifier and signified, the narrative often gestures to some abstract and ineffable realm that inexorably works against an overall focus and authorial omniscience. Observing Adela and Ronny's civilized decision to call off their engagement, there is 'a little green bird . . . so brilliant and neat [to Adela] that it might have hopped straight out of a shop'. Such a limitation of vision and desire is hardly condoned;

indeed, Forster suggests the perils of too much assumed knowledge gleaned from the wide savannahs of Hastings. This hardly fits them for the role of hero and heroine. Stylistically, the passage is striking in that it shifts gear so rapidly from this apparently gentle comedy of manners to a more elliptical mode:

> The bird in question dived into the dome of the tree. It was of no importance, yet they would have liked to identify it, it would somehow have solaced their hearts. But nothing in India is identifiable, the mere asking of a question causes it to disappear or to merge in something else.
> 'McBryde has an illustrated bird book,' [Ronny] said dejectedly.
> (*PI*, 77–8)

For a moment India ceases to have a topographical identity, and then the comedy resumes – but between humans (and specifically Europeans) who are rendered curiously bereft of certainty and who are fatally denied our sympathies. If this is still humour, then it is of the gallows variety. It is a turn or modulation that is more prevalent in *Passage* than in any of his other work. Normality cannot now be reassembled with the promise of graphic definition.

What does operate to lend the text some consistency of address is a narratorial 'voice', but even this power affords no clear translation of 'ou-boum'; it can only depict it as an echo, and India as vast and occasionally cavernous. The small green bird remains just that – the choice of a particular genus would hardly be relevant here – as it is mentioned only in order to be elusive. As David Lodge points out, *Passage* is in fact 'a symbolist novel disguised as a realistic one' (Lodge 1977: 97) and, in his analysis of the book's opening depiction of the environs of Chandrapore (1977: 96–9), Lodge explores the quiet way in which contiguous, not similar or logically connected, details work to defy a reader's sense of having grasped a totality. In this, the narrative is deliberately bad at spelling out just what contains the muddle of colonialist India. Like the agnostic's sense of God (or Gods), the uncertainty is instinctive as well as intellectual.

Recently, a renewed engagement with the form of Forster's fiction has found a writer more attuned to postmodernist taste than might have been thought possible in the 1980s. For Fredric Jameson, in his extended reading of the opening passages from *Howards End* (in Deane *et al.*, 1990), Forster's own brand of imperialism is evident in his style of representing near-anarchy only to suggest a designing hand behind the infinite: Empire in the human (and so excusable) form of the

Wilcoxes. This is only *suggested*, however, as these figures are rendered incomplete,

> for we are only able to see that face, the 'Imperial type,' turn inward, toward the internal metropolitan reality. The other pole of the relationship, what defines him fundamentally and essentially in his 'imperial' function – the persons of the colonized – remains structurally occluded, and cannot but so remain . . .
>
> (Deane *et al.* 1990: 58)

But that is *Howards End* from 1910, a text that remains eventually landlocked in its aspirations. What cost Forster so much effort in the writing of *Passage* – and what steered him eventually away from fiction – is the effort to dispense with this structural safety-net. As Lionel Trilling noted in 1944, he 'refuses to be conclusive. No sooner does he come to a conclusion than he must unravel it again' (Trilling 1944: 16; see also Paul Armstrong 1992). Is the irony contained? Is the apparent mystery/muddle presided over by Godbole and which crystallizes Mrs Moore's eventual fear of nihilism eventually dispersed by some providential hand (authorial or divine)? Do we accept without demur the narrator's own verdict on the narrative 'scheme' of the work: 'Looking back at the great blur of the last twenty-four hours, no man could say where was the emotional centre of it, any more than he could locate the heart of a cloud' (*PI*, 306)? Or can we, indeed, in identifying a consistent Forsterian attitude, locate a hidden agenda to the work, freed of its metonymic turns and narrative surprises ? We can at least conclude that these sorts of question are not ones that are part of the preliminary encounter with *A Passage to India*.

Notes

Introduction

1 'Classic realism' is Colin MacCabe's phrase, and an account of its 'hierarchy of discourses' and its effects of verisimilitude and closure can be found in his *James Joyce and the Revolution of the Word* (1978). See also Catherine Belsey's *Critical Practice* (1980), especially pp. 67–84.

2 Leavis came to believe that the academic study of English offered the only hope of spiritual survival in the godless wasteland of contemporary civilization. In a lecture on 'Literature and the University', printed in *English Literature in Our Time and the University* (1969), he argued for the university as 'a centre of consciousness for the community', its own centre to be found in 'an English school' [i.e. department] whose

> focus of cultural continuity can only be English. English literature, magnificent and matchless in diversity and range, and so full and profound in its registration of changing life, gives us a continuity that is not yet dead. There is no other; no other access to anything approaching a full continuity of mind spirit and sensibility – which is what we desperately need.
>
> (Leavis 1969: 59–60)

3 The importance for human communication of the rhetorical figures of *metonymy* (based on contiguity) and *metaphor* (based on similarity) was proposed by the linguistician Roman Jakobson. More recently, David Lodge (1977) has explored their implications for literary texts and modes, arguing

for an affinity between metonymy and realism, on the one hand, and metaphor and modernism, on the other. Thus, for example, *Bleak House*, which refers to an actual location in the novel, is a 'metonymic' title (though with metaphoric/symbolic overtones), while *The Rainbow*, which points to the symbolic dimensions of Lawrence's narrative (though an actual rainbow does appear in it), is a metaphoric one.

4 I am thinking of his *Writing Degree Zero* (Barthes 1967), which explored 'the multiplication of modes of writing' (1967: 90) and argued that in the modern period 'Literature is openly reduced to the problematics of language . . . Form is the first and last arbiter of literary responsibility' (1967: 88–9).

5 Furbank (1977–8: II, 132) records that after writing *Howards End* Forster was 'bored with writing about marriage and the relations of men and women'.

6 Bakhtin argued that every utterance, even the most seemingly self-absorbed and monological, is engaged in a 'dialogical' encounter with other utterances, heard or unheard, without which it would be unintelligible. For a fuller account of his ideas, see the essays in Holquist (1981).

7 See the references in note 1 above. This is the view of Barbara Rosecrace (1982), who finds in the novel 'a somber and impersonal voice' that 'speaks of uncertainty in secure accents'. But although Rosecrace's reading subordinates the text's confusions and uncertainties to an authoritative narrative 'voice', her stress on 'impersonality' suggests a Forster closer to the proto-modernist (and anti-humanist) fictions of the later Henry James and the early James Joyce: 'Forster's narrative language, his detached tone and remote perspective, dominate the novel, and the view they project testifies to the artist's degree of withdrawal from the world he has created' (1982: 234–5). Consider how closely this echoes the aesthetic theory expounded by Stephen Dedalus in Joyce's *Portrait of the Artist as a Young Man* (1916):

> The personality of the artist, at first a cry or a cadence or a mood and then a fluid and lambent narrative, finally refines itself out of existence, impersonalizes itself, so to speak. The esthetic image in the dramatic form is life purified in and reprojected from the human imagination. The mystery of esthetic, like that of material creation, is accomplished. The artist, like the God of creation, remains within or behind or beyond or above his handiwork, invisible, refined out of existence, indifferent, paring his fingernails.
>
> (Joyce 1992: 233)

For Frederick Crews, too, the novel 'passes beyond humanistic morality', though for him this leads to 'a basically metaphysical critique of man's fate' (Crews 1962: 179).

8 If this account of the resistance to theory reads like a parody, consider the

response to the (really quite innocuous) collection of theoretical essays edited by Peter Widdowson, *Re-Reading English* (1982). See Tony Davies, 'Damning the Tides: the New English and the Reviewers', in Green (1987: 91–102).

9 'The end of history' is the title of a recent book by the American political philosopher Francis Fukuyama. The 'end of ideology' was announced some years ago by his compatriot Daniel Bell.

10 The Sardinian revolutionary and political theorist argued that 'all men are "philosophers" ', exponents of 'the "spontaneous philosophy" which is proper to everybody'. See Gramsci (1971: 9, 323).

11 Roland Barthes, exploring the experience of reading, distinguishes between *plaisir* (pleasure) and *jouissance* (rapture). The first, based on repetition and containment, and associated with the solid, reassuringly familiar kind of realist fiction he calls *textes de plaisir*, is enjoyable and unthreatening, a 'good read' inducing 'euphoria, fulfillment, comfort' (*Le Plaisir du Texte*, Paris 1973: 34). The second, based on surprise, contradiction and excess, is provoked by texts – 'modernist', 'postmodernist' or whatever – whose form and meaning refuse to be reduced to a recognizable pattern, remaining tantalizingly open and unresolved. Although associated with different types of writing, the two are just as importantly modes of reading. Recent feminist, psychoanalytic and materialist criticism has shown that even the most cosily 'pleasurable' and closed of texts can be reopened and its meanings destabilized by a radical rereading. See, for example, the discussion of formula romance by Janice Radway (1987) and the discussion of Jane Austen's *Mansfield Park* in Said (1993: 95–116).

1 The Politics of Desire

1 As Said points out:

> The period of immense advance in the institutions and content of Orientalism coincides exactly with the period of unparalleled European expansion; from 1815 to 1914 European direct colonial domination expanded from about 35 percent of the earth's surface to about 85 percent of it.
>
> (Said 1978: 41).

2 This explains the Western response to the Arabs and Islam evident even today:

> it was in the Near Orient, the lands of the Arab Near East, where Islam was supposed to define cultural and racial characteristics, that the British and the French encountered each other and 'the Orient' with the greatest intensity, familiarity and complexity.
>
> (Said 1978: 41).

3 See J.A. Symonds's *Studies of the Greek Poets* (1873) and *Sketches in Italy and Greece* (1874), and Walter Pater's *Studies in the History of the Renaissance* (1873), 'The Age of Athletic Prizemen' (1874) and *Plato and Platonism* (1893) (see Pater 1920a; 1920b; 1922).

4 It is significant that the legislation on homosexuality in the nineteenth century was tied up with regulating prostitution. Both the 1885 and 1898 Acts were concerned primarily with prostitution. The Vagrancy Act was intended to control soliciting for immoral purposes, while the Criminal Law Amendment Act sought to provide protection for women and girls. However, whereas the Criminal Law Amendment Act raised the age of sexual consent for girls from thirteen to sixteen, it had an extremely adverse effect on the lives of homosexuals. See Jeffrey Weeks, *Coming Out: Homosexual Politics in Britain from the Nineteenth Century to the Present* (1983).

5 Henry Richard Charles Somerset, born in 1849, was the second son of the eighth Duke of Beaufort. He became Member of Parliament for Monmouthshire in 1871 and Comptroller of the Royal Household in 1874. In 1872 he married Isabel, daughter of the third and last Earl Somers. On learning of her husband's affair with a commoner, his wife and mother-in-law made the affair a public scandal. Lord Henry was shunned by his family and refused legal custody of his child. He resigned from his public offices in 1879 and went to the Continent, whence he returned only after his beloved Harry's death in New Zealand in 1902. See *Love in Earnest: Some Notes on the Lives and Writings of English 'Uranian' Poets from 1889 to 1930* (Smith 1970: 25–27).

6 Cited by Salter (1975: 26).

7 *Goldsworthy Lowes Dickinson* (1973); *HD*; *AH*.

8 See Gardner (1973). For other views on Forster's novel as a critique of the Raj, see also Bradbury (1970); and G.K. Das, *E.M. Forster's India* (1977).

9 Homo-erotic desire is displaced in *Howards End* on to the plane of marriage and heterosexual relations. While ostensibly focusing on marriage and social issues, the narrator nevertheless endows greater value to the relation-ship of the two Schlegel sisters and the friendship between Margaret and Mrs Wilcox than to Margaret's marriage to Mr Wilcox. The news of Margaret's marriage arouses hostility and protest (*HE*, 169). Leonard Bast represents the deterioration of the homo-erotic ideal and the novel is con-cerned with the barriers that prevent the Wilcox men from relating to Leonard. Although the novel does not encompass friendship between men, the narrative ends with the vision of friendship, projected into the future, between Helen's baby son and Tom, the farm boy (*HE*, 333).

10 In *Where Angels Fear to Tread*, the characters' journeys to Italy are bound up with Dante's almost classical ideal of love expounded in *La Vita Nuova*, while *A Room with a View* contains references to Phaethon and Persephone and to Michelangelo.

11 'The Blue Boy', review of W.G. Archer's *The Loves of Krishna* in *The Listener*, LVII, 1459 (14 March 1957), p. 444.

12 Men bathing together as a homo-erotic motif derives from Walt Whitman in 'Song of Myself' from *Leaves of Grass* (1973; first published in 1855). The most significant rendering of the scene of men bathing in Forster is found in the twelfth chapter of *A Room with a View*. The manuscripts of *The Longest Journey* contained a chapter in which Stephen bathes in a river and walks naked through the woods; see 'The Manuscripts of *The Longest Journey*', Appendix C to *The Longest Journey* (*LJ*, 332–4). In *Howards End*, where homo-erotic desire is repressed, the bathing scene is accordingly aborted (*HE*, 216).

13 In the draft manuscripts of *A Room with a View* Mr Beebe takes care of George who has a delicate constitution (see *LN*, 106–11). In *The Longest Journey* Stephen bandages Rickie when he breaks his thumb nail on the horse's neck and later holds him gently as Rickie falls asleep on his horse (*LJ*, 108–11). For his part, Rickie takes care of Stephen when he arrives drunk at Dunwood House (*LJ*, 248–9). Ultimately, of course, Rickie dies in trying to save his brother from being run over by a train (*LJ*, 282). Finally, in *Maurice* when Clive falls ill, Maurice tenderly nurses his friend back to health (*M*, 97).

14 Carpenter was influenced by Whitman, and both writers combined the socialist ideal of comradeship with the vision of sexual love between men. Carpenter believed social and sexual freedom to be inextricably linked and these ideas are explored fully in his long poem *Towards Democracy* (1911; first published in 1883). The title is derived from Whitman's *Democratic Vistas* (1871). Carpenter, like Whitman before him and Forster after him, interprets democracy in terms not just of political equality but also of sexual liberation. Although, in 1886, Carpenter was one of the founding members of the Sheffield Socialist Society, the emphasis on emotional fulfilment gave Carpenter's socialism a tinge of mysticism. Carpenter, of course, was able to combine socialism with homosexual love most effectively in his own life. In 1881, Carpenter settled at Millthorpe in Derbyshire, and near Sheffield; he lived among working-class men, and made a living by selling the produce from his small farm in the Chesterfield market. In 1898, he formed a lasting relationship with George Merrill, who was born and bred in Sheffield slums. They lived together till Merrill's death in 1928 and their lifestyle represented a practical realization of Carpenter's social and sexual ideals. For a further exposition of Carpenter's philosophy see also *Love's Coming-of-Age: A Series of Papers on the Relation of Sexes* (1896), *England's Ideal, and Other Papers on Social Subjects* (1887), and *Civilisation: its Cause and Cure, and Other Essays* (1889).

15 As is indicated in Beauman (1993: 323); in *The Manuscripts of A Passage to India* (ed. Oliver Stallybrass, 1978 (vol. 6a of the Abinger edn)), it is clear that Forster originally left no doubt that the assault took place. At MS B

48–9 (*MPI*, 242–3), held at the Humanities Research Center at Austin, Texas, it is clear that the assailant is not Aziz, but see also the jottings on B 8v: 'Aziz and Janet drift into one another's arms – then apart' (*MPI*, 580).

16 The specific seductiveness of India lies in that it accommodates male friend-ship. Forster's India is 'the East, where the friends of friends are a reality, where everything gets done some time, and sooner or later everyone gets his share of happiness' (*PI*, 131). Forster does not condemn England's col-onization of India, but deplores the fact that the opportunity for friendship was being lost due to political conflict. Fielding says to Adela:

> 'The first time I saw you, you were wanting to see India, not Indians, and it occurred to me: Ah, that won't take us far. Indians know whether they are liked or not – they cannot be fooled here. Justice never satisfies them, and that is why the British Empire rests on sand.'
>
> (*PI*, 248)

The narrative of *A Passage to India* works on the premise that, 'between people of distant climes there is always the possibility of romance' (*PI*, 256), and Forster explores this possibility in the text in spite of the political circumstances.

2 Law and Order

1 P.N. Furbank's more extensive biography of Forster, *E.M. Forster: A Life* (1977–8), similarly, if with greater elaboration, identifies the novelist, emphasizing for example, not only Forster's pacifism during the First World War, but also his personally ambivalent relationship to England's imperial mission.

2 The term 'post-colonial' is used here with a hyphen to mark its historical reference to the period following decolonization and to distinguish it from, even while acknowledging its strong associations with, the unhyphenated term 'postcolonial' as indicating a theoretical approach elaborated from out of the economic, political and cultural conditions of post-colonialism.

3 In *The Wretched of the Earth*, Frantz Fanon describes the colonial world as a 'world cut in two' (Fanon 1965: 29). In a much-cited analysis, Fanon distinguishes between the 'settler's town' and the 'native town':

> The settler's town is a strongly-built town, all made of stone and steel. It is a brightly-lit town; the streets are covered with asphalt, and the garbage cans swallow all the leavings, unseen, unknown and hardly thought about. The settler's feet are never visible, except perhaps in the sea; but there you're never close enough to see them. His feet are protected by strong shoes although the streets of his town are clean and even, with no holes or stones. The settler's town is a well-fed town, an easy-going town; its belly is always full of

good things. The settler's town is a town of white people, of foreigners.

The town belonging to the colonized people, or at least the native town, the Negro village, the medina, the reservation, is a place of ill fame, peopled by men of evil repute. They are born there, it matters little where or how; they die there, it matters not where, or how. It is a world without spaciousness; men live there on top of each other. The native town is a hungry town, starved of bread, of meat, of shoes, of coal, of light. The native town is a crouching town, a town on its knees, a town wallowing in the mire. It is a town of niggers and dirty arabs.

(Fanon 1965: 30)

4 For a fuller discussion of the significance of the punkah wallah, see Sharpe (1987).

3 Of Mimicry and English Men

1 As if in testimony to this unassimilability, even within the text, Forster does not spell the names consistently. Thus all other references to 'Jamila' record the name 'Jemila'.
2 For a critique of Bhabha, see, for example, Benita Parry (Parry 1987). Spivak addresses Parry's critique in her contribution to *Literary Theory Today* (Collier and Geyer Ryan 1990: 219–44).
3 In 'Articulating the Archaic' (Collier and Geyer Ryan 1990: 203–18), Bhabha briefly applies his theory to Forster, to read the writing of cultural difference through the text's production of colonial Otherness. For Bhabha, the 'culturally unassimilable words and scenes of nonsense', such as the Marabar Caves, 'suture the colonial text in a hybrid time and truth that survives and subverts the generalizations of literature and history' (Collier and Geyer Ryan 1990: 208). My reading, turned back upon the enunciation of the colonizer in the performance of narrative, thus follows very different lines.
4 For a fuller discussion of this practice, and of its analogues in Forster's other Indian writings, see my chapters on Forster in London (1990).
5 See, in particular, the discussion of mimicry in 'The Power of Discourse and the Subordination of the Feminine' in Irigaray (1985: 68–85.)
6 For one of the most interesting readings of these intersections in *Passage*, see Silver (1988).
7 For a discussion of the 'exchange of women', see Gayle Rubin ('The Traffic in Women: Notes on the "Political Economy" of Sex', in Reiter 1975: 157–210), whose coinage, 'the traffic in women', I borrow here. See also Eve Sedgwick, whose crucial work on male homosocial desire (Sedgwick 1985) informs the terms of my argument throughout this section. For

other readings of the exchange of women, see Irigaray's discussions, 'Women on the Market' and 'Commodities among Themselves', in Irigaray (1985: 170–97). Brenda Silver also comments on this circuit of exchange in *Passage* (Silver 1988).

8 Aziz's response, for example, to the scientific treatises on sex found in European manuals – 'Science seemed to discuss everything from the wrong end. It didn't interpret his experiences when he found them in a German manual, because by being there they ceased to be his experiences' (*PI*, 94) – echoes the homosexual Maurice's revulsion at Mr Ducie's diagrams of the sexual process, diagrams that 'bore no relation to his experiences': 'he knew that the subject was serious and related to his own body. But he could not himself relate it; it fell to pieces as soon as Mr Ducie put it together, like an impossible sum' (*M*, 7).

9 One of the few explicitly feminist critiques of the novel; that of Frances Restucchia (1989) falls into this latter category. While it offers an oscillating position for the feminist critic, between a reading of the novel's misogyny and its construction of a space of subversive femininity, both readings have problematic 'racial' implications. The first connects the novel's misogynistic effects to Forster's surrender to 'Oriental indeterminacy', while the second appropriates the Caves' 'Otherness' for a white European middle-class feminism (gynesis).

10 In *Nation and Narration* (1990), Bhabha works through these distinctions in a somewhat different context: in the act of 'writing the nation'. He distinguishes between the 'pedagogical', associated with the certainties of a 'nationalist' criticism (with 'the people' conceived as a 'self-generating' image and a priori historical presence) and the 'performative', associated with the repetitive sliding between discursive positions (with 'the people' as constructed in the enunciatory present of the performance of narrative). For Bhabha, the performative intervenes in the sovereignty of the pedagogical, producing the split subject of cultural discourse that emerges in the contestation of these two modes of narrative authority.

4 Representing the Unrepresentable

1 See, for example, Oliver Stallybrass's introduction to the Penguin edition of *A Passage to India* (Forster 1989: 22–7), and Ebbatson and Neale (1986: 33–7 and 98–113).

2 There are so many feminist literary theory books that it is difficult to suggest just one which gives an overview: Toril Moi's *Sexual/Textual Politics* (Moi 1985) is perhaps the most accessible.

3 Kate Millett (1977) was perhaps the first to articulate this concern fully. For an excellent anthology of more sophisticated analyses of representation

theory in practice, see Rosemary Betterton (1987) and also the discussion of Anglo-American feminist theory in Moi (1985, 19–88).

4 See the discussion in Mills *et al.* (1989: 51–82) for a description of this tendency.

5 For a discussion of a type of analysis which tries to move beyond representation analysis and images of women using Foucauldian discourse theory rather than psychoanalysis, see my *Discourses of Difference* (Mills 1991: 67–107).

6 For a general analysis of feminist work on Freud, see Mitchell (1974). For a good introductory guide to Jacques Lacan's work see Grosz (1990); and for an analysis which uses Julia Kristeva's work to describe representational practices, see Schaffer (1988). See also Moi (1986: 137–270).

7 All the various meanings of 'play' are called into action in this use of the term, both the sense of playfulness and that of a certain 'give' or malleability in an object or material.

8 For an analysis of this tendency in women's experimental writing, see my article 'No Poetry for Ladies: Gertrude Stein, Julia Kristeva and Modernism' in Murray (1989: 85–107).

9 For an excellent analysis of this crisis of legitimation in current literary theory, especially in relation to colonial discourse theorizing, see Robert Young (1990: especially 1–27).

10 The novels of Paul Scott, Flora Annie Steele and John Masters also deal with this theme, but it is referred to constantly even if obliquely in many other texts dealing with the colonial situation.

11 See Pratt (1992: 90–107) for an analysis of the way white women are used to symbolize the 'moral' side of colonialism.

12 Gandhi began his *hartal* (general strike) and *sattyagraha* (passive resistance) campaigns in 1919. He was arrested in 1922 and released in 1924, the year of publication of *A Passage to India*; India did not gain independence until 1947.

13 Perhaps this can be most clearly seen when considering the film which was made by David Lean (1984), where the novel is converted into a Hollywood classic realist film and the moments of undecidability within the book are translated into clarity.

14 James Morris (1973: esp. 468–89) describes several of these views; for a full discussion of the memsahib, see Mills (1991: 58–63).

References

Unless otherwise stated, place of publication is London.

Adams, Stephen (1980) *The Homosexual as Hero in Contemporary Fiction.* Plymouth.

Ahmed, Aijaz (1987) Jameson's rhetoric of otherness, *Social text.* 17: 3–25.

Althusser, Louis (1971) *Lenin and Philosophy* (1st edn, 1969).

Ardener, Shirley (1978) *Defining Females: The Nature of Women in Society.*

Armstrong, Isobel (ed.) (1992) *New Feminist Discourses: Critical Essays on Theories and Texts.*

Armstrong, Nancy (1987) *Desire and Domestic Fiction.* New York.

Armstrong, Paul B. (1992) Reading India: E.M Forster and the politics of interpretation, *Twentieth Century Literature*, 38: 365–85.

Barker, Francis (ed.) (1983) *The Politics of Theory.* Colchester.

Beauman, Nicola (1993) *Morgan: A Biography of E.M. Forster.*

Beer, John (ed.) (1985) *A Passage to India: Essays in Interpretation.*

Belsey, Catherine (1980) *Critical Practice.*

Belsey, Catherine and Moore, Jane (eds) (1989) *The Feminist Reader: Essays in Gender and the Politics of Literary Criticism.*

Betterton, Rosemary (ed.) (1987) *Looking On: Images of Femininity in the Arts and Media.*

Bhabha, Homi (1983) The other question, *Screen*, 24: 18–35.

Bhabha, Homi (1984) Of mimicry and man: The ambivalence of colonial discourse, *October*, 28: 125–33.

Bhabha, Homi (1985) Signs taken for wonders: Questions of ambivalence and authority under a tree outside Delhi, May 1817, *Critical Inquiry*, 12: 144–65.

Bhabha, Homi (1989) Location, intervention, incommensurability: A conversation with Homi Bhabha, *Emergences*, 1: 63–88.

Bhabha, Homi (ed.) (1990) *Nation and Narration*.

Booth, Wayne C. (1961) *The Rhetoric of Fiction*. Chicago.

Bradbury, Malcolm (ed.) (1966) *E.M. Forster: A Collection of Critical Essays*.

Bradbury, Malcolm (ed.) (1970) *E.M. Forster: A Passage to India, A Casebook*.

Brown, E.K. (1950) *Rhythm in the Novel*.

Carpenter, Edward (1911) *Towards Democracy*. Manchester.

Chaudhuri, Nirad (1954) Passage to and from India, *Encounter*, 11: 19–24.

Collier, Peter and Ryan, Helga Geyer (eds) (1990) *Literary Theory Today*. Ithaca, NY.

Crews, Frederick (1962) *E.M. Forster: The Perils of Humanism*.

Das, G.K. and Beer, John (eds) (1979) *E.M. Forster: A Human Exploration*.

Deane, Seamus, Eagleton, Terry, Jameson, Fredric and Said, Edward (1990) *Nationalism, Colonialism and Literature*. Minneapolis, MN.

Ebbatson, Roger and Neale, Catherine (1989) *E.M. Forster: A Passage to India* (Penguin Masterguide). Harmondsworth.

Fanon, Frantz (1965) *The Wretched of the Earth*, trans. Constance Farrington. Harmondsworth (1st French edn 1961).

Fanon, Frantz (1967) *Black Skin, White Masks*, trans. Charles Lam Markmann. New York.

Forster, E.M. (1936) *Abinger Harvest*.

Forster, E.M. (1962) *Aspects of the Novel* (1st edn 1927).

Forster, E.M. (1965) *Two Cheers for Democracy* (1st edn 1951).

Forster, E.M. (1971) *Maurice*.

Forster, E.M. (1972) *The Life to Come and Other Stories*, ed. Oliver Stallybrass.

Forster, E.M. (1972) *Where Angels Fear to Tread*, ed. Oliver Stallybrass (1st edn 1905).

Forster, E.M. (1973) *Howards End*, ed. Oliver Stallybrass (1st edn 1910).

Forster, E.M. (1977) *The Lucy Novels: Early Sketches for a Room with a View*, ed. Oliver Stallybrass.

Forster, E.M. (1978) *The Manuscripts of a Passage to India*.

Forster, E.M. (1978) *A Passage to India*, ed. Oliver Stallybrass (1st edn 1924).

Forster, E.M. (1983) *Hill of Devi and Other Indian Writings*, ed. Elizabeth Heine.

Forster, E.M. (1984) *The Longest Journey*, ed. Elizabeth Heine (1st edn 1907).

Forster, E.M. (1989) *A Passage to India*, ed. Oliver Stallybrass. Harmondsworth.

Foucault, Michel (1972) *The Archaeology of Knowledge*, trans. A.M. Sheridan Smith (1st French edn 1969).

Furbank, P.N. (1970) The personality of E.M. Forster, *Encounter*, 35: 61–8.

Furbank, P.N. (1977–8) *E.M. Forster: A Life* (2 vols).

Gardner, Philip (ed.) (1973) *E.M. Forster: The Critical Heritage*.

Gramsci, Antonio (1971) *Selections from the Prison Notebooks*, ed. Q. Hoare and G. Nowell Smith.

Green, Michael (ed.) (1987) *English and Cultural Studies: Broadening the Context* (Essays and Studies).

Grosz, Elizabeth (1990) *Jacques Lacan: A Feminist Introduction.*

Guha, Ranajit (ed.) (1982) *Subaltern Studies I.* Delhi.

Guha, Ranajit (1983a) *Elementary Aspects of Peasant Insurgency in Colonial India.* Delhi.

Guha, Ranajit (ed.) (1983b) *Subaltern Studies II.* Delhi.

Guha, Ranajit (ed.) (1984) *Subaltern Studies III.* Delhi.

Guha, Ranajit (ed.) (1985) *Subaltern Studies IV.* Delhi.

Guha, Ranajit (ed.) (1987) *Subaltern Studies V.* Delhi.

Guha, Ranajit (ed.) (1989) *Subaltern Studies VI.* Delhi.

Guha, Ranajit and Spivak, Gayatri Chakravorty (1988) (eds) *Selected Subaltern Studies.* Delhi.

Herz, Judith and Martin, Robert K. (eds) (1982) *E.M. Forster: Centenary Revaluations.*

Holquist, Michael (ed.) (1981) *The Dialogic Imagination.* Austin, TX.

Hulme, Peter (1986) *Colonial Encounters: Europe and the Native Caribbean, 1492–1797.*

Irigaray, Luce (1985) *This Sex Which Is Not One*, trans. Catherine Porter. Ithaca, NY (1st edn 1977).

Iser, Wolfgang (1978) *The Act of Reading: A Theory of Aesthetic Response* (1st edn 1976).

James, Henry (1968) *Selected Literary Criticism*, ed. Morris Shapira. Harmondsworth.

Jardine, Alice (1985) *Gynesis: Configurations of Woman and Modernity.* Ithaca, NY.

Jenkyns, Richard (1980) *The Victorians and Ancient Greece.* Oxford.

Joyce, James (1992) *A Portrait of the Artist as a Young Man*, ed. Seamus Deane (orig. pub. 1914–15). Harmondsworth.

Kabbani, Rana (1986) *Europe's Myths of Orient: Devise and Rule.*

Kermode, Frank and Hollander, John (eds) (1973) *Modern British Literature.* New York.

King, Francis (1978) *E.M. Forster and his World.*

Kipling, Rudyard (1940) *Rudyard Kipling's Verse: The Definitive Edition.*

Kirkpatrick, B.J. (ed.) (1985) *A Bibliography of E.M. Forster* (1st edn 1965). Oxford.

Kristeva, Julia (1980) *Desire in Language: A Semiotic Approach to Literature and Art*, ed. Leon S. Roudiez and trans. Alice Jardine, Thomas Gora and Leon S. Roudiez. Oxford.

Leavis, F.R. (1962) *The Common Pursuit* (chapter on Forster, originally published 1938).

Lodge, David (1977) *The Modes of Modern Writing: Metaphor, Metonymy, and the Typology of Modern Literature.*

London, Bette (1990) *The Appropriated Voice: Narrative Authority in Conrad, Forster, and Woolf.* Ann Arbor, MI.

Macherey, Pierre (1978) *A Theory of Literary Production*, trans. Geoffrey Wall (1st edn 1966).

Meyers, Jeffrey (1977) *Homosexuality and Literature, 1890–1930*.

Millett, Kate (1977) *Sexual Politics* (1st edn 1969).

Mills, Sara (1991) *Discourses of Difference: Women's Travel Writing and Colonialism*.

Mills, Sara, Pearce, Lynne, Spaull, Sue and Millard, Elaine (eds) (1989) *Feminist Reading/Feminists Reading*. Hemel Hempstead.

Mitchell, Juliet (1974) *Psychoanalysis and Feminism*. Harmondsworth.

Moi, Toril (1985) *Sexual/Textual Politics*.

Moi, Toril (1986) *The Kristeva Reader*. Oxford.

Morris, James (1973) *Heaven's Command: An Imperial Progress*. Harmondsworth.

Murray, David (ed.) (1989) *Literary Theory and Poetry*.

Parry, Benita (1972) *Delusions and Discoveries: Studies on India in the British Imagination, 1880–1930*.

Parry, Benita (1987) Problems in current theory of colonial discourse, *Oxford Literary Review*, 9: 27–58.

Pater, Walter (1920a) *The Renaissance: Studies in Art and Poetry* (1st edn 1873).

Pater, Walter (1920b) *Plato and Platonism: A Series of Lectures* (1st edn 1893).

Pater, Walter (1922) The age of athletic prizemen: A chapter in Greek art, *Greek Studies: A Series of Essays* (1st edn 1895).

Pemble, John (1987) *The Mediterranean Passion: Victorians and Edwardians in the South*. Oxford.

Pratt, Mary Louise (1992) *Imperial Eyes: Travel Writing and Transculturation*.

Radway, Janice A. (1987) *Reading the Romance: Women, Patriarchy and Popular Fiction* (orig. pub. 1984).

Reiter, Rayna R. (ed.) (1975) *Toward an Anthropology of Women*. New York.

Restucchia, Frances L. (1989) 'A Cave of My Own': E.M. Forster and sexual politics, *Raritan*, 9: 110–28.

Rosecrace, Barbara (1982) *Forster's Narrative Vision*. Ithaca, NY.

Rowbotham, Sheila and Weeks, Jeffrey (1977) *Socialism and the New Life: The Personal and Sexual Politics of Edward Carpenter and Havelock Ellis*.

Said, Edward (1978) *Orientalism*.

Said, Edward (1984) *The World, The Text, and The Critic* (1st edn 1983).

Said, Edward (1993) *Culture and Imperialism*.

Salter, Donald (1975) That is my ticket: The homosexual writings of E.M. Forster, *London Magazine*. 15(2): 5–33.

Schaffer, Kay (1988) *Women and the Bush: Forces of Desire in the Australian Cultural Tradition*. Cambridge.

Scott, Paul (1966) How well have they worn, *Times* (London), 6 January: 15.

Scott, Paul (1976) *The Raj Quartet*.

Sebeok, Thomas A. (ed.) (1975) *The Tell-Tale Sign: A Survey of Semiotics*. Lisse, Netherlands.

Sedgwick, Eve Kosofsky (1985) *Between Men: English Literature and Male Homosocial Desire*. New York.

Sharpe, Jennifer (1987) 'Scenes of an Encounter: A Double Discourse of Colonialism and Nationalism', Ph.D. dissertation, University of Texas at Austin.

Showalter, Elaine (1985) (ed.) *The New Feminist Criticism: Essays on Women, Literature and Theory*.

Silver, Brenda R. (1988) Periphrasis, power, and rape in *A Passage to India, Novel*, 22: 86–105.

Smith, Timothy d'Arch (1970) *Love in Earnest: Some Notes on the Lives and Writings of English 'Uranian' Poets from 1889 to 1930*.

Spivak, Gayatri Chakravorty (1985) Can the subaltern speak? Speculations on widow sacrifice, *Wedge*, 7/8: 120–30.

Sprinker, Michael (ed.) (1992) *Edward Said: A Critical Reader*. Oxford.

Stape, J.H. (1993) *E.M. Forster: Interviews and Recollections*.

Stone, Wilfrid (1966) *The Cave and the Mountain*.

Symonds, J.A. (1873) *Studies of the Greek Poets*.

Symonds, J.A. (1893) *In the Key of Blue and Other Prose Essays*.

Thomson, George H. (1967) *The Fiction of E.M. Forster*. Detroit.

Trilling, Lionel (1944) *E.M. Forster* (1st edn 1943).

Trollope, Joanna (1983) *Britannia's Daughters: Women of the British Empire*.

Viswanathan, Gauri (1989) *Masks of Conquest: Literary Study and British Rule in India*. New York.

Weeks, Jeffrey (1983) *Coming Out: Homosexual Politics in Britain from the Nineteenth Century to the Present* (1st edn 1977).

Whitman, Walt (1973) *Leaves of Grass*, ed. Sculley Bradley and Harold W. Blodgett. New York.

Williams, Raymond (1977) *Marxism and Literature*. Oxford.

Young, Robert (1990) *White Mythologies: Writing History and the West*.

Further Reading

1 The Politics of Desire

Firstly, two studies that provide a broad cultural context for homo-eroticism in this period:

Jeffrey Meyers, *Homosexuality and Literature, 1890–1930* (London, 1977)
   This is one of the earliest attempts in modern criticism to study the theme of homosexuality in literature. However, the main limitation of this book is that it never quite manages to integrate its treatment of homosexuality with specifically literary analysis. Although Meyers' study is now dated in terms of both language and style, it is still significant as a pioneering work.

Jeffrey Weeks, *Coming Out: Homosexual Politics in Britain, from the Nineteenth Century to the Present* (London, 1983; 1st edn, 1977)
   A more theoretical study than that by Meyers (1977), full of careful distinctions between various 'gay' groupings and how Forster derived some of his ideas of male bonding from privately published work.

Here also are three readings that emphasize Forster's indeterminacy:

Gillian Beer, Negation in *A Passage to India*, in Beer (1985)
   This stresses the syntactical and semantic choices that Forster chose to illustrate his sense of the immense void that surrounds human powers of decision and volition.

Jeffrey Heath, A voluntary surrender: Imperialism and imagination in *A Passage to India*, *University of Toronto Quarterly*, 59 (1989–90), 287–309

An intricate account of how an apparently non-imperialist text can display certain imperialist assumptions. The clash between the deep structure of the plot and the surface sentiments provides some of the drama of the novel.

Wendy Moffat, *A Passage to India* and the limits of certainty, *Journal of Narrative Technique*, 20 (1990), 331–41
As the title suggests, this is a careful investigation into Forster's ambiguity, and its roots in an appreciation of cultural collapse.

Lastly, I would advise a glance at one chapter from Alan Sinfield's *Faultlines: Cultural Materialism and the Politics of Dissident Reading* (Oxford, 1992): 'Cultural Imperialism' (pp. 254–302). Although primarily about American cultural politics, this has a great deal concerning the present British social climate in which Forster's fiction is now read (post-*Maurice*).

2 Law and Order

In addition to the works cited in the essay, the following works are recommended for the various historical and political contextualizations to this reading of *A Passage to India*.

Edward Said, *Orientalism* (New York, 1978)
The pioneering study of Western constructions of the 'Orient' as constitutive part, precedent and sequel, to the history of colonialism.

Partha Chatterjee, *Nationalist Thought and the Colonial World: A Derivative Discourse* (London, 1986)
A reading of the discourses of colonialism and nationalism with particular reference to India.

Kumkum Sangari and Sudesh Vaid (eds), *Recasting Women: Essays in Indian Colonial History* (New Brunswick, NJ, 1990) and Stree Shakti Sanghtana, *'We Were Making History': Women and the Telangana Uprising* (London, 1989)
Both of these texts propose alternative research and reading strategies for writing women's history generally and the histories of Indian women in particular.

Gayatri Chakravorty Spivak, *The Post-colonial Critic: Interviews, Strategies, Dialogues*, ed. Sarah Harasym (New York and London, 1990)
A collection of interventions by Spivak on questions of colonialism – post- and neo-feminism, subaltern studies, the international division of labour, and pedagogy.

Vron Ware, *Beyond the Pale: White Women, Racism and History* (London and New York, 1992)
See especially Part Three, 'Britannia's Other Daughters: Feminism in the Age of Imperialism'.

3 Of Mimicry and English Men

Homi K. Bhabha, (ed.), *Nation and Narration* (London, 1990)

A series of wide-ranging essays that reassess traditional understandings of the nation and its authority by turning attention to the speakers and narratives through which a sense of nationhood is evoked. The book focuses on the role of language (and ambivalence of language) in articulating a concept of the nation that is itself necessarily ambivalent. It provides theoretical and historically- and nation-specific analyses that highlight social contexts of cultural representation.

Judith Butler, Performative acts and gender constitution: An essay in phenomenology and feminist theory, in Sue-Ellen Case (ed.), *Performing Feminisms: Feminist Critical Theory and Theatre* (Baltimore, MD, 1990, 270–82)

A lucid and concise introduction to Butler's influential intervention in feminist understandings of gender. It articulates theoretical and philosophical bases for viewing gender as a performative act and for assessing implications of the destabilizing of gender as interpretive category. For elaboration of these ideas, see also Judith Butler, *Gender Trouble: Feminism and the Subversion of Identity* (New York, 1990). Other essays in *Performing Feminisms* provide useful applications of the concept of performance to feminist analyses of film, theatre and performance art and to the theorizing of feminism and femininity.

Henry Louis Gates Jr, 'Race,' writing, and difference, *Critical Inquiry*, 12, no. 1, Autumn 1985

A series of essays that explore the way ideas of difference are inscribed in the concept of 'race', as it functions in popular and academic usages, and the way ideas about racial difference structure literary texts. Essays include reassessments of the biological and ideological understandings of race, as well as readings of specific verbal and visual texts as they participate in and perpetuate structures of power and domination. Explores colonial and postcolonial texts and contexts as well as American representations of racial difference.

Luce Irigaray, *This Sex Which is Not One*, trans. Catherine Porter (Ithaca, NY, 1985)

A series of widely ranging essays on the status of woman in Western philosophical thought and psychoanalytic theory. Especially useful for its probing analysis of male-centred structures of language and thought and its experimental performance of feminine discourse. It introduces the idea of 'mimicry' as a strategy for illuminating and contesting women's exclusion from dominant systems of representation.

Edward W. Said, *Orientalism* (New York, 1978)

This work set the terms for most subsequent discussion of colonialism as representational as well as political practice. It offers detailed elaboration and powerful critique of 'Orientalism' as a set of discursive practices (operating in a variety of institutional and cultural contexts) for 'knowing' and dominating the East, and hence bolstering the idea of European superiority.

Eve Kosofsky Sedgwick, *Between Men: English Literature and Male Homosocial Desire* (New York, 1985)

This book provides both a theoretical paradigm for reading the sexual and social relations between men, as they are historically constituted, and a series of readings of literary texts ranging from Shakespeare to Dickens. It introduces and elaborates the key critical concept of 'homosocial desire' to cover the continuum of culturally pervasive relationships between men (such as male bonding) that distinguish themselves from homo-erotic attachments and that work to exclude women.

4 Representing the Unrepresentable

Two books offer an analysis which seems to come close to an awareness of Jardine's position and yet set it within a knowledge of historical processes:

A. Parker, M. Russo, D. Somner, P. Yaeger (eds), *Nationalisms and Sexualities* (London, 1993)

This collection of essays attempts to analyse a wide range of constructions of national identity and the way that they map on to gendered identities. Although not all of the essays are concerned with colonialism and gender, many of them pose interesting questions about the way gender and national identity intermesh.

Mary Louise Pratt, *Imperial Eyes: Travel Writing and Transculturation* (London, 1992)

This study forms an analysis of a wide range of travel writing, particularly about South America. Pratt is concerned to add different methodologies to the conventional one of colonial control, and instead focuses on the 'contact zone', that is, the way in which indigenous people shaped and resisted the colonial power.

Most surveys of the British Empire are centred on male exploration and 'adventure'. There is one work which takes exception to this rule:

Nirad Chaudhuri and M. Strobel (eds), *Western Women and Imperialism: Complicity and Resistance* (Indianapolis, 1992)

Here, also, is one early feminist approach to Forster's work:

Bonnie Blumenthal Finkelstein, *Forster's Women: Eternal Differences* (New York, 1975)

This work takes seriously the Bloomsbury ethic that self-development is of paramount importance. Forster's 'androgynous' vision is liberating. The section on *Passage* can be found on pp. 117–36.

Lastly, an essay that develops some of the valuable connections first explored by Brenda Silver (1988):

Jenny Sharpe, The unspeakable limits of rape: Colonial violence and counter-insurgency, *Genders*, 10 (1991), 25–46

Index

ENGLISH PEOPLE
THE EXPERIENCE OF TEACHING AND LEARNING ENGLISH
IN BRITISH UNIVERSITIES

Colin Evans

English People is a portrait of the subject 'English' as it is experienced by teachers and students in British Higher Education. The author has interviewed staff and students in the Universities of Cardiff, Newcastle, Oxford and Stirling and in the former Polytechnic of North London (now the University of North London). These 'English People' speak of the impact of Theory, of Feminism, of the experience of reading and writing, of the problems of teaching literature, of the peculiarities of Oxford and of compulsory Anglo-Saxon, of post-colonial literature and of academic leadership in a time of financial pressure.

English People is also an example of the way in which nations attempt to produce unity out of ethnic diversity by using the national education system and especially the subject which has the name of the national language. It questions whether 'English' can still produce unity and whether it has unity itself. Is 'English', like the British Isles, a varied archipelago and not a land mass? Has it deconstructed itself out of existence?

The book is about students and teachers who have made this choice of subject and career, and is fascinating reading for past, present and aspiring students and teachers of English, in universities, colleges and schools. It is also relevant to anyone interested in Higher Education and its organization.

Contents
Part 1: Joining – Origins – Choice – Reading and writing – Teaching and learning – Life in an institution – Part 2: Dividing – Male/female – Theory – Discipline – English, Englishes and the English – Postface – Appendix – Notes – Bibliography – Index.

256pp   0 335 09359 0 (Paperback)   0 335 09361 2 (Hardback)

HEART OF DARKNESS
Anthony Fothergill

Heart of Darkness, one of the crucial literary works of the last hundred years, is also one of the most commented on. This *Guide* does not try to add yet one more account of what the novel is 'really about', though it does introduce readers to the characteristic approaches the work has received, and helps them to adjudicate these. Rather, by a close and questioning scrutiny of the text, it draws attention to the way the work raises the major theoretical issue of Reading itself. How do we read, how do we make meanings? And how do we represent these? The active process of reading the work seems to mimic the journey Marlow makes into the African interior: pitfalls and snags, alluring desires, frustrating delays and shocking glimpses of meaning characterize both. The *Guide* suggests ways in which this can help us understand Marlow's own comprehending and telling of his experiences. For him, too, reading is inescapable. Thematic concerns like the portrayal of colonialism, the confrontation of the 'Civilized' with the 'Savage', the representation of the 'Other' (for Marlow, the Black or the woman) are all given fresh life when seen through this perspective. The importance of recognizing that Marlow's 'reading' – and Conrad's writing – always occurs within culture, within the historical and political assumptions and parameters of Conrad's own time, is emphasized, and helps readers towards a fuller awareness of their own activity.

Contents
Meanings and readings – Stories and histories – Senses of place – Colonialism; semi-colonialism – 'Civilization' and 'savagery': Marlow imagining the other – Endings: crying, dying, lying . . . and telling stories – In lieu of concluding . . . – Notes – Suggestions for further reading – Index.

144pp   0 335 15257 0 (Paperback)   0 335 15258 9 (Hardback)

NARRATIVE AND IDEOLOGY
Jeremy Tambling

Jeremy Tambling asks why it matters that everything we read, from newspapers to novels, comes in the form of stories. Literary criticism has often forgotten the importance of the plot in its concern with themes and characters, but this study begins with the primacy of the story. It also asks how narratives are shaped by cultural and social assumptions – how they are always ideological. He asks, what are narratives and why are they important?

This study works through discussion of specific examples to ask how different types of writing produce different narratives, to ask about the twentieth-century breakdown of narrative, to discuss whether there are any 'master plots' to which all narratives conform. Is it, indeed, possible to think outside narrative and the way it shapes thought and expectations?

With detailed attention to all the elements of the plot, this is an important introduction to the significance of narrative in literature and in life.

Contents
Narrative and ideology – 'Fanny and Annie' – Who narrates? Part 1 – Who narrates? Part 2 – Narrative plots: 'Character' and 'action' – Ideology and the pleasure of the text – Time and ideology: 'The garden of forking paths' – In defence of narrative – Instead of a conclusion – Notes – Suggestions for further reading – Index of names.

136pp   0 335 09354 X (Paperback)   0 335 09355 8 (Hardback)

WOMEN IN LOVE

Graham Holderness

Women in Love is now regarded as D.H. Lawrence's masterpiece. However, when it was first published (in an American edition in 1920) it aroused considerable resistance, bafflement, hostility and anger, even from some of Lawrence's closest admirers. According to Swinnerton in the *Manchester Guardian*:

> The principal difficulty of the book is that it is difficult to read. It is full of absurdities . . . The difficulty arises from the static quality of the book, the lack of momentum. It arises also from the intrinsic similarity of all the characters.

These and similar charges have been echoed by many subsequent readers and students even though *Women in Love* has been accepted by literary and educational establishments since the 1950s as a major classic. It also continues to provoke the critics, being accused at times by Marxists of simplistic ahistoricism, and of crude male chauvinism by feminists.

Graham Holderness invites us to explore with him the text's difficulties, controversies, intensities and pleasures. He traces the novel's narrative roots in nineteenth century realism and its technical leaps into modernism. He discusses the status of ideas in the text, its sexual politics, its relationship to myth and to Lawrence's perception of the First World War. He opens out the densities, richness and internal contradictions of this great novel.

Contents

Character, narrative – Ideas, language – Creativity, dissolution – Sexual politics: homosexuality, feminism – Metaphysic, apocalypse – Biography, history – Notes – Suggestions for further reading – Index.

152pp   0 335 15253 8 (Paperback)   0 335 15254 6 (Hardback)